# SCIENCE
# &RELIGION

## A NEW INTRODUCTION
### SECOND EDITION

Alister E. McGrath

WILEY-BLACKWELL

A John Wiley & Sons, Ltd., Publication

This second edition first published 2010
© 2010 Alister E McGrath
Edition history: Blackwell Publishers Ltd (1e, 1999)

Blackwell Publishing was acquired by John Wiley & Sons in February 2007. Blackwell's publishing program has been merged with Wiley's global Scientific, Technical, and Medical business to form Wiley-Blackwell.

*Registered Office*
John Wiley & Sons Ltd, The Atrium, Southern Gate, Chichester, West Sussex, PO19 8SQ, United Kingdom

*Editorial Offices*
350 Main Street, Malden, MA 02148-5020, USA
9600 Garsington Road, Oxford, OX4 2DQ, UK
The Atrium, Southern Gate, Chichester, West Sussex, PO19 8SQ, UK

For details of our global editorial offices, for customer services, and for information about how to apply for permission to reuse the copyright material in this book please see our website at www.wiley.com/wiley-blackwell.

The right of Alister E McGrath to be identified as the author of this work has been asserted in accordance with the Copyright, Designs and Patents Act 1988.

*Library of Congress Cataloging-in-Publication Data*

McGrath, Alister E., 1953–
    Science and religion : an introduction / Alister E. McGrath. – 2nd ed.
        p. cm.
    Includes bibliographical references and index.
    ISBN 978-1-4051-8790-9 (hardcover : alk. paper) – ISBN 978-1-4051-8791-6 (pbk. : alk. paper)
1. Religion and science.   I. Title.
    BL240.3.M44 2010
    201′.66--dc22

                                                                                2009020180

A catalogue record for this book is available from the British Library.

Set in 10.5/13 pt Adobe Caslon by SNP Best-set Typesetter Ltd., Hong Kong
Printed in Singapore by Ho Printing Singapore Pte Ltd

01   2010

# Contents

# Preface

The study of science and religion is one of the most fascinating areas of human inquiry. It brings together two of the most significant forces in contemporary society. The remarkable surge in books and television documentaries dealing with God and physics, spirituality and science, and the great mysteries of human nature and destiny are a clear sign that there is growing interest in this area. Many colleges, seminaries, and universities now offer courses dealing with the general theme of science and religion, which often attract large and appreciative audiences.

Yet there is a problem here. To make sense of the dialogue between sciences and religion, it is necessary to know something about both. A major difficulty facing the field of "science and religion" studies concerns the extent of prior knowledge of those interested in this area of study. To appreciate the complex interaction of the natural sciences and religion, it is necessary to have at least a good general working knowledge of at least one religion and one major natural science, preferably physics or biology. Many of those who would like to explore this fascinating field find themselves discouraged through this lack of prior knowledge.

This book aims to deal with this situation by assuming that its readers know little, if anything, about the natural sciences or religion, and aims to introduce everything on the basis of the assumption of very limited knowledge on the part of its readers. The main themes and issues in the study of religion and the natural sciences are carefully explored and explained without making unrealistic assumptions about what its readers are likely to know already. Those with some previous knowledge in the areas of science or religion will therefore find that they are from time to time presented with material with which they are already familiar. It is hoped that this will not prove tedious. In any case, the particular concern of this volume is to explore the interface of science and religion. Those who already have some knowledge of science or religion should therefore find that material with which they are already familiar is handled in new ways, so that its connections with our theme become clear.

My own interest in this field goes back for more than 30 years. I began my studies at Oxford University in 1971 by studying chemistry, focusing on quantum theory, before going on to gain my doctorate in molecular biophysics. After this, I studied theology at both Oxford and Cambridge Universities, focusing particularly on the historical interaction of science and religion, particularly during the sixteenth and nineteenth centuries. It is my hope that my own experience of relating the two areas of study may be of value to others seeking to do the same.

This work represents a major revision of the first edition of this work, which benefited considerably from the feedback of its many users. It is hoped that this second edition represents an improvement on its predecessor, both in terms of the scope and level of its coverage. Both the author and publisher welcome comments and criticism, which will be of value to them in developing future editions of this work.

Alister E. McGrath
King's College, London
January, 2009

# How To Use This Book

This book is an introduction to the dialogue between science and religion. It assumes that you know little, if anything, about either science or religion, and sets out to explore this exciting and important field as if you were encountering it for the very first time.

This emphasis on *accessibility* means that this book includes lots of explanatory material that you will not find in other works of this kind. Years of teaching experience have helped me to realize that students who are new to this field often need far more help than is often appreciated. All the material that is included in this volume has been tested on students and modified to make sure it is easily understood. You should find that you are able to cope with the entire book without undue difficulty, even if you have relatively little scientific or religious background knowledge.

Some readers who already have a background in relevant fields may find that they can skip sections, or read them through very quickly. Yet they may find that other sections introduce them to material which they have not come across before, and will welcome the entry-level introduction to those areas that this work provides.

This book is an introduction, not a comprehensive textbook. It is a starting point for your exploration of the field, but it cannot hope to deal with the questions raised in detail. Its discussions of complex issues – such as the nature of realism – must be seen as opening the door to further reflection. They are intended to help you become familiar with issues, but cannot deal with them in depth. For this reason, each chapter includes a short list of suitable works for further reading, which will be helpful and accessible to readers who wish to take their thinking further.

It is not necessary to read the material in the order in which it is presented in this work. Each chapter has been designed to be self-contained, and has been written in such a way that it can be understood without the need for additional information. This occasionally means that there is some repetition of material within this book, and it is hoped that readers will be able to overlook this minor irritation. However, readers will find that they will get the most out of this work by reading the material in the order in which it is arranged. For example, some readers may prefer to omit the historical material altogether. However, they will find that they gain more from later chapters if they possess the background information which is provided in these chapters.

As is customary in this field, this book concentrates on the dialogue between Christianity and the natural sciences. This interaction has been of major importance historically in the shaping of western culture, and also shapes most courses on science and religion taught in western universities. However, a brief introduction is also provided to the issues found in four other world religions, for those wishing to broaden their horizons.

Finally, as already noted, the work aims to direct students to more advanced works that will allow them to take their reading and thinking further. Each chapter includes a short section for further reading, identifying the best recent works in these areas. Rather than provide extended reading lists, a selection of works of proven value have been identified as suitable next areas for exploration of the field. All major citations in the text are sourced, so that readers can follow them through if they wish to study them in their original context.

Both the author and publisher intend to ensure that this work is kept up-to-date, accessible, and relevant, and welcome comments from users which will help them plan future editions of this work. User feedback was of enormous importance in developing the second edition of this work, and both author and publisher are very grateful for the many comments they received which enabled the numerous improvements which it includes.

# Chapter

# 1

## Introducing the Dialogue Between Science and Religion

W hy study the interaction of science and religion? The fact that you are reading this book in the first place suggests that you probably think it that it is worth your while to explore their mutual relationship. Yet it is important to begin any engagement with the burgeoning field of science and religion studies by considering its importance and potential benefits, and also clarifying what it is that is being studied.

Religion and science are two of the most powerful cultural and intellectual forces in today's world. Some scientists and religious believers see them as locked in mortal combat: science and religion are thus at war with each other, and that war will continue until one of them is eradicated. Although this view tends to be associated particularly with dogmatic atheist scientists, such as Peter Atkins (born 1940) or Richard Dawkins (born 1941), they are also encountered among religious believers. Some fundamentalist Christians and Muslims, for example, see science as a threat to their faith. A good example of this can be found in the criticisms of evolution made by conservative Protestant Christians, who see it as undermining the biblical creation accounts.

We shall explore the origins of this "warfare" model of the interaction between science and religion later in this work. Although it is influential culturally, it is not seen by historians of science as being particularly reliable or defensible. If anything, science now seems to be opening up religious questions, rather than closing them down, or declaring them to be meaningless. It is increasingly being recognized that natural science can "throw up questions that point beyond itself and transcend its power to answer" (Polkinghorne, 1988, p. 23). Commenting on the scientific search for the origins of the universe, the astronomer Robert Jastrow notes how modern science finds itself asking precisely the same questions as those posed in earlier generations by religious thinkers.

> It is not a matter of another year, another decade of work, another measurement, or another theory; at this moment, it seems as though science will never be able to raise the curtain on the mystery of creation. For the scientist who has lived by his faith in the power of reason, the story ends like a bad dream. He has scaled the mountains of ignorance; he is about to conquer the highest peaks; as he pulls himself over the final rock, he is greeted by a band of theologians who have been sitting there for centuries. (Jastrow, 1978, pp. 115–16)

The dialogue between science and religion sets out to ask whether, in what ways, and to what extents, these two conversation partners might learn from each other. Given the cultural importance of both science and religion, the exploration of how they relate to each other has the potential for both conflict and enrichment. Despite the risks to both sides, it remains profoundly worthwhile. Why? Three reasons are often given for this judgment.

1   Neither science nor religion can claim to give a total account of reality. It is certainly true that some on each side have offered grand visions of their discipline being able to answer every question about the nature of the universe and the meaning of life – as, for example, in Richard Dawkins's notion of "universal Darwinism." These, however, are not regarded as representative by their peers. Nor is the notion of "nonoverlapping magisteria," as developed by writers such as the late Stephen Jay Gould (1941–2002), acceptable. This envisages that science and religion occupy well-defined domains or areas of competency, which do not overlap or intersect.

Science and religion are perhaps better thought of as operating at different levels, often reflecting on similar questions, yet answering them in different ways. Historians suggest that both science and religion lose their way when they play at being what they are not. There are some scientists who declare they have displaced religion (evident in recent "scientific atheism"), just as there are religious activists who claim to have displaced science (evident in modern "creationism"). Science does not answer every question that we might have about the world. Neither does religion. Yet taken together they can offer a stereoscopic view of reality denied to those who limit themselves to one discipline's perspective on things. The science and religion dialogue allows us to appreciate the distinct identities, strengths, and limits of each conversation partner. It also offers us a deeper understanding of things than either religion or science could offer unaided.

2   Both science and religion are concerned about making sense of things. Although many religions, including Christianity, can be argued to place an emphasis upon the transformation of the human situation, most set out to offer explanations of the world. Why are things the way they are? What explanations may be offered for what we observe? What is the "bigger picture" which makes sense of our observations and experience? Scientific and religious explanations generally take different forms, even when reflecting on the same observations. Perhaps most importantly, science tends to ask "how" questions, where religion asks "why." Science seeks to clarify mechanisms; religions offer meaning.

These approaches do not need to be seen as being in competition, or as being mutually incompatible. They operate at different levels. While some scientists hold that explaining how things happen is the best answer to life's biggest questions, most would argue for a clear distinction between "explanation" and "meaning." One of the most influential discussions of this point is found in Roy Baumeister's classic work *Meanings of Life* (1991). For Baumeister, "meaning" transcends "explanation." Baumeister suggested that four basic needs – purpose, efficacy, value, and self-worth – appeared to underlie the human quest for meaning, understood as "shared mental representations of possible relationships among things, events, and relationships" (1991, p. 15).

3   In recent years there has been a significant increase in awareness within the scientific community of the broader issues raised by its research, and limits placed upon that community's ability to answer them. An obvious example concerns ethical questions. Is science able to determine what is right and what is wrong? Most scientists would affirm that their discipline is fundamentally amoral – that is, that the scientific method does not extend to moral questions. For example, Richard Dawkins succinctly confirmed that "science has no methods for deciding what is ethical" (Dawkins, 2003, p. 34). Stephen Jay Gould made a similar point in his important essay "Nonmoral Nature":

> Our failure to discern a universal good does not record any lack of insight or ingenuity, but merely demonstrates that nature contains no moral messages framed in human terms. Morality is a subject for philosophers, theologians, students of the humanities, indeed for all thinking people. The answers will not be read passively from nature; they do not, and cannot, arise from the data of science. The factual state of the world does not teach us how we, with our powers for good and evil, should alter or preserve it in the most ethical manner. (Gould, 1994, p. 42)

This has led to growing interest in complementarian approaches to such issues. Natural scientists seem increasingly willing to complement scientific understandings of the world with additional approaches that permit or encourage the ethical,

**Figure 1.1** Stephen Jay Gould (Jon Chase/ Harvard News Office)

aesthetical, and spiritual enhancement of their approaches. Religion is being seen increasingly as an important dialogue partner in allowing the natural sciences to engage with questions which are raised, yet not answered, by scientific research. Debates about the ethics of biotechnology, for example, often raise important questions which science cannot answer – such as when a human "person" comes into existence, or what constitutes an acceptable quality of life.

Other reasons may easily be added for encouraging such a conversation. Yet it is important to appreciate that there are also difficulties associated with the dialogue between science and religion. The most obvious of these is the outright refusal on the part of some "scientific atheists" on the one hand, or religious fundamentalists on the other, to engage in any dialogue. For both sides of this highly polarized argument, science and religion are enemies, and those who engage in dialogue are either traitors or appeasers. Both the atheist scientific writer Richard Dawkins and the biblical creationist Henry Morris, for example, represent this extreme position, arguing that there is a war between science and religion. Antireligious and antiscientific bias or prejudice remain a significant obstacle to a fruitful dialogue.

Yet other concerns should also be noted, of which the following are the most important.

First, the term "science" covers a wide range of disciplines, each with its own distinctive methodology. To speak of the dialogue between "science and religion" seems to imply that there is some uniform entity called "science," whereas in fact there are many scientific disciplines, each with its own distinctive sphere of study and associated method of investigation. As we shall see later in this study, the interaction of physics and religion is significantly different from that of biology and religion. The term "science" thus needs to be qualified or further defined before the question can be answered properly.

Second, in much the same way, the term "religion" is very vague, referring to a wide variety of movements. Christianity, Islam, and Hinduism, for example, adopt quite different attitudes towards the natural world, and especially its capacity to disclose or point to God. It is virtually impossible to generalize about "religion," when it embraces such a wide variety of viewpoints. It is remarkably difficult to offer a viable

definition of what constitutes a "religion." Since there is no generally accepted definition of religion, it is often difficult to know whether the dialogue should include
worldviews with religious elements (such as Confucianism). Developing this point
further, a significant variety of viewpoints on the relation of faith and science can be
found within any single religion. For example, Christianity consists of a number of
important groups, including Catholicism, Orthodoxy, and Protestantism, each of
which in turn consists of subgroups. This raises the possibility of a significant number
of different religious attitudes towards science.

Thirdly, many would question whether the dialogue is best thought of in terms of
"science and *religion*." The term "religion" designates a broad range of activities, attitudes, and beliefs, and is not purely about ideas. Some writers have argued that the
real dialogue between science and religion takes place at the level of methods and
ideas. If this is so, we should really speak about a dialogue between science and *theology*. This point has been developed by a number of writings, including some by the
leading British theologian Thomas F. Torrance (1913–2007).

These are all important points to bear in mind as we explore the important and
intellectually exciting interaction between science and religion. We begin by sketching
some historical background, before moving on to look at the big debates of the present.

## For Further Reading

Baumeister, Roy F. *Meanings of Life*. New York: Guilford Press, 1991.
Clayton, Philip (ed.). *Oxford Handbook of Science and Religion*. Oxford: Oxford University Press,
    2006.
Dear, Peter R. The Intelligibility of Nature: How Science Makes Sense of the World. Chicago:
    University of Chicago Press, 2006.
Polkinghorne, John. *Science and Creation: The Search for Understanding*, 2nd edn. Philadelphia,
    PA: Templeton Foundation Press, 2006.
Watts, Fraser, and Kevin Dutton (eds). *Why the Science and Religion Dialogue Matters*.
    Philadelphia, PA: Templeton Foundation Press, 2006.

# I History

*Three Landmark Debates*

Many are attracted to study the relation of science and religion because of its contemporary relevance. What are the implications of the "big bang" for belief in a creator God? Do the latest developments in evolutionary psychology undermine or reinforce traditional religious arguments for the existence of God based on desire? Part of the sheer excitement of this field is the fact that it engages live debates, issues that are of immediate relevance.

Why, then, study past debates? Surely this is irrelevant to contemporary concerns. Why look at the past, when so much is happening in the present? This is a real concern, and must be taken seriously. For many natural scientists, for example, there is little point in reflecting on the history of their disciplines. They are developing so rapidly that older ideas become outdated with alarming speed. To study history seems to be about disengaging from the real world, and entering a very different world that bears little relation to ours. As L. P. Hartley wrote at the beginning of *The Go-Between*, "The past is a foreign country: they do things differently there."

Yet anyone wishing to understand the interaction of science and religion needs to become familiar with three major landmarks – the astronomical debates of the sixteenth and early seventeenth centuries; the rise of the Newtonian worldview in the late seventeenth and eighteenth century; and the Darwinian controversy of the nineteenth. The issues raised by these developments are found again and again in contemporary debates.

Part I aims to introduce these landmark debates, indicating the points at issue and their significance for our theme. As these three debates are constantly referred to in the literature concerning the theme of "science and religion" – as they are also in the present text – readers must consider it essential to master the basic ideas and developments which are discussed in this part. For this reason, it has been placed at the opening of the work.

Yet many, while recognizing the practical force of this point, will still want to ask why they should bother studying history at all. Before looking at these three specific debates, we shall pause and give some thought to the place of history in the interaction between science and religion.

# Chapter

# 2

# Why Study History?

What is the point of referring back to the past when we are meant to be talking about themes concerning science and religion in the twenty-first century? Why study the past, when there is so much of importance and interest in the present? This is a fair question, and merits a careful answer. To explore the importance of this point, we shall consider the origins of the widespread popular belief that science and religion are permanently at loggerheads – the so-called "warfare" model of the interaction of science and religion. This is still deeply embedded in popular thinking.

## The Historical Origins of the "Warfare" Model of Science and Religion

In the eighteenth century, a remarkable synergy developed between religion and the sciences in England. Newton's "celestial mechanics" was widely regarded as at worst consistent with, and at best a glorious confirmation of, the Christian view of God as creator of a harmonious universe. Many members of the Royal Society of London – founded to advance scientific understanding and research – were strongly religious in their outlooks, and saw this as enhancing their commitment to scientific advancement.

Yet all this changed in the second half of the nineteenth century. The general tone of the later nineteenth-century encounter between religion (especially Christianity)

**Figure 2.1** John William Draper (Draper Family Collection, Archives Center, National Museum of American History, Smithsonian Institution)

**Figure 2.2** Andrew Dickson White (Courtesy of the Division of Rare and Manuscript Collections, Cornell University Library)

and the natural sciences was set by two works – John William Draper's *History of the Conflict Between Religion and Science* (1874) and Andrew Dickson White's *The Warfare of Science with Theology in Christendom* (1896). The crystallization of the "warfare" metaphor in the popular mind was unquestionably catalyzed by such vigorously polemical writings.

As a generation of historians has now pointed out, the notion of an endemic conflict between science and religion, so aggressively advocated by White and Draper, is itself socially determined, created in the lengthening shadows of hostility towards individual clergy and church institutions. The interaction of science and religion has been influenced more by their social circumstances than by their specific ideas. The Victorian period itself gave rise to the social pressures and tensions which engendered the myth of permanent warfare between science and religion.

A significant social shift can be discerned behind the emergence of this "conflict" model. From a sociological perspective, scientific knowledge was advocated by particular social groups to advance their own specific goals and interests. There was growing competition between two specific groups within English society in the nineteenth century: the clergy and the scientific professionals. The clergy were widely regarded as an elite at the beginning of the nineteenth century, with the "scientific parson" a well-established social stereotype. With the appearance of the professional scientist, however, a struggle for supremacy began, to determine who would gain the cultural ascendancy within British culture in the second half of the nineteenth century. The "conflict" model has its origins in the specific conditions of the Victorian era, in which an emerging professional intellectual group sought to displace a group which had hitherto occupied the place of honor.

The "conflict" model of science and religion thus came to prominence at a time when professional scientists wished to distance themselves from their amateur colleagues, and when changing patterns in academic culture necessitated demonstrating its independence from the church and other bastions of the establishment. Academic freedom demanded a break with the church; it was a small step towards depicting the church as the opponent of learning and scientific advance in the late nineteenth century, and the natural sciences as its strongest advocates. This naturally led to earlier incidents – such as the Galileo debate – being read and interpreted in the light of this controlling paradigm of the warfare of science and religion.

It will be clear that the idea that science and religion are in permanent conflict thus reflects the agendas and concerns of a specific period. Yet that moment is now past, and its agendas can be set to one side, allowing a more informed and dispassionate assessment of things. The study of history allows us both to account for the origins of this deeply problematic understanding of the relation of science and religion, and to assess its reliability. Above all, it allows us to move beyond it, and construct more informed and positive approaches to the interaction of these two distinct domains of thought.

## There Is No "Master Narrative" for Science and Religion

The relationship between science and religion has always been complex. There is no "master narrative" which describes their relationship – such as the notoriously inaccurate "warfare" narrative, which posits that science and religion have always been engaged in a fight to the death. Every generation has given careful thought to the big questions of life, both scientific and religious. The scientific revolution witnessed both tension and collaboration between traditional religious viewpoints, and innovative scientific theories.

To illustrate this complex picture, let us consider the Christian doctrine of creation, which shaped the intellectual world of early modern Europe, and encouraged people to think of a regular, ordered universe, which reflected the wisdom of its creator. Intense study of the created order was a means of gaining an increased appreciation of the "mind of God." There was thus a positive religious motivation for undertaking scientific research. Yet this same traditional doctrine of creation generated tensions, especially as Charles Darwin's narrative of human origins began to gain the ascendancy in the late nineteenth century. On a literal reading of the opening chapters of the Christian Bible, Darwin's theory seemed to be incorrect. Tensions emerged, which remain to this day.

It is also important to appreciate that science is, almost by definition, a subversive activity, challenging all kinds of vested interests and power groups. The physicist Freeman Dyson penned an important essay entitled "The Scientist as Rebel," in which he pointed out that many scientists have found themselves engaged in a "rebellion against the restrictions imposed by the locally prevailing culture" (Dyson, 1995, p. 1).

This can easily be illustrated from the history of the interaction of science and culture. For the Arab mathematician and astronomer Omar Khayyam (1048–1122), science was a rebellion against the intellectual constraints of Islam; for nineteenth-century Japanese scientists, science was a rebellion against the lingering feudalism of their culture; for the great Indian physicists of the twentieth century, their discipline was a powerful intellectual force directed against the fatalistic ethic of Hinduism (not to mention British imperialism, which was then dominant in the region). And in western Europe, scientific advance inevitably involved confrontation with the culture of the day – including its political, social, and religious elements. In that the West has been dominated by Christianity, it is thus unsurprising that the tension between science and western culture has often been viewed as a confrontation between science and Christianity. In fact, the real tension is between scientific innovation and cultural traditionalism.

## The Essentialist Fallacy About Science and Religion

Some writers take the view that the relation between science and Christian theology is permanently defined, at least in its fundamental respects, by the essential nature of the two disciplines. It is argued that, once the essential nature of the two disciplines is grasped, their mutual relationship can be inferred as a matter of course.

This view is found particularly in writers who are hostile to religion. "The *real* war is between rationalism and superstition. Science is but one form of rationalism, while religion is the most common form of superstition" (Jerry Coyne, quoted in Dawkins,

2006, p. 67). However, it is not limited to those who advocate the "warfare" model, being also encountered in the writings of those who argue that science and religion are essentially collaborative.

Underlying these "essentialist" accounts of the interaction of science and religion is the assumption that each of these terms designates something fixed, permanent, and essential. This means that their mutual relationship is determined by something essential to each of the disciplines, which is not affected by the contingencies of history or culture.

This tendency to attribute fixed and unchanging defining qualities to both science and religion has been successfully challenged by a series of rigorous historical studies. These have demonstrated the diversity, occasional inconsistency, and sheer complexity of understandings of the mutual relationship of science and religion since about the year 1500. No single account or "metanarrative" may be offered of this relationship, precisely because the variety of relationships that have existed reflect prevailing social, political, economic, and cultural factors.

There are three main difficulties with the "essentialist" approach, all of which are shown up by historical scholarship.

1   It treats "science" and "religion" as essentially fixed and unchanging entities, whose relationship is permanently defined by their subject matter.
2   It assumes that this relationship may be universally defined in terms of the "warfare" imagery which became popular during the nineteenth century, for reasons we explored earlier. This is then used as a controlling metanarrative, a prism through which all related intellectual engagements throughout history are to be viewed, permanently adversarial.
3   It fails to draw a distinction between the institution of the Christian church and the ideas of Christian theology, especially during the late Middle Ages, and fails to appreciate that the political decisions of the former often rest on considerations which have little to do with the latter. To critique the leading ideas of Christian theology on the basis of the actions of certain late medieval ecclesiastical figures is to assume a simple, direct, and linear connection between these entities which rarely existed in practice.

## Dispelling Myths About Science and Religion

Certain stereotypes about science and religion remain prevalent in western culture. These often rest on misunderstandings or misreading of history. The study of history helps clear the air for the dialogue between science and religion by neutralizing the purely negative perceptions of this relationship which are often perpetuated in the media. An obvious example is the controversy surrounding Galileo Galilei's views on the solar system. The Galileo affair is often portrayed as yet another illustration of the perennial war between science and religion. Yet things were much more complicated.

Galileo and his heliocentric theories were initially well received within papal circles. It is generally agreed that Galileo's positive reputation in ecclesiastical circles until a surprisingly late date was linked to his close relationship with the papal favorite, Giovanni Ciampoli. When Ciampoli fell from grace in the spring of 1632, Galileo found his position seriously weakened, perhaps to the point of being fatally compromised. Without the protection of Ciampoli, Galileo became vulnerable to those who wished to discredit him. Sadly, Galileo and his theories became interlocked with papal politics, and the wider political and ecclesiastical conflicts of his age.

A second example of a stereotypical account of the relation of science and religion which can be defused by serious historical scholarship concerns the famous meeting of the British Association at Oxford on June 30, 1860. The British Association had always seen one of its most significant objectives as being to popularize science. As Charles Darwin's *Origin of Species* had been published the previous year, it was natural that it should be a subject of discussion at the 1860 meeting. Darwin himself was in ill health, and was unable to attend the meeting in person. Samuel Wilberforce, Bishop of Oxford, was pitted against Thomas Henry Huxley. According to the popular legend, repeated uncritically in many biographies of Darwin, Wilberforce attempted to pour scorn on the theory of evolution by suggesting that it implied that humans were recently descended from monkeys. Would Huxley, he asked, prefer to think of himself being descended from an ape on his grandfather's or grandmother's side? He was then duly rebuked by Huxley, who turned the tables on him, showing him up to be an ignorant and arrogant cleric. Wilberforce had, in fact, written an extensive review of the *Origin of Species*, pointing out some serious weaknesses. Darwin regarded this review as significant, and modified his discussion at several points in response to Wilberforce's criticisms. Nevertheless, by 1900 the legend was firmly established, and went some way towards reinforcing the "conflict" or "warfare" model of the interaction of science and religion.

The classic statement of this legend is actually quite late. It dates from 1898, and takes the form of an autobiographical memory from Mrs Isabella Sidgwick, published in *Macmillan's Magazine*. This account is inconsistent with accounts published or in circulation closer to the time of the meeting itself. A review in the *Athenaeum*, published shortly after the event, expressed the consensus at that time. Wilberforce and Huxley, it declared, "have each found foemen worthy of their steel, and made their charges and countercharges very much to their own satisfaction and the delight of their respective friends." One of Huxley's most recent and empathetic biographers,

Adrian Desmond, argues that it is ridiculous to speak of Huxley being a "victor" in this situation. Yet the legend still lingers!

## The Importance of Biblical Interpretation

Finally, we may note one issue that recurs throughout the history of the interaction of science and religion – the importance of biblical interpretation. Conflict between science and religion often arises when scientific advance is seen to conflict with the prevailing modes of biblical interpretation. Two obvious examples may be given to illustrate the importance of this point.

The Copernican debate centered on the question of whether the earth rotated around the sun (the "heliocentric" model) or the sun around the earth (the "geocentric" model). One or two passages in the Christian Bible seemed to point to the earth being stationary and the sun rotating – for example, references to the sun standing still (Joshua 10: 12), or to the foundations of the earth being "immovable" (Psalm 96: 10). A "common sense" or "literal" reading of these texts pointed to a geocentric view of the solar system. But was this what was actually intended? Was this simply a conventional way of speaking, which was not intended to have metaphysical implications?

Similarly, the Darwinian controversy raised some important questions about how the Genesis creation accounts were to be understood. Were they literal accounts of the origins of the universe and humanity, which taught that the universe originated about six thousand years ago? Or were they to be interpreted in terms of a more extended vision of creation? In this case, Darwinism found itself pitted against very literal approaches to the interpretation of the Genesis creation narratives. These had developed within English-speaking Protestantism since the early eighteenth century, and had been assumed to be normative. Darwinism called that into question.

Yet it must not be supposed that the advance of science has constantly challenged traditional biblical interpretation, as is sometimes suggested. Traditional Christian views of creation, for example, speak of the cosmos coming into being from nothing. Yet the western scientific tradition, from Aristotle until the 1940s, tended to treat the universe as something that was permanent or eternal. The idea that it had a chronological beginning was seen as absurd. The rise of what is now known as the "standard cosmological model" in the last 50 years is based on the notion that the universe is not eternal, but that it came into being at a definite point. Here we have a situation in which a traditional Christian interpretation of the Bible resonates with modern cosmology.

In this chapter, we have considered some general principles which emerge from the study of the interaction of science and religion. In the three chapters which follow, we shall consider three great episodes of importance to our themes, beginning with the Copernican controversy of the sixteenth century.

## For Further Reading

Brooke, John Hedley. *Science and Religion: Some Historical Perspectives*. Cambridge, UK: Cambridge University Press, 1991.

Dyson, Freeman. "The Scientist as Rebel." In John Cornwell (ed.), *Nature's Imagination: The Frontiers of Scientific Vision*, pp. 1–11. Oxford: Oxford University Press, 1995.

Ferngren, Gary B. (ed.). *Science and Religion: A Historical Introduction*. Baltimore: Johns Hopkins University Press, 2002.

Lindberg, David C., and Ronald L. Numbers. *God and Nature: Historical Essays on the Encounter Between Christianity and Science*. Berkeley: University of California Press, 1986.

Welch, Claude. "Dispelling Some Myths About the Split Between Theology and Science in the Nineteenth Century." In W. Mark Richardson and Wesley J. Wildman (eds), *Religion and Science: History, Method, Dialogue*, pp. 29–40. New York: Routledge, 1996.

# Chapter

# 3 Debate 1

## *Copernicus, Galileo, and the Solar System*

The great Austrian psychoanalyst Sigmund Freud declared that humanity had been the subject of three "narcissistic wounds" in the modern age, each of which challenged the human sense of self-importance. The first wound, Freud argued, was inflicted by the Copernican revolution, which showed that human beings did not stand at the center of the universe, but were at its periphery. The second was the Darwinian demonstration that humanity did not even have a unique place on the planet earth. The third, Freud somewhat immodestly suggested, was his own demonstration that humanity was not even the master of its own limited realm. According to Freud, each of these revolutions added to the pain and wounds inflicted by its predecessor, forcing a radical reevaluation of the place and significance of humanity. We shall consider the religious importance of Freud's views later in this work. Yet it is highly appropriate to open this account by looking at the first of these "wounds" – the Copernican revolution.

Every age is characterized by a series of settled beliefs, which undergird its world-view. The Middle Ages is no exception. One of the more important elements in the medieval worldview was the belief that the sun and other celestial bodies – such as the moon and the planets – rotated around the earth. This "geocentric" view of the universe was treated as self-evidently true. The Bible was interpreted in the light of this belief, with geocentric assumptions being brought to the interpretation of a number of passages. Most living languages still bear witness to this geocentric world-view. For example, even in modern English, it is perfectly acceptable to state that "the sun rose at 7.33 a.m." – despite the fact that this reflects the belief that the sun rotates around the earth. As the truth or falsity of the geocentric model of the solar system made little difference to everyday life anyway, there was little popular interest in challenging it.

The model of the universe which was most widely accepted during the early Middle Ages was devised by Claudius Ptolemy, an astronomer who worked in the Egyptian city of Alexandria during the first half of the second century. In his *Amalgest*, Ptolemy brought together existing ideas concerning the motions of the moon and planets, and argued that these could be understood on the basis of the following assumptions:

1   The earth is at the center of the universe;
2   All heavenly bodies rotate in circular paths around the earth;
3   These rotations take the form of motion in a circle, the center of which in turn moves in another circle. This central idea, which was originally due to Hipparchus, is based on the idea of *epicycles* – that is, circular motion imposed upon circular motion.

Increasingly detailed and precise observation of the movement of the planets and stars caused increasing difficulties for this theory. Initially, the discrepancies could be accommodated by adding additional epicycles. By the end of the fifteenth century, the model was so complex and unwieldy that it was close to collapse. But what could replace it?

During the sixteenth century, the geocentric model of the solar system was abandoned in favor of a heliocentric model, which depicted the sun as lying at its center, with the earth being seen as one of a number of planets orbiting around it. This represented a radical departure from the existing model, and must be regarded as one of the most significant changes in the human perception of reality to have taken place in the last millennium. Although it is customary to refer to this shift in thinking as "the Copernican revolution," it is generally agreed that three individuals were of major importance in bringing about the acceptance of this change.

Nicolaus Copernicus (1473–1543), a Polish scholar, argued that the planets moved in concentric circles around the sun. The earth, in addition to rotating about the sun, also rotated on its own axis. The apparent motion of the stars and planets was thus due to a combination of the

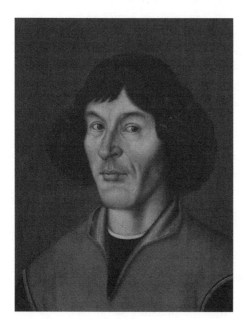

**Figure 3.1** Copernicus (akg-images/Erich Lessing)

rotation of the earth on its own axis, and its rotation around the sun. The model possessed a simplicity and elegance which compared favorably with the increasingly cumbersome Ptolemaic model. Nevertheless, it still proved incapable of explaining all known observational data. The theory would require further modification before it would find acceptance.

The Danish researcher Tycho Brahe (1546–1601), based at an observatory on an island near Copenhagen, carried out a series of precise observations on planetary motion over the period 1576–92. These observations would form the basis for Johann Kepler's modified model of the solar system. Kepler acted as assistant to Tycho when the latter was forced to relocate to Bohemia following the death of Frederick II of Denmark.

Johann Kepler (1571–1630) focused his attention on the observation of the motion of the planet Mars. The Copernican model, which assumed that planets orbit in circles around the sun, was unable to account for the observed motion of the planet. In 1609, Kepler was able to announce that he had uncovered two general laws governing the motion of Mars. First, Mars rotated in an elliptical orbit, with the sun at one of its two foci. Second, the line joining Mars to the sun covers equal areas in equal periods of time. By 1619, Kepler had extended these two laws to the remaining planets, and uncovered a third law: the square of the periodic time of a planet (that is, the time taken by the planet to complete one orbit around the sun) is directly proportional to the cube of its mean distance from the sun.

Kepler's model represented a significant modification of Copernicus's ideas. It must be stressed that Copernicus's radical new model was simply not able to explain the observational data, despite its conceptual elegance and simplicity, on account of his flawed assumption that orbits were necessarily circular. This assumption, interestingly, seems to have derives from classical Euclidian geometry; Copernicus never really freed himself completely from classic Greek ways of thinking. Circles were perfect geometrical figures, whereas ellipses were distorted. Why should nature make use of deformed geometry?

The publication of Copernicus's treatise *On the Revolutions of the Heavenly Bodies* in May 1543 caused a mild sensation, although the final acceptance of the model would have to wait for the detailed work by Kepler in the first two decades of the seventeenth century. As we noted, the older model (often referred to as a "geocentric" theory) was widely accepted by theologians of the Middle Ages, who had become so familiar with reading the text of the Bible through geocentric spectacles that they had some difficulty coping with the new approach.

Early published defenses of the Copernican theory (such as G. J. Rheticus's *Treatise on Holy Scripture and the Motion of the Earth*, which is widely regarded as the earliest known work to deal explicitly with the relation of the Bible and the Copernican theory) thus had to deal with two issues. First, they had to set out the observational evidence which led to the conclusion that the earth and other planets rotated around the sun. Second, they had to demonstrate that this viewpoint was consistent with the Bible, which had long been read as endorsing a geocentric view. As we noted above, the observational evidence was only finally accounted for in the light of Kepler's modification of Copernicus's model. But what of the theological aspects of that model? What of the radical shift which it proposed from an earth-centered universe?

There is no doubt that the rise of the heliocentric theory of the solar system caused theologians to reexamine the manner in which certain biblical passages were interpreted. However, at this stage, we may distinguish three broad approaches within the Christian tradition of biblical interpretation. In what follows, we shall note these, and consider their importance to the science and religion dialogue.

First, there is a *literal* approach, which argues that the passage in question is to be taken at its face value. For example, a literal interpretation of the first chapter of Genesis would argue that creation took place in six periods of 24 hours.

Secondly, there is a nonliteral or *allegorical* approach, which stresses that certain sections of the Bible are written in a style which it is not appropriate to take absolutely literally. During the Middle Ages, three nonliteral senses of Scripture were recognized; this was regarded by many sixteenth-century writers as somewhat elaborate. This view regards the opening chapters of Genesis as poetic or allegorical accounts, from which theological and ethical principles can be derived; it does *not* treat them as literal historical accounts of the origins of the earth.

Thirdly, there is an approach based on the idea of *accommodation*. This has been by far the most important approach in relation to the interaction of biblical interpretation and the natural sciences. The approach argues that revelation takes place in culturally and anthropologically conditioned manners and forms, with the result that it needs to be appropriately interpreted. This approach has a long tradition of use within Judaism and subsequently within Christian theology, and can easily be shown to have been influential within the patristic period. Nevertheless, its mature development can be found within the sixteenth century. This approach argues that the opening chapters of Genesis use language and imagery appropriate to the cultural conditions of its original audience; it is not to be taken "literally," but is to be interpreted to a contemporary readership by extracting the key ideas which have been expressed in forms and terms which are specifically adapted or "accommodated" to the original audience.

The third approach proved to be of especial importance during the debates over the relation between theology and astronomy during the sixteenth and seventeenth centuries. The noted reformer John Calvin (1509–64) may be regarded as making two major and positive contributions to the appreciation and development of the natural sciences. First, he positively encouraged the scientific study of nature; second, he eliminated a major obstacle to the development of that study, through his understanding of the way in which the Bible was to be interpreted in terms of "accommodation" (as explained above). His first contribution is specifically linked with his stress upon the orderliness of creation; both the physical world and the human body testify to the wisdom and character of God. Calvin thus commends the study of both astronomy and medicine. They are able to probe more deeply than theology into the natural world, and thus uncover further evidence of the orderliness of the creation and the wisdom of its creator. It may thus be argued that Calvin gave a new religious motivation to the scientific investigation of nature.

Calvin's second major contribution was to eliminate a significant obstacle to the development of the natural sciences – biblical literalism. Calvin points out that the Bible is primarily concerned with the knowledge of Jesus Christ. It is not an astronomical, geographical, or biological textbook. And when the Bible is interpreted, it must be borne in mind that God "adjusts" to the capacities of the human mind and heart. God has to come down to our level if revelation is to take place. Revelation thus presents a scaled-down or "accommodated" version of God to us, in order to meet our limited abilities. Just as a human mother stoops down to reach her child, so God stoops down to come to our level. Revelation is an act of divine condescension.

The impact of both these ideas upon scientific theorizing, especially during the seventeenth century, was considerable. For example, in his preface to William Gilbert's treatise on magnetism (1600), the English writer Edward Wright defended Copernicus's heliocentric theory of the solar system against biblical literalists by arguing, in the first place, that Scripture was not concerned with physics, and in the second, that its manner of speaking was "accommodated to the understanding and way of speech of the common people, like nurses to little children" (quoted in Hooykaas, 1972, pp. 122–3). Both these arguments derive directly from Calvin, who may be argued to have made a fundamental contribution to the emergence of the natural sciences in this respect.

Fresh controversy broke out over the heliocentric model of the solar system in Italy during the early decades of the seventeenth century. In this case, the debate centered on the views of Galileo Galilei (1564–1642), who mounted a major defense of the Copernican theory of the solar system. This eventually led to the Catholic church condemning Galileo, in what is widely regarded as a clear error of judgment on the part of some ecclesiastical bureaucrats. Galileo's views had initially been received sympathetically

**Figure 3.2** Galileo. Portrait by Justus Sustermans (Galleria Palatina, Palazzo Pitti, Florence, Italy/The Bridgeman Art Library)

within senior church circles, partly on account of the fact that he was held in high regard by a papal favorite, Giovanni Ciampoli. Ciampoli's fall from power led to Galileo losing support within papal circles, and is widely regarded as opening the way to Galileo's condemnation by his enemies.

Although the controversy centering on Galileo is often portrayed as science versus religion, or libertarianism versus authoritarianism, the real issue concerned the correct interpretation of the Bible. Appreciation of this point is thought to have been hindered in the past on account of the failure of historians to engage with the theological (and, more precisely, the hermeneutical) issues attending the debate. In part, this can be seen as reflecting the fact that many of the scholars interested in this particular controversy were scientists or historians of science, who were not familiar with the intricacies of the debates on biblical interpretation of this remarkably complex period. Nevertheless, it is clear that the issue which dominated the discussion between Galileo and his critics was that of how to interpret certain biblical passages. The issue of accommodation was of major important to that debate, as we shall see.

To explore this point, we may turn to a significant work published in January 1615. In his *Letter on the Opinion of the Pythagoreans and Copernicus*, the Carmelite friar Paolo Antonio Foscarini argued that the heliocentric model of the solar system was not incompatible with the Bible. Foscarini did not introduce any new principles of biblical interpretation in his analysis; rather, he sets out and applies traditional rules of interpretation:

> When Holy Scripture attributes something to God or to any other creature which would otherwise be improper and incommensurate, then it should be interpreted and explained in one or more of the following ways. First, it is said to pertain metaphorically and proportionally, or by similitude. Second, it is said … according to our mode of consideration, apprehension, understanding, knowing, etc. Thirdly, it is said according to vulgar opinion and the common way of speaking. (cited in Blackwell, 1991, pp. 94–5)

The second and third ways which Foscarini identifies are generally regarded as types of "accommodation," the third model of biblical interpretation we noted earlier. As we have seen, this approach to biblical interpretation can be traced back to the first Christian centuries, and was not regarded as controversial.

Foscarini's innovation did not lie in the interpretative method he adopted, but in the biblical passages to which he applied it. In other words, Foscarini suggested that certain passages, which many had interpreted literally up to this point, were to be interpreted in an accommodated manner. The passages to which he applied this approach were those which seemed to suggest that the earth remained stationary, and the sun moved. Foscarini argued as follows:

Scripture speaks according to our mode of understanding, and according to appearances, and in respect to us. For thus it is that these bodies appear to be related to us and are described by the common and vulgar mode of human thinking, namely, the earth seems to stand still and to be immobile, and the sun seems to rotate around it. And hence Scripture serves us by speaking in the vulgar and common manner; for from our point of view it does seem that the earth stands firmly in the center and that the sun revolves around it, rather than the contrary. (cited in Blackwell, 1991, p. 95)

Galileo's growing commitment to the Copernican position led him to adopt an approach to biblical interpretation similar to Foscarini's.

The real issue was how to interpret the Bible. Galileo's critics argued that some biblical passages contradicted him. For example, they argued, Joshua 10: 12–13 spoke of the sun standing still at Joshua's command. Did not that prove beyond reasonable doubt that it was the sun which moved around the earth? In his *Letter to the Grand Countess Christina*, Galileo countered with an argument that this was simply a common way of speaking. Joshua could not be expected to know the intricacies of celestial mechanics, and therefore used an "accommodated" way of speaking.

The official condemnation of this viewpoint was based on two considerations. In the first place, Scripture is to be interpreted according "to the proper meaning of the words." The accommodated approach adopted by Foscarini is thus rejected in favor of a more literal approach. As we have stressed, both methods of interpretation were accepted as legitimate, and had a long history of use within Christian theology. The debate centered on the question of which was appropriate to the passages in question.

Second, the Bible is to be interpreted "according to the common interpretation and understanding of the Holy Fathers and of learned theologians." In other words, it was being argued that nobody of any significance had adopted Foscarini's interpretation in the past; it was therefore to be dismissed as an innovation. It followed that the views of both Foscarini and Galileo were to be rejected as innovations, without any precedent in Christian thought.

This second point is of major importance, and needs to be examined more carefully, in that it is to be set against the long-standing and bitter debate between Protestantism and Roman Catholicism, fuelled during the seventeenth century by the Thirty Years War (1618–48), over whether the former was an innovation or a recovery of authentic Christianity. The idea of the unchangeability of the catholic tradition became an integral element of Roman Catholic polemic against Protestantism. As Jacques-Bénigne Bossuet (1627–1704), one of the most formidable apologists for Roman Catholicism, put this point in 1688:

The teaching of the church is always the same ... The gospel is never different from what it was before. Hence, if at any time someone says that the faith includes something which yesterday was not said to be of the faith, it is always heterodoxy, which is any doctrine different from orthodoxy. There is no difficulty about recognizing false doctrine; there is no argument about it. It is recognized at once, whenever it appears, simply because it is new. (cited in Chadwick, 1957, p. 20)

These same arguments were widely used at the opening of the century, and are clearly reflected and embodied in the official critique of Foscarini. The interpretation which he offered had never been offered before – and it was, for that reason alone, wrong.

It will therefore be clear that this critical debate over the interpretation of the Bible must be set against a complex background. The highly charged and politicized atmosphere at the time seriously prejudiced theological debate, for fear that the concession of any new approach might be seen as an indirect concession of the Protestant claim to legitimacy. To allow that Roman Catholic teaching on any matter of significance had "changed" was potentially to open the floodgates which would inevitably lead to demands for recognition of the orthodoxy of central Protestant teachings – teachings that the Roman Catholic church had been able to reject as "innovations" up to this point.

It was thus inevitable that Galileo's views would meet with resistance. The key factor was that of theological innovation: to concede Galileo's interpretation of certain biblical passages would seriously undermine the Catholic criticisms of Protestantism, which involved the assertion that Protestantism introduced new (and therefore erroneous) interpretations of certain biblical passages. Sadly, it was only a matter of time before Galileo's views would be rejected. From this brief analysis, it will be clear that the Galileo controversy was set against a complex polemical background, involving tensions between Protestant and Catholic over the interpretation of Scripture, and the doctrinal heritage of the past. Galileo had the misfortune to get caught up in the crossfire and undercurrents of this debate.

In this chapter, we have considered the importance of the growing realization that the earth did not stand at the center of the universe for scientific and religious thought. In the following chapter, we shall consider the scientific and religious aspects of the growing realization that the known universe could be regarded as a vast, complex, and regular piece of machinery. We therefore turn to consider the achievement of Isaac Newton, and the emergence of the mechanical worldview.

## For Further Reading

Biagioli, Mario. *Galileo, Courtier: The Practice of Science in the Culture of Absolutism*. Chicago: University of Chicago Press, 1993.

Blackwell, Richard J. *Galileo, Bellarmine, and the Bible*. Notre Dame, IN: University of Notre Dame Press, 1991.

Brooke, John Hedley. "Matters of Fact and Faith: The Galileo Affair." *Journal of the History of Astronomy,* 27 (1996): 68–74.

Finocchiaro, Maurice A. *Retrying Galileo, 1633–1992*. Berkeley, CA: University of California Press, 2005.

Moss, Jean Dietz. *Novelties in the Heavens: Rhetoric and Science in the Copernican Controversy*. Chicago: University of Chicago Press, 1993.

# 4

# Debate 2

## *Newton, the Mechanical Universe, and Deism*

Scholars routinely speak of the "scientific revolution" which swept through western Europe during the seventeenth century. It is difficult to say precisely when this revolution began. Some would argue that its origins lie in the work of Copernicus and Galileo, which we looked at in the previous chapter. Others would argue that it began much earlier, having its roots in trends in late medieval universities, or the new attitudes of the Renaissance.

Others suggest that a fundamental philosophical change lay behind the scientific revolution. The work of Francis Bacon (1561–1626) argued that knowledge began with experience of the world. The proper starting point of scientific knowledge is observation of phenomena, which is followed by the attempt to derive general principles to explain those observations. Despite these difficulties of definition, there is virtually universal agreement that Sir Isaac Newton (1642–1727) played a pivotal role in the scientific revolution. In this chapter, we shall consider some of his achievements, and their religious implications.

As we saw in the previous chapter, the emergence of the heliocentric model of the solar system had clarified issues of geometry; issues of mechanics, however, remained unresolved. Kepler had established that the square of the periodic time of a planet is directly proportional to the cube of its mean distance from the sun. But what was the basis of this law? What deeper significance did it possess? Could the motion of the earth, moon, and planets all be accounted for on the basis of a single principle? Part of the genius of Isaac Newton lay in his demonstration that a single principle could be seen as lying behind what was known about "celestial mechanics." Such was the force of Newton's demonstration of the mechanics of the solar system that the poet Alexander Pope (1688–1744) was moved to write the following lines as Newton's epitaph:

> Nature and Nature's Law lay hid in Night
> God said, *Let Newton be!*, and all was Light.

Newton is often presented as a noble monument to rationality and cosmic order, a beacon of scientific orthodoxy in the midst of a still superstitious society. In fact, the reality is somewhat more complicated. Papers which remained undiscovered until the twentieth century offer a more complex picture of Newton as someone of almost pathological loneliness, who came close to madness, was obsessed with alchemy, and was fascinated by theological heresies. Newton may well have ushered in the modern world through his discoveries, but he belonged to the world that has now been left behind. Yet despite these many foibles, Newton remains one of the most significant

**Figure 4.1** Isaac Newton. Portrait by Sir Godfrey Kneller (Petworth House, West Sussex, UK/The Bridgeman Art Library)

figures in the history of science in general, and its relation to religion in particular.

The most helpful way to understand Newton's demonstration of the laws of planetary motion is to think of him establishing a series of principles which govern the behavior of objects on earth, and subsequently extrapolating these same principles to the motion of the planets. For example, consider the famous story of Newton noticing an apple falling to the earth. The same force which attracted the apple to the earth could, in Newton's view, operate between the sun and the planets. The gravitational attraction between the earth and an apple is precisely the same force which operates between the sun and a planet, or the earth and the moon.

Newton initially concentrated his attention on uncovering the laws which governed motion. His three laws of motion established the general principles relating to terrestrial motion. The critical development lay in his assumption that these same laws could be applied to celestial as much as to terrestrial mechanics. Newton began work on his planetary theory as early as 1666. Taking his laws of motion as his starting point, he addressed Kepler's three laws of planetary motion. It was a relatively simple matter to demonstrate that Kepler's second law could be understood if there exists a force between the planet and the sun, directed towards the sun. The first law could be explained if it was assumed that the force between the planet and sun was inversely proportional to the square of the distance between them. This force could be determined mathematically, on the basis of what would later be termed "the Law of Universal Gravitation," which can be stated as follows: any two material bodies, *P* and *P′*, with masses *m* and *m′*, attract each other with a force *F*, given by the formula

$$F = Gmm'/d^2$$

where *d* is their distance apart, and *G* is the constant of gravitation. It should be noted that Newton did not need to determine the precise value of *G* to explain Kepler's laws.

Newton applied the laws of motion to the orbit of the moon around the earth. On the basis of the assumption that the force which attracted an apple to fall to the earth also held the moon in its orbit around the earth, and that this force was inversely proportional to the square of the distance between the moon and the earth, Newton was able to calculate the period of the moon's orbit. It proved to be incorrect by a factor of roughly 10 percent. Yet this error arose through an inaccurate estimate of the distance between the earth and the moon. Newton had simply used the prevailing estimate of this distance; on using a value which was more accurate, determined by the French astronomer Jean Picard in 1672, theory and observation proved to be in agreement.

Newton's theories were grounded on the basic concepts of mass, space, and time. Each of these concepts can be measured, and are capable of being handled mathematically. Although Newton's emphasis on mass has now been replaced by an interest in momentum (the product of mass and velocity), these basic themes continue to be of major significance in classical physics. On the basis of his three fundamental concepts, he was able to develop precise ideas of acceleration, force, momentum, and velocity.

It is not our intention to provide a full historical analysis of precisely how and when Newton arrived at his conclusions, nor to set them out in detail. The important point to appreciate is that Newton was able to demonstrate that a vast range of observational data could be explained on the basis of a set of universal principles. Newton's successes in explaining terrestrial and celestial mechanics led to the rapid development of the idea that nature and the universe could be thought of as a great machine, operating according to fixed laws. This is often referred to as a "mechanistic worldview."

The religious implications of this will be clear. The idea of the world as a machine immediately suggested the idea of *design*. Newton himself was supportive of this interpretation. Although later writers tended to suggest that the mechanism in question was totally self-contained and self-sustaining – and therefore did not require the existence of a God – this view was not widely held in the 1690s. Perhaps the most famous application of Newton's approach is found in the writings of William Paley (1743–1805), who compared the complexity of the natural world with the design of a watch. Both implied design and purpose, and so pointed to a creator. Newton's work was thus initially seen as a splendid confirmation of the existence of God.

Newton's emphasis upon the regularity of the world was one of the reasons behind a significant development in the ways in which God was pictured and understood. Traditionally, Christian theology and iconography drew on biblical images of God, such as a king or shepherd. The Scientific Revolution led to a new image of God capturing the imagination of many during the seventeenth century – namely, God as a clockmaker. One clock in particular was singled out as a worthy analogue of the celestial machine – the great cathedral clock of Strasbourg. This clock, rebuilt in 1574, displayed information about the time, the location of the planets, the phases of the moon, and other astronomical information. These were displayed using a series of dials and other visual effects.

Yet it was not long before the estrangement of celestial mechanics and religion began to set in. Celestial mechanics seemed to many to suggest that the world was a self-sustaining mechanism which had no need for divine governance or sustenance for its day-to-day operation. The image of God as a "clockmaker" (and the associated natural theology which appealed to the regularity of the world) came to be seen as leading to a purely naturalist understanding of the universe, in which God had no continuing role to play. The scene was set for the rise of the important religious movement generally known as "Deism."

Newton's emphasis on the regularity of nature is seen by most scholars as one of the factors which encouraged the rise of Deism. The term "Deism" (from the Latin *deus*, "god") refers to a view of God which maintains God's creatorship, but denies a continuing divine involvement with, or special presence within, that creation. It is thus often contrasted with "theism" (from the Greek *theos*, "god"), which allows for continuing divine involvement within the world. The term "Deism" is generally used to refer to the views of a group of English thinkers during the "Age of Reason," in the late seventeenth century and early eighteenth centuries. In his influential study *The Principal Deistic Writers* (1757), John Leland grouped together a number of writers – including Lord Herbert of Cherbury, Thomas Hobbes, and David Hume – under the broad and newly coined term "Deist." Whether these writers would have approved of this designation is questionable. Close examination of their religious views shows that they have relatively little in common, apart from a general skepticism about several traditional Christian ideas, such as the necessity of divine revelation. The Newtonian worldview offered Deists a highly sophisticated way of defending and developing their views, by allowing them to focus on the wisdom of God in creating the world.

Deism can be regarded as a weaker form of Christianity which placed particular emphasis on the regularity of the world. It rapidly gained a sophisticated following in late seventeenth-century England, especially at a time when traditional Christianity was seen as intellectually weak. Deism can be seen as a culturally adapted form of

Christianity, which reduced the Christian faith to a reaffirmation of God as creator of the world, and the basis of human morality.

John Locke's *Essay Concerning Human Understanding* (1690) developed an idea of God which became characteristic of much later Deism. Locke argued that "reason leads us to the knowledge of this certain and evident truth, that there is an eternal, most powerful and most knowing Being" (Book 3, chapter X, §6). The attributes of this being are those which human reason recognizes as appropriate for God. Having considered which moral and rational qualities are suited to the deity, Locke argues that "we enlarge every one of these with our idea of infinity, and so, putting them together, make our complex idea of God" (Book 2, chapter 23, §33). In other words, the idea of God is made up of human rational and moral qualities, projected to infinity.

Its critics, however, saw Deism as having reduced God to a mere clockmaker. God wound the world up, like a clock, and then left it to run, unattended. Newton, it must be noted, never suggested that God was unable to intervene in the workings of the universe. He merely noted that there was no reason to suggest that he did. Having established a regular universe, governed by fixed laws, there was no need for special divine action to keep it going.

We see here how the rise of the mechanical worldview (a scientific development) has religious implications. The Newtonian model of the universe seemed to resonate with a particular way of thinking about God. More importantly, it suggested that this God could be known and studied without the need for any specifically religious beliefs, or the study of religious texts, such as the Bible. A religion of nature could be developed, appealing from the regularity of the mechanism of the universe to the wisdom of its constructor.

This line of argument can be found in Matthew Tindal's *Christianity as Old as Creation* (1730), which argued that Christianity was nothing other than the "republication of the religion of nature." God is understood as the extension of accepted human ideas of justice, rationality, and wisdom. This universal religion is available at all times and in every place, whereas traditional Christianity rested upon the idea of a divine revelation which was not accessible to those who lived before Christ. Tindal's views were propagated before the modern discipline of the sociology of knowledge created skepticism of the idea of "universal reason," and are an excellent model of the rationalism characteristic of the movement, and which later became influential within the Enlightenment.

The ideas of English Deism percolated through to the continent of Europe through translations (especially in Germany), and through the writings of individuals familiar with and sympathetic to them, such as Voltaire in his *Philosophical Letters*. Enlightenment rationalism is often considered to be the final flowering of the bud of English Deism. For our purposes, however, it is especially important to note the obvious consonance between Deism and the Newtonian worldview. As we noted earlier, Deism owed its growing intellectual acceptance in part to the successes of the Newtonian mechanical view of the world.

If God was being excluded from the mechanics of the world, there were many who suggested that divine design and activity was still to be found in the biological realm. Did not this show evidence of design? One of the most influential writers to suggest that this was the case was John Ray (1627–1705). In his *Wisdom of God Manifested in the Works of Creation* (1691), Ray argued that the beauty and regularity of the created order, including plants and animals, pointed to the wisdom of their creator. Ray, it must be emphasized, worked with a static view of creation. He understood the phrase "Works of Creation" to mean "the Works created by God at first, and by Him conserv'd to this Day in the same State and Condition in which they were at first made."

The most famous appeal to God as the designer and maker of the natural world, especially its biological aspects, was due to William Paley, Archdeacon of Carlisle, who compared God to one of the mechanical geniuses of the Industrial Revolution. God had directly created the world in all its intricacy. Paley accepted the viewpoint of his age – namely, that God had constructed (Paley prefers the word "contrived") the world in its finished form, as we now know it. The idea of any kind of development seemed impossible to him. Did a watchmaker leave his work unfinished? Certainly not!

Paley argued that the present organization of the world, both physical and biological, could be seen as a compelling witness to the wisdom of a creator god. Paley's *Natural Theology; or Evidences of the Existence and Attributes of the Deity, Collected from the Appearances of Nature* (1802) had a profound influence on popular English religious thought in the first half of the nineteenth century, and is known to have been read by Darwin. Paley was deeply impressed by Newton's discovery of the regularity of nature, which allowed the universe to be thought of as a complex mechanism, operating according to regular and understandable principles. Nature consists of a series of biological structures which are to be thought of as being "contrived" – that is, constructed with a clear purpose in mind.

Paley used his famous analogy of the watch on a heath to emphasize that contrivance necessarily presupposed a designer and constructor: "Every indication of contrivance, every manifestation of design, which existed in the watch, exists in the works of nature" (*Natural Theology*, chapter 1). Indeed, Paley argues, the difference is that nature shows an even greater degree of contrivance than the watch. Paley is at his best when he deals with the description of mechanical systems within nature, such as the immensely complex structure of the human eye and heart. Yet Paley's argument (like John Ray's before him) depended on a static worldview, and simply could not cope with the dynamic worldview underlying Darwinism.

It is at this point that we need to turn to consider the nineteenth-century Darwinian controversy, which opened up a new area of scientific debate, with important implications for some traditional religious beliefs.

## For Further Reading

Byrne, Peter A. *Natural Religion and the Nature of Religion: The Legacy of Deism.* London: Routledge, 1989.

Dijksterhuis, E. J. *The Mechanization of the World Picture: Pythagoras to Newton.* Princeton, NJ: Princeton University Press, 1986.

Force, James E. "The Breakdown of the Newtonian Synthesis of Science and Religion: Hume, Newton and the Royal Society." In R. H. Popkin and J. E. Force (eds), *Essays on the Context, Nature and Influence of Isaac Newton's Theology*, pp. 143–63. Dordrecht: Kluwer Academic Publishers, 1990.

Hall, A. Rupert. *Isaac Newton: Adventurer in Thought.* Cambridge, UK: Cambridge University Press, 1996.

Harrison, Peter. "Natural Theology, Deism, and Early Modern Science." In Arri Eisen and Gary Laderman (eds), *Science, Religion, and Society: An Encyclopedia of History, Culture and Controversy*, pp. 426–33. New York: Sharp, 2006.

# Chapter

# 5

# Debate 3

## *Darwin and the Biological Origins of Humanity*

The publication of Charles Darwin's *Origin of Species* (1859) is rightly regarded as a landmark in nineteenth-century science. On December 27, 1831, HMS *Beagle* set out from the southern English port of Plymouth on a voyage that lasted almost five years. Its mission was to complete a survey of the southern coasts of South America, and afterwards to circumnavigate the globe. The small ship's naturalist was Charles Darwin (1809–82). During the long voyage, Darwin noted some aspects of the plant and animal life of South America, particularly the Galapagos Islands and Tierra del Fuego, which seemed to him to require explanation, yet which were not satisfactorily accounted for by existing theories. The opening words of *Origin of Species* set out the riddle that he was determined to solve:

> When on board H.M.S. Beagle, as naturalist, I was much struck with certain facts in the distribution of the organic beings inhabiting South America, and in the geological relations of the present to the past inhabitants of that continent. These facts, as will be seen in the latter chapters of this volume, seemed to throw some light on the origin of species – that mystery of mysteries, as it has been called by one of our greatest philosophers. (Darwin, 1859, p. 1)

One popular account of the origin of species, widely supported by the religious and academic establishment of the early nineteenth century, held that God had somehow created everything more or less as we now see it. The success of the view owed much to the influence of William Paley, whose approach we considered in chapter 4. God was the divine watchmaker, responsible for the design and construction of such fabulously complex structures as the human eye.

Darwin knew of Paley's views, and initially found them persuasive. However, his observations on the *Beagle* raised some questions. On his return, Darwin set out to develop a more satisfying explanation of his own observations and those of others. Although Darwin appears to have hit on the basic idea of evolution through natural selection by 1842, he was not ready to publish. Such a radical theory would require massive observational evidence to be marshaled in its support.

Four features of the natural world seemed to Darwin to require particularly close attention, in the light of problems and shortcomings with existing explanations.

**Figure 5.1** Charles Darwin (c.1875/Elliott& Fry/ akg-images)

1   The forms of certain living creatures seemed to be adapted to their specific needs. Paley's theory proposed that these creatures were individually designed by God with those needs in mind. Darwin increasingly regarded this as a clumsy explanation.

2   Some species were known to have died out altogether – to have become extinct. This fact had been known before Darwin, and was often explained on the basis of "catastrophe" theories, such as a "universal flood," as suggested by the biblical account of Noah.

3   Darwin's research voyage on the *Beagle* had persuaded him of the uneven geographical distribution of life forms throughout the world. In particular, Darwin was impressed by the peculiarities of island populations.

4   Many creatures possess "rudimentary structures" (sometimes also referred to as "vestigial structures"), which have no apparent or predictable function. Examples of these structures include the nipples of male mammals, the rudiments of a pelvis and hind limbs in snakes, and wings on many flightless birds. How might these be explained on the basis of Paley's theory, which stressed the importance of the individual design of species? Why should God design redundancies?

These aspects of the natural order could all be explained on the basis of Paley's theory. Yet the explanations offered seemed cumbersome and strained. What was originally a relatively neat and elegant theory began to crumble under the weight of accumulated difficulties and tensions. There had to be a better explanation. Darwin offered a wealth of evidence in support of the idea of biological evolution, and proposed a mechanism by which it might work – *natural selection*.

Darwin's radical theory of natural selection can be seen as the culmination of a long process of reflection on the origins of species. Among the studies which prepared the way for Darwin's theory, particular attention should be paid to Charles Lyell's *Principles of Geology* (1830). The prevailing popular understanding of the history of the earth from its creation took the form of a series of catastrophic changes. Lyell argued for what he called "uniformitarianism" (a term coined by the geologist James Hutton in 1795), in which the same forces which can now be observed at work within the natural world are argued to have been active over huge expanses of time in the past. Darwin's theory of evolution works on a related assumption: that forces which lead to the development of new breeds of plants or animals in the present operate over very long periods of time in the past.

The major rival to Darwin's theory was due to the eighteenth-century Swedish naturalist Carl von Linné (1707–78), more generally known by the Latinized form of his name, "Linnaeus." Linnaeus argued for the "fixity of species." In other words, the present range of species which can be observed in the natural world represents the way things have been in the past, and the way they will remain. Linnaeus's detailed classification of species conveyed the impression to many of his readers that nature was fixed from the moment of its origination. This seemed to fit in rather well with a traditional and popular reading of the Genesis creation accounts, and suggested that the botanical world of today more or less corresponded to that established in creation. Each species could be regarded as having been created separately and distinctly by God, and endowed with its fixed characteristics.

The main difficulty here, pointed out by the French naturalist Georges Buffon and others, was that the fossil evidence suggested that certain species had become extinct. In other words, fossils were found which contained the preserved remains of plants (and animals) which now had no known counterpart on the earth. Did not this seem to contradict the assumption of the fixity of species? And if old species died out, might not new ones arise to replace them? Other issues seemed to cause some difficulty for the theory of special creation – for example, the irregular geographical distribution of species.

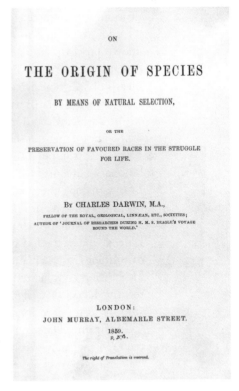

**Figure 5.2** Title page of *The Origin of Species* (© Bettmann/CORBIS)

In his *Origin of Species*, Darwin set out with great care why the idea of "natural selection" should be considered the best mechanism to explain how the evolution of species took place, and how it is to be understood. The key point is that natural selection is proposed as nature's analogue to the process of "artificial selection" in stock-breeding. Darwin was familiar with these issues, especially as they related to the breeding of pigeons. The first chapter of the *Origin of Species* therefore considers "variation under domestication" – that is, the way in which domestic plants and animals are bred by agriculturists. Darwin notes how selective breeding allows farmers to create animals or plants with particularly desirable traits. Variations develop in successive generations through this process of breeding, and these can be exploited to bring about inherited characteristics which are regarded as being of particular value by the breeder. In the second chapter, Darwin introduces the key notions of the "struggle for survival" and "natural selection" to account for what may be observed in both the fossil records and the present natural world.

Darwin then argues that this process of "domestic selection" or "artificial selection" offers a model for a mechanism for what happens in nature. "Variation under domestication" is presented as an analogue of "variation under nature." A process of "natural selection" is argued to occur within the natural order which is analogous to a well-known process, familiar to English stockbreeders and horticulturalists: "As man can produce and certainly has produced a great result by his methodical and unconscious means of selection, what may not nature effect?" (Darwin, 1859, p. 83).

Darwin's theory of natural selection suggested that one could speak of *directionality* within nature, without implying that there was either *progression* or *purpose*. The choice of the phrase "natural selection" proved controversial, as it seemed to some of Darwin's critics that it implied that nature somehow actively or intentionally chose which evolutionary outcomes were to be preferred. This is not what Darwin intended. He was simply making the point that some process similar to "artificial selection" seemed to operate within nature itself. Darwin offered a completely naturalistic mechanism for evolution, which did not depend upon nature actively choosing its own outcomes. Indeed, one of the most significant implications of Darwin's theory is that any notion of teleology or purpose within nature becomes very difficult to sustain. As Thomas H. Huxley commented in an essay in *The Natural History Review* in 1864, after reading Darwin's *Origin of Species*, it was clear that "teleology, as commonly understood, had received its deathblow at Mr Darwin's hands."

In the end, Darwin's theory had many weaknesses and loose ends. For example, it required that new distinct biological species should evolve; yet the evidence for this was conspicuously absent. Darwin himself devoted a large section of *The Origin of Species* to detailing difficulties with his theory, noting in particular the "imperfection of the geological record," which gave little indication of the existence of intermediate species, and the "extreme perfection and complication" of certain individual organs, such as the eye. Nevertheless, he was convinced that these were difficulties which could be tolerated on account of the clear explanatory superiority of his approach. Yet even though Darwin did not believe that he had adequately dealt with all the problems which required resolution, he was confident that his explanation was the best available:

> A crowd of difficulties will have occurred to the reader. Some of them are so grave that to this day I can never reflect on them without being staggered; but, to the best of my judgement, the greater number are only apparent, and those that are real are not, I think, fatal to my theory. (Darwin, 1859, p. 171)

Darwin's theories, as set out in the *Origin of Species* (1859) and the *Descent of Man* (1871), hold that all species – including humanity – result from a long and complex process of biological evolution. The religious implications of this will be clear. Traditional Christian thought regarded humanity as being set apart from the rest of nature, created as the height of God's creation, and alone endowed with the "image of God." Darwin's theory suggested that human nature emerged gradually, over a long period of time, and that no fundamental biological distinction could be drawn between human beings and animals in terms of their origins and development.

So what religious issues were raised by Darwin's theory? It will be evident from the historical account just presented that Darwin's account of the origin of species raises serious problems for a static understanding of the biological order. As we noted in chapter 4, this underlies William Paley's arguments for the existence of God, based on an appeal to the intricacies of the biological realm. Paley's most noted critic in recent years is the Oxford zoologist Richard Dawkins, who argues that Darwin's approach eliminates any notion of God creating or designing the world. Everything can be accounted for, he argues, by the blind forces of natural selection. In his *Blind Watchmaker* (1987), Dawkins relentlessly points out the failings of Paley's viewpoint, and the explanatory superiority of Darwin's approach, especially as it has been modified through the neo-Darwinian synthesis. Dawkins argues that Paley's approach is based on a static view of the world, rendered obsolete by Darwin's theory.

Dawkins himself is eloquent and generous in his account of Paley's achievement, noting with appreciation his "beautiful and reverent descriptions of the dissected machinery of life." Without in any way belittling the wonder of the biological "watches" that so fascinated and impressed Paley, Dawkins argued that his case for God – though made with "passionate sincerity" and "informed by the best biological scholarship of his day" – is "gloriously and utterly wrong." The "only watchmaker in nature is the blind forces of physics" (Dawkins, 1986, p. 5). For Dawkins, Paley is typical of his age; his ideas are entirely understandable, given his historical location prior to Darwin. But nobody, Dawkins argues, could share these ideas now. Paley is obsolete.

This, then, is perhaps one of the most obvious religious issues raised by the rise of Darwinism – the undermining of an argument for the existence of God which had played a major role in British religious thought, both popular and academic, for more than a century. Of course, the argument could easily be restated in more appropriate forms – a development which took place during the second half of the nineteenth century, when many Christian writers stressed that evolution could be seen as the means by which God providentially directed what was now understood as an extended process, rather than a single event.

A further religious issue concerned the interpretation of the Bible. Many of the controversies concerning science and religion have focused on the issue of biblical interpretation. The Copernican controversy, for example, raised the question of whether the Bible actively promoted a geocentric view of the universe, or whether it had simply been interpreted in this way for sufficiently long for this impression to have become widespread. A similar issue emerged with the debate concerning Darwinism.

It is of importance to note that Darwinism became of special concern to Christians in cultures which had been particularly influenced by literal readings of the book of Genesis. Such readings are known to have been widespread within popular Protestantism in Britain and the United States in the first half of the nineteenth century, even though more nuanced interpretative schemes had been proposed by Protestant academics in both countries. Despite these more sophisticated interpretations of the Genesis creation accounts, at the popular level it was widely assumed that the "common sense" reading of the Bible led to a six-day understanding of the creation of the world and humanity. Darwinism posed a significant challenge, both to this specific reading of the book of Genesis, as well as to existing models of biblical interpretation in general. Were the six days of the Genesis creation account to be taken literally, as periods of 24 hours? Or as indefinite periods of time? And was it legitimate to suggest that vast periods of time might separate the events of that narrative? Or was the Genesis creation account to be interpreted as a historically and culturally conditioned narrative, reflecting ancient Babylonian myths, which could not be taken as a scientific account of the origins of life in general, and humanity in particular? The debates are many, and continue to this day.

A third point at which Darwin's theories raise difficulties for traditional Christian theology concerned the status of humanity. For most Christians, humanity was the height of God's creation, distinguished from the remainder of the created order by being created in the image of God. On this traditional reading of things, humanity is to be located within the created order as a whole, yet stands above it on account of its unique relationship to God. Yet Darwin's *Origin of Species* posed an implicit, and *The Descent of Man* an explicit, challenge to this view. Humanity had emerged, over a vast period of time, from within the natural order.

If there was one aspect of his own theory of evolution which left Charles Darwin feeling unsettled, it was its implications for the status and identity of the human race. In every edition of the *Origin of Species*, Darwin consistently stated that his proposed mechanism of natural selection did not entail any fixed or universal law of progressive development. Furthermore, he explicitly rejected Lamarck's theory that evolution demonstrated an "innate and inevitable tendency towards perfection." The inevitable conclusion must therefore be that human beings (now understood to be participants within, rather than merely observers of, the evolutionary process) cannot in any sense be said to be either the "goal" or the "apex" of evolution.

This was not an easy idea for Darwin, or for his age, to accept. The conclusion to the *Descent of Man* speaks of humanity in exalted terms, while nevertheless insisting upon its "lowly" biological origins:

> Man may be excused for feeling some pride at having risen, though not through his own exertions, to the very summit of the organic scale; and the fact of his having thus risen, instead of having been aboriginally placed there, may give him hope for a still higher destiny in the distant future. But we are not here concerned with hopes or fears, only with the truth as far as our reason permits us to discover it; and I have given the evidence to the best of my ability. We must, however, acknowledge, as it seems to me, that man with all his noble qualities ... still bears in his bodily frame the indelible stamp of his lowly origin. (Darwin, 1871, p. 405)

Most Darwinists would insist that it is a corollary of an evolutionary worldview that we must recognize that we are animals, part of the evolutionary process. Darwinism thus critiques the absolutist assumptions concerning the place of humanity within nature that lies behind "speciesism" – a somewhat cumbersome term introduced by Richard Ryder, and given wider currency by the Australian ethicist Peter Singer (born 1946), currently Ira W. DeCamp Professor of Bioethics at Princeton University. This has raised considerable difficulties beyond the realm of traditional religion, in that many political and ethical theories are predicated on the assumption of the privileged status of humanity within nature, whether this is justified on religious or secular grounds.

So how have Christians responded to the challenges of Darwin's theory of natural selection? During the century and a half since the publication of Darwin's *Origin of Species*, at least four categories of response have emerged, which will be considered below.

1  Young Earth Creationism. This position represents the continuation of the "common reading" of Genesis, which was widely encountered in popular and at least some academic writing before 1800. On this view, the earth was created in its basic form between 6,000 and 10,000 years ago. Young earth creationists

generally read the first two chapters of the book of Genesis in a way that allows for no living creatures of any kind before Eden, and no death before the Fall. Most young earth creationists hold that all living things were created simultaneously, within the timeframe proposed by the Genesis creation accounts, with the Hebrew word *yom* ("day") meaning a period of 24 hours. The fossil records, which point to a much greater timescale and to the existence of extinct species, are often understood to date from the time of Noah's flood. This viewpoint is often, but not universally, stated in forms of a 144-hour creation and a universal flood. Perhaps the most noted young earth creationist was Henry Madison Morris (1918–2006), the founder of the Institute for Creation Research, which has played an important advocational role in resisting evolutionary thought in American churches and schools.

2  Old Earth Creationism. This view has a long history, and is probably the majority viewpoint within conservative Protestant circles. It has no particular difficulty with the vast age of the world, and argues that the "young earth" approach requires modification in at least two respects. First, that the Hebrew word *yom* may need to be interpreted as an "indefinite time participle" (not unlike the English word "while"), signifying an indeterminate period of time which is given specificity by its context. In other words, the word "day" in the Genesis creation accounts is to be interpreted as a long period of time, not a specific period of 24 hours. Second, that there may be a large gap between Genesis 1.1 and Genesis 1.2. In other words, the narrative is not understood to be continuous, but to make way for the intervention of a substantial period of time between the primordial act of creation of the universe, and the emergence of life on earth. This viewpoint is advocated by the famous *Schofield Reference Bible*, first published in 1909, although the ideas can be traced back to writers such as the earlier nineteenth-century Scottish divine Thomas Chalmers (1780–1847).

3  Intelligent Design. This movement, which has gained considerable influence in the United States in recent years, argues that the biosphere is possessed of an "irreducible complexity" which makes it impossible to explain its origins and development in any method other than positing intelligent design. Intelligent design does not deny biological evolution; its most fundamental criticism of Darwinism is teleological – that evolution has no goal. The Intelligent Design movement argues that standard Darwinism runs into significant explanatory difficulties, which can only be adequately resolved through the intentional creation of individual species. Its critics argue that these difficulties are overstated, or that they will in due course be resolved by future theoretical advances. Although the movement avoids direct identification of God with this intelligent designer (presumably for political reasons), it is clear that this assumption is intrinsic to its working methods.

The movement is particularly associated with Michael Behe (born 1952), author of *Darwin's Black Box*, and William A. Dembski (born 1960), author of *Intelligent Design: The Bridge Between Science and Theology*. Both Dembski and Behe are fellows of the Discovery Institute, based in Seattle.

4   Evolutionary Theism. A final approach argues that evolution is to be understood as God's chosen method of bringing life into existence from inorganic materials, and creating complexity within life. Whereas Darwinism gives a significant place to random events in the evolutionary process, evolutionary theism sees the process as divinely directed. Some evolutionary theists propose that each level of complexity is to be explained on the basis of "God working within the system," perhaps at the quantum level. Others, such as Howard van Till (born 1938), adopt a "fully gifted creation" perspective, arguing that God built in the potential for the emergence and complexity of life in the initial act of creation, so that further acts of divine intervention are not required. Van Till argues that the character of divine creative action is not best expressed in terms of "reference to occasional interventions in which a new form is imposed on raw materials that are incapable of attaining that form with their own capabilities," bur rather by reference to "God's giving being to a creation fully equipped with the creaturely capabilities to organize and/ or transform itself into a diversity of physical structures and life-forms" (van Till, 1999, p. 175). Variations on such approaches are found elsewhere, as in the writings of Arthur Peacocke (1924–2006).

These terms are, of course, open to criticism. Writers such as the philosopher of biology Francisco Ayala (born 1934), for example, have pointed out that "creationism" and "intelligent design" can be interpreted in thoroughly mainline ways, open to biological evolution. Others have pointed out that the term "evolutionary theism" might be taken to suggest that its adherents do not believe in the divine creation of all things. In fact, evolutionary theism holds that creation is to be understood both as event and process, rather than as a simple event in the past.

## For Further Reading

Brooke, John Hedley. *Science and Religion: Some Historical Perspectives*. Cambridge, UK: Cambridge University Press, 1991.

Dawkins, Richard. *The Blind Watchmaker: Why the Evidence of Evolution Reveals a Universe Without Design*. New York: W. W. Norton, 1986.

Dennett, Daniel C. *Darwin's Dangerous Idea: Evolution and the Meaning of Life*. New York: Simon & Schuster, 1995.

Moore, James R. *The Post-Darwinian Controversies: A Study of the Protestant Struggle to Come to Terms with Darwin in Great Britain and America, 1870-1900.* Cambridge, UK: Cambridge University Press, 1979.

Roberts, Jon H. *Darwinism and the Divine in America : Protestant Intellectuals and Organic Evolution, 1859-1900.* Madison, WI: University of Wisconsin Press, 1988.

# II

# Science and Religion
*General Themes*

In the first part of this work, we considered three major debates of considerable importance to the dialogue between science and religion. Each of them opened up questions of significance for this dialogue – for example, the key role played by biblical interpretation, particularly in the Copernican and Darwinian debates. In the second part of this work, we shall consider some further general themes of importance for an informed interaction between science and religion. For example, what are we to make of the widespread belief that science proves its beliefs, whereas religion merely asserts them, often in very dogmatic ways? What do the two mean when they speak of "explanation"? And how do they make use of models or analogies in the process of representing and experiencing the real world?

In what follows, we shall consider a series of 12 general themes of interest to the dialogue between science and religion. Each is introduced, and illustrated with reference to helpful and illuminating debates or discussions which it is hoped will help readers gain a better understand of the field. Detailed discussion of more specific fields of scientific research – for example, cosmology, or evolutionary psychology – follows in the third major part of this work.

# Chapter

# 6   Models of Interaction Between Science and Religion

How are we to understand the complex relationship between science and religion? It is not an easy matter to analyze. There are considerable variations between the different natural sciences in terms of their methods and approaches. The term "religion" is notoriously difficult to define, and there are considerable differences between and within individual religions. Any attempt to generalize about the relationship between science and religion is therefore bound to encounter serious difficulties. Nevertheless, the effort is generally regarded as worthwhile. Are they enemies, strangers, friends, or partners?

One of the most influential categorizations of approaches to the relation of science and religion is due to Ian Barbour (born 1923), regarded by many as the pioneer of studies in science and religion. Barbour's typology of "ways of relating science and religion" first appeared in 1988, and remains the most widely used typology in the field. Barbour lists four broad types of relations: conflict, independence, dialogue, and integration. To begin with, we shall set out and illustrate Barbour's fourfold scheme, before noting some questions that might be raised concerning it.

## Conflict

Historically, the most significant understanding of the relation between science and religion is that of "conflict," or perhaps even "warfare." This strongly confrontational model continues to be deeply influential at the popular level, even if its appeal has diminished considerably at a more scholarly level. "The war between science and theology in colonial America has existed primarily in the cliché-bound minds of historians" (Numbers, 1985, p. 64). This influential model was expounded in two influential works published in the later part of the nineteenth century – John William Draper's *History of the Conflict Between Religion and Science* (1874) and Andrew Dickson White's *History of the Warfare of Science with Theology in Christendom* (1896). Today, the best-known representative of this approach is Richard Dawkins, who argued in a speech to the American Humanist Association that "faith is one of the world's great evils, comparable to the smallpox virus but harder to eradicate." Science and religion are implacably opposed. Science represents reason, and religion superstition.

Yet this model is not restricted to antireligious scientists. It is widespread within conservative religious groups within Christianity and Islam, who are often virulently hostile to the idea of biological evolution. The creationist Henry M. Morris (1918–2006) published a sustained critique of modern evolutionary theory with the title *The Long War Against God* (1989). In an appreciative foreword to the book, a conservative Baptist pastor declares that "modern evolutionism is simply the continuation of Satan's long war against God." Morris even invites us to imagine Satan imagining the idea of evolution as a means of dethroning God.

Yet many of the historical episodes that are traditionally placed in this category, or held to represent its manifestation, can be interpreted in other ways. The Galileo controversy, for example, is still presented as a classic example of "science against religion," even though it is now seen as much more complex and nuanced. Similarly, Darwin's theory of evolution is often presented as antireligious, even though Darwin himself was adamant that it was not. Indeed, in 1889 the Anglican theologian Aubrey Moore remarked that "Darwinism appeared, and, under the disguise of a foe, did the work of a friend." The issue of whether science and religion are in conflict all too often seems to rest on complex issues of interpretation.

# Independence

The Darwinian controversy caused many to distrust the "warfare" or "conflict" model. In the first place, it was seen to be historically questionable. Yet in the second, there was growing concern to prevent any alleged "conflict" from damaging either science or religion. This led many to insist that the two fields had to be regarded as completely independent of each other. This approach insists that science and religion are to be seen as independent, autonomous fields of study or spheres of reality, each with its own distinct rules and language. Science has little to say about religious beliefs, and religion has little to say about scientific study.

This approach is found in the 1981 policy statement of the National Academy of Science, which declared that "religion and science are separate and mutually exclusive realms of human thought whose presentation in the same context leads to misunderstanding of both scientific theory and religious belief." It is also found in Stephen Jay Gould's model of "nonoverlapping magisteria" (NOMA), which can be seen as based on the affirmation of mutual respect and the recognition of differing methodologies and domains of interpretation between science and religion:

> I believe, with all my heart, in a respectful, even loving concordat between our magisteria – the NOMA solution. NOMA represents a principled position on moral and intellectual grounds, not a mere diplomatic stance. NOMA also cuts both ways. If religion can no longer dictate the nature of factual conclusions properly under the magisterium of science, then scientists cannot claim higher insight into moral truth from any superior knowledge of the world's empirical constitution. This mutual humility has important practical consequences in a world of such diverse passions. (Gould, 2001, pp. 9–10)

A variant of this approach is provided by the American theologian Langdon Gilkey (1919–2004). In his 1959 work *Maker of Heaven and Earth*, Gilkey argues that theology and the natural sciences represent independent and different ways of approaching reality. The natural sciences are concerned with asking "how" questions, where theology asks "why" questions. The former deals with secondary causes (that is, interactions within the sphere of nature), while the latter deals with primary causes (that is, the ultimate origin and purpose of nature).

This independence model appeals to many scientists and theologians because it gives them freedom to believe and think what they like in their own respective fields ("magisteria," to use Gould's phrase), without forcing them to relate these magisteria. However, as Ian Barbour points out, this inevitably compartmentalizes reality. "We do not experience life as neatly divided into separate compartments; we experience it in wholeness and interconnectedness before we develop particular disciplines to study different aspects of it" (Barbour, 1990, p. 16). In other words, the circles overlap and interlock; they are not completely separate.

## Dialogue

A third way of understanding the relation between science and religion is to see them as engaged in a dialogue, leading to enhanced mutual understanding. As the late Pope John Paul II commented in 1998, "the church and the scientific community will

**Figure 6.1** John Paul II (AP/PA Photos)

inevitably interact; their options do not include isolation." So what form might their interaction take? How might they complement each other? For John Paul II, the answer was clear: "Science can purify religion from error and superstition; religion can purify science from idolatry and false absolutes. Each can draw the other into a wider world, a world in which both can flourish."

This point was further developed by the "Dialogue Group" of scientists and Catholic bishops in the United States, who declared that "science and religion can offer complementary insights on complex topics like the emerging bio-technologies." We see here a recognition that the moral limitations placed on the natural sciences by virtue of the amoral character of the scientific method leads to a realization of the need to supplement the scientific discussion from other sources.

This dialogue respects the distinct identity of its participants, while exploring shared presuppositions and assumptions. Ian Barbour regards this model as the most satisfactory of the possible range of approaches. It is also found throughout the recent writings of John Polkinghorne, who points out a series of significant parallels between the two magisteria. For example, both science and religion involve at least some degree of personal judgment, in that both deal with data that is "theory laden." Similarly, both involve a series of what might be termed "fiduciary" assumptions – for example, that the universe is rational, coherent, ordered, and whole. A similar concern underlies Alister E. McGrath's *Scientific Theology* (2001–3), which aims to enhance the intellectual rigor of Christian theology through an extended dialogue with the natural sciences, especially in relation to issues of methods of investigating and representing reality.

## Integration

A fourth understanding of the way in which science and religion interact can be found in the writings of the Cambridge theologian Charles Raven (1885–1964). In his *Natural Religion and Christian Theology* (1953), Raven argued that the same basic methods had to be used in every aspect of the human search for knowledge, whether religious or scientific: "The main process is the same, whether we are investigating the structure of an atom or a problem in animal evolution, a period of history or the religious experience of a saint" (Raven, 1953, vol. 2, p. 10). Raven vigorously resists any attempt to divide the universe into "spiritual" and "physical" components, and insists that we must "tell a single tale which shall treat the whole universe as one and indivisible" (vol. 2, p. 10). Barbour himself is very sympathetic to this approach, and sees process thought as a catalyst to this process of integration. A similar outlook is found in the later writings of Arthur Peacocke, who interprets evolution as God's manner of creation.

It is important to note that Barbour tends to present these four options as stages in an intellectual journey of discovery, perhaps analogous to John Bunyan's classic *The Pilgrim's Progress*. The intellectual wayfarer might begin with Conflict, followed by a brief and unsatisfactory flirtation with Independence, and finally finding a satisfactory resting place in Dialogue or (preferably) some form of Integration. Both the Conflict and Independence models are *wrong*, Barbour argues, whereas the Dialogue and Integration approaches are *right*. Inevitably, those who are interested in trying to find a reliable and unbiased account of the possibilities will find Barbour slightly unsettling at this point.

So what difficulties are raised by this simple taxonomy? The most obvious is that it is inadequate to do justice to the complexity of history. As Geoffrey Cantor and Chris Kenny point out, history bears witness to a series of "complications that cannot be incorporated in simplistic taxonomies" (2001, p. 774). It is difficult to refute this point. Barbour's fourfold scheme is useful precisely because it is so simple. Yet its simplicity can be a weakness, as much as a strength.

More seriously, the model is purely intellectual in its approach, concerning how ideas are held together. What about the social and cultural aspects of the matter, which play such an important role in any attempt to understand how the interaction of science and religion works out in practice, either in the past or the present? There has been a growing trend in recent scholarship to shift the analysis away from a purely intellectual approach to the interaction of science and religion, and consider their symbolic and social dimensions, where the interaction is much more nuanced.

Furthermore, the historical context often needs close examination. Supposed tensions and conflicts between science and religion, such as the Galileo controversy, often turn out to have more to do with papal politics, ecclesiastical power struggles, and personality issues than with any fundamental tensions between faith and science. Historians of science have made it clear that the interaction of science and religion is determined primarily by the specifics of their historical circumstances, and only secondarily by their respective subject matters. There is no universal paradigm for the relation of science and religion, either theoretically or historically. The case of Christian attitudes to evolutionary theory in the late nineteenth century makes this point particularly evident. As the Irish geographer and intellectual historian David Livingstone makes clear in a ground-breaking study of the reception of Darwinism in two very different contexts – Belfast, Northern Ireland and Princeton, New Jersey – local issues and personalities were often of decisive importance in determining the outcome, rather than any fundamental theological or scientific principles.

Nevertheless, despite its limitations, the framework set out by Barbour remains helpful as a means of approaching the field of science and religion studies. It represents a useful description of possible approaches, but should not be pressed too far in terms of a rigorous analysis of the issues. Perhaps it could be thought of as a useful sketch of the terrain, rather than as a detailed and precise map.

We are now ready to begin to consider some specific issues that arise in any attempt to explore the relationship between science and religion. The first question that we shall explore concerns the idea of "explanation." What role does explanation play in science or Christian theology?

## For Further Reading

Barbour, Ian G. *Issues in Science and Religion*. Englewood Cliffs, NJ: Prentice-Hall, 1966.

Cantor, Geoffrey, and Chris Kenny. "Barbour's Fourfold Way: Problems with His Taxonomy of Science-Religion Relationships." *Zygon*, 36 (2001): 765–81.

Evans, John H., and Michael S. Evans. "Religion and Science: Beyond the Epistemological Conflict Narrative." *Annual Review of Sociology*, 34 (2008): 87–105.

Gould, Stephen Jay. "Nonoverlapping Magisteria" *Natural History* 106 (1997): 16–22.

Livingstone, David N. "Darwinism and Calvinism: The Belfast–Princeton Connection." *Isis* 83 (1992): 408–28.

# Chapter

# 7

# Science, Religion, and the Explanation of Things

Human beings long to make sense of things – to identify patterns in the rich fabric of nature, to offer explanations for what happens around them, and to reflect on the meaning of their lives. Both the scientific and religious communities aim to make sense of what is observed. They set out to wrestle with the ambiguities of experience, in order to offer the "best explanations" for what is observed. Both the sciences and religion may therefore be described as offering interpretations of experience. This is not to say that either science or religion may be reduced to such interpretations, but is simply to note that both possess an explanatory dimension. This being the case, a comparison of the way in which the two disciplines deal with making sense of the complexities of experience is of considerable interest to our study.

So what do we mean when we talk about "explanation," whether in science or religion? The important point that needs to be made before proceeding further is that the notions of "knowledge" and "understanding" are not identical. To know that something exists or has happened is not the same as understanding why this is the case. "Knowing that *A* exists" and "understanding why *A* exists" are very different things. This is often expressed in terms of causal explanation. *A* happened, and it caused *B*. For example, the extinction of the dinosaurs is held to be explained by the "K-T event," usually interpreted as an asteroid hitting the earth at the end of the Cretaceous period, 65 million years ago, throwing up a dust layer that encircled the earth and drastically altering climactic conditions. (The unusual term "K-T event" is the generally used abbreviation for the more cumbersome "Cretaceous-Tertiary Mass Extinction event.")

Science offers explanations of what is observed. So how are such "explanations" to be understood? In recent years, three particularly significant discussions of explanation have emerged:

1   Paul Humphreys' model of causal explanation. On this approach, *A* can be considered an explanation of *B* if *A* can be said to cause *B*.
2   Peter Lipton's account of the nature of explanatory loveliness, which sets a causal approach to explanation within the framework of "inference to the best explanation." While not denying the importance of causal explanations, Lipton sees these as a special case within the overall quest for the "best" explanation.
3   The account of explanatory unification offered by Michael Friedman and Paul Kitcher. This holds that *A* may be said to explain *B* if it offers a broader framework of reference which allows *B* to be seen in a new way, which makes sense of its distinct features.

All three of these approaches have merits, although it is now widely believed that the method of "inference to the best explanation" can accommodate them all.

Recent years have seen a growing interest within the philosophy of science in the idea of "inference to the best explanation." This represents a decisive move away from older positivist understandings of the scientific method, still occasionally encountered in popular accounts of the relation of science and religion, which holds that science is able to – and therefore ought to – offer evidentially and inferentially infallible evidence for its theories. This approach, found at many points in the writings of Richard Dawkins, is now realized to be deeply problematic. It is particularly important to note that scientific data are capable of being interpreted in many ways, each of which has evidential support. In contrast, positivism tended to argue that there was a single unambiguous interpretation of the evidence, which any right-minded observer would discover.

Since there are many explanations, the question of how the best such explanation is to be identified becomes of acute importance. An early anticipation of this approach can be found in the American pragmatist philosopher Charles Peirce (1839–1914), son of a noted Harvard astronomer, and himself a scientific practitioner. For Peirce, scientific thinking is characterized by a specific form of "abductive inference," described in a 1903 lecture "On Pragmatism and Abduction" as follows:

> The surprising fact, *C*, is observed;
> But if *A* were true, *C* would be a matter of course.
> Hence, there is reason to suspect that *A* is true.

A related approach is found in Norwood R. Hanson's reflections on the advance of scientific knowledge. Hanson (1924–67), in a 1961 article titled "Is There a Logic of Scientific Discovery," suggested the following three-step process:

1   The observation of some "surprising" or "astonishing phenomena," which represent anomalies within existing ways of thinking. This "astonishment" may arise because the observations are in conflict with existing theoretical accounts.

2   The realization that these phenomena would not seem to be astonishing if a certain hypothesis (or set of hypotheses) *H* pertained. These observations would be expected on the basis of *H*, which would act as an explanation for them.

3   There is therefore good reason for proposing that *H* be considered to be correct.

Like Peirce, Hanson thus identifies astonishing or surprising observations as a fundamental motivation in the enterprise of scientific discovery. Is there a theoretical standpoint from which these observations would not be astonishing, or even merely anomalous, but would be *expected*?

It should therefore come as no surprise that the question of "inference to the best explanation" has come to the fore in recent discussions of the philosophy of science, both in terms of the analysis of past episodes in scientific advance, and of the application of the scientific method in the present. Older models of the scientific method – such as Carl Hempel's deductive-nomological explanation – are increasingly being discarded, or subsumed under the framework of "inference to the best explanation."

The importance of this approach for the natural sciences can be illustrated from a well-known historical example: Charles Darwin's appeal to the novel concept of natural selection as the "best explanation" of an accumulated body of observations concerning natural history. For Darwin, four features of the natural world in particular seemed to require particularly close attention, in the light of problems and shortcomings with existing explanations, especially the idea of "special creation" offered by earlier religious apologists such as William Paley (1743–1805). While this theory offered explanations of these observations, they seemed increasingly cumbersome and forced. A better explanation, Darwin believed, had to lie to hand. None of these were "proofs" of natural selection; nevertheless, they possessed a cumulative force in suggesting it was the best explanation of observation. Although we noted these earlier (pp. 34–5), when considering the Darwinian controversies, it will be helpful to set these observations out once more.

1   Many creatures possess "rudimentary structures," which have no apparent or predictable function – such as the nipples of male mammals, the rudiments of a pelvis and hind limbs in snakes, and wings on many flightless birds. How might these be explained on the basis of Paley's theory, which stressed the importance of the individual design of species? Why should God design redundancies? Darwin's theory accounted for these with ease and elegance.

2   Some species were known to have died out altogether. The phenomenon of extinction had been recognized before Darwin, and was often explained on the basis of

"catastrophe" theories, such as a "universal flood," as suggested by the biblical account of Noah. Darwin's theory offered a neater account of the phenomenon.

3   Darwin's research voyage on the *Beagle* had persuaded him of the uneven geographical distribution of life forms throughout the world. In particular, Darwin was impressed by the peculiarities of island populations, such as the finches of the Galapagos islands. Once more, the doctrine of special creation could account for this, yet in a manner that seemed forced and unpersuasive. Darwin's theory offered a much more plausible account of the emergence of these specific populations.

4   Various forms of certain living creatures seemed to be adapted to their specific needs. Darwin held that these could best be explained by their emergence and selection in response to evolutionary pressures. Paley's theory of special creation proposed that these creatures were individually designed by God with those specific needs in mind.

All these aspects of the natural order could be explained on the basis of William Paley's theory, which we noted earlier. Yet the explanations offered seemed more than a little cumbersome and contrived. What was originally a relatively neat and elegant theory began to crumble under the weight of accumulated difficulties and tensions. There had to be a better explanation, which would account for these observations more satisfactorily than the alternatives which were then available.

Darwin was quite clear that his theory of natural selection was not the only explanation of the biological data which could be adduced. He did, however, believe that it possessed greater explanatory power than its rivals, such as the doctrine of independent acts of special creation. "Light has been thrown on several facts, which on the belief of independent acts of creation are utterly obscure" (Darwin, 1859, p. 203). Darwin's theory had many weaknesses and loose ends. Nevertheless, he was convinced that these were difficulties which could be tolerated on account of the clear explanatory superiority of his approach. Yet even though Darwin did not believe that he had adequately dealt with all the problems which required resolution, he was confident that his explanation was the best available. In the sixth edition of the *Origin of Species*, he responded to some theoretical objections to his approach as follows.

> It can hardly be supposed that a false theory would explain, in so satisfactory a manner as does the theory of natural selection, the several large classes of facts above specified. It has recently been objected that this is an unsafe method of arguing; but it is a method used in judging the common events of life, and has often been used by the greatest natural philosophers. (Darwin, 1872, p. 421)

While recognizing that it lacked rigorous proof, Darwin clearly believed that his theory could be defended on the basis of criteria of acceptance and justification that were

**Figure 7.1** 1890 HMS *Beagle* in the Straits of Magellan (© Bettmann/CORBIS)

already widely used in the natural sciences, and that its explanatory capacity was itself a reliable guide to its truth.

So how do we decide which is the best of these possible explanations of what is observed? What criteria might be appropriate to determine which of these competing abductions is indeed the "best"? For example, is the best explanation the *likeliest* (that is, the one best supported by the scientific data), or the *loveliest* (that is, the one which provides the most understanding of the scientific data)?

This discussion is increasingly being linked to the notion of the "unification of scientific theory." It is now thought that a hallmark of a successful explanation is its ability to bring together a series of phenomena that were once thought to be distinct, but could not be viewed as part of the same explanation. Successful unificationist explanations identify connections or relationships between phenomena that were previously thought to be unrelated. Examples of the unification of explanation are to be found in Descartes's unification of algebra and geometry, Isaac Newton's unification of terrestrial and celestial theories of motion, James Clerk Maxwell's unification of electricity and magnetism, the integration of Darwinian and Mendelian insights in neo-Darwinism, and Einstein's demonstration of the unity of physics. Not all attempts to achieve unification have been successful; to date, for example, the unification of quantum and relativity theory still remains a distant goal.

So how does this relate to explanation in religion? On the basis of the older positivist approach to scientific explanation, there was clearly little common ground between the two communities. However, the growing realization of the centrality of "inference to the best explanation" to the scientific method has opened up new possibilities of understanding. For example, the philosopher of religion Basil Mitchell (born 1917) sets out a widely held consensus within the Christian tradition on this question:

> It would be somewhat perverse to deny that both within a system of religious belief and in the individual's approach to such a system there appear what look like explanations or demands for explanation. The perplexed individual who asks "What is this all for, what does it mean?" is ostensibly looking for some explanation of the "changes and chances of this transitory life." And if he becomes persuaded that all these things have a purpose in the providence of God, then it would seem that he has found an explanation. (Mitchell, 1973, pp. 100–1)

Similarly, Richard Swinburne (born 1934) argues that God is the best explanation for the complex patterns of phenomena that we observe in the natural world. The existence of God, he argues, may be inferred legitimately and securely from what is observed in the world of everyday experience.

Yet the suggestion that religion is concerned with explaining things needs careful exploration. After all, many would point out, religion often seems more concerned with the salvation of souls rather than the explanation of reality. In the case of Christianity, the emphasis of the New Testament is not upon offering some explanatory account of the world, but upon the transformation of human existence through the life, death, and resurrection of Jesus of Nazareth. The gospel is thus about salvation, the transformation of the human situation, rather than an explanation of the natural world.

Alvin Plantinga (born 1932) is one of a number of philosophers of religion who suggest that explanation is not of primary importance for Christianity. Why, he asks, should explanatory potential be seen as of fundamental importance in this matter?

> Suppose theistic belief is explanatorily idle: why should that compromise it, or suggest that it has low epistemic status? If theistic belief is not proposed as an explanatory hypothesis in the first place, why should its being explanatorily idle, if indeed it is, be held against it? (Plantinga, 2000, p. 370)

Similarly, the philosopher of religion D. Z. Phillips (1934–2006) also marginalizes the explanatory aspects of belief in God. Religion does not require explanation, nor does it offer explanations.

Yet while the emphasis of the Christian faith may not fall on explanation, there is little doubt that it has explanatory capacity. The New Testament points to the potential transformation of humanity through faith. While much of this transformation is described using the language of salvation and redemption, it is clearly also understood to extend to the human mind and its encounter with reality. Paul urges his readers not to "be conformed to this world," but rather to "be transformed by the renewing of [their] minds" (Romans 12: 2). This points to the capacity of the Christian faith to bring about a radical change in the way in which we understand and inhabit the world.

This changed way of seeing the world is described by Augustine of Hippo (354–430) as the "healing of the eye of the heart" by divine grace: "Our whole business in this life is to heal the eye of the heart so that God might be seen." While it may be informed and reinforced through the church's ministry of word and sacrament, Augustine insists that this is to be understood, fundamentally and characteristically, as a divine act of grace, accomplishing something that lies beyond the capacity of unaided human nature. In his careful study *Explanation from Physics to Theology*, Philip Clayton (born 1956) brings out the significance of "the meaning dimension" in religion. A number of different levels of explanation may be discerned; nevertheless, a phenomenological approach to the question definitely discloses an explanatory imperative within the religious traditions.

From this discussion, it will be clear that there are important parallels – but not an identity – between religious and scientific notions of explanation. In particular, the notion of "inference to the best explanation," which is now widely regarded as the basic philosophy of the natural sciences, appears to have considerable importance for Christian apologetics. Perhaps for this reason, it is coming to play an increased role in Christian approaches to natural theology – a matter we shall return to in chapter 14.

In the meantime, however, we shall move on to consider another general issue that often arises in any discussion of the relation of science and religious faith. Can the existence of God be *proved*, in the way that the chemical formula for water can be shown to be $H_2O$? We shall consider this important question about faith, proof, and evidence in the following chapter.

## For Further Reading

Clayton, Philip. *Explanation from Physics to Theology: An Essay in Rationality and Religion.* New Haven, CT: Yale University Press, 1989.

Dear, Peter R. *The Intelligibility of Nature: How Science Makes Sense of the World.* Chicago: University of Chicago Press, 2006.

Lipton, Peter. *Inference to the Best Explanation*, 2nd edn. London: Routledge, 2004.

McGrath, Alister E. *A Fine-Tuned Universe: The Quest for God in Science and Theology*. Louisville, KY: Westminster John Knox, 2009.

Prevost, Robert. *Probability and Theistic Explanation*. Oxford: Clarendon Press, 1990.

Swinburne, Richard. *The Existence of God*, 2nd edn. Oxford: Clarendon Press, 2004.

# Chapter

# 8

# Science, Religion, and Proofs for God's Existence

One of the most interesting issues in science and religion concerns the nature of "proofs" of theories – whether the theory in question is Einstein's theory of relativity, or the Christian affirmation of the existence of God. When I first began to study science as a teenager, back in the 1960s, I was encouraged to think that science proved its findings with total conviction. The chemical composition of water, for example, could be proved to be $H_2O$. It is a commonplace for those committed to the outmoded "warfare" model of the relation of science and religion to contrast them at this point. Science and religion are often placed at opposite ends of the scale on the question of evidence. Richard Dawkins, a vigorous (though not especially well-informed) advocate of this approach, argues that science proves things by an appeal to evidence, where religion runs way from the evidence. "Faith," he tells us, "means blind trust, in the absence of evidence, even in the teeth of evidence" (Dawkins, 1989, p. 198).

In chapter 7, we considered the place of explanation in the natural sciences and Christian theology. In the case of the natural sciences, the question is how to make sense of an accumulation of observations of the natural world. What "big picture" makes most sense out of these observations? As we saw in the previous chapter, this usually involves the process of "inference to the best explanation." Yet this is always understood to be a *provisional* assessment – what the noted psychologist William James (1842–1910) called a "working hypothesis," which was open to revision as evidence mounted and reflection proceeded. Today, on the basis of the evidence available to us, we might accept this scientific theory; tomorrow, on the basis of new evidence or revised interpretations of old evidence, we might accept a quite different scientific theory.

As Michael Polanyi (1891–1976), a chemist and noted philosopher of science pointed out, natural scientists find themselves having to believe some things that they know will later be shown to be wrong – but not being sure *which* of their present beliefs would turn out to be erroneous.

Scientific theorizing offers what is believed to be the best account of the experimental observations currently available. Radical theory change takes place either when it is believed that there is a better explanation of what is currently known, or when new information comes to light which forces us to see what is presently known in a new light. Unless we know the future, it is impossible to take an absolute position on the question of whether any given theory is "right." We simply don't know which of today's theories will be discarded as interesting failures by future generations. Yet this does not prevent scientists from committing themselves to a given theory, believing that it is right (while knowing it may prove to be inadequate or wrong in the longer term).

**Figure 8.1** Michael Polanyi

This emphasis on the *provisionality* of scientific theories severely undermines the outdated positivism that often accompanies the "warfare" model of the relation of science and religion. Often, it is not so much a case of "science has proved this to be true" as "most scientists currently believe that this is true (but they might change their minds as and when more evidence accumulates)." This is not in any way a criticism of the natural sciences. It is simply a recognition of how the scientific method works. Historians of science regularly point to a group of theories which were scientific orthodoxy in their age, and are now regarded as clearly incorrect.

To explore the importance of this point, let us ask a question: is Darwin's theory of evolution correct? The best answer to this question would be that Darwin's theory, as modified by his successors, is currently believed to be the best explanation of a vast body of biological data. Yet as more and more data builds up, there is a possibility that what Thomas Kuhn calls a "paradigm shift" may take place. In other words, there may be a radical theory shift away from Darwinism towards some new theory, at present unknown. Richard Dawkins, an enthusiastic advocate of Darwinism, is quite clear about this point:

> Darwin may be triumphant at the end of the twentieth century, but we must acknowledge the possibility that new facts may come to light which will force our successors of the

twenty-first century to abandon Darwinism or modify it beyond recognition. (Dawkins, 2003, p. 81)

So what about religious beliefs, especially those grounded in an interaction with the natural world? The most interesting question here is whether belief in God can be proved, in a way similar to the proof of a scientific theory. It is widely agreed that there are three general categories of arguments for the existence of God which are of particular importance in relation to the natural sciences. These are generally referred to as the cosmological, teleological, and *kalam* arguments, although there is some debate about whether the third is to be regarded as a distinct category or argument in its own right, or a category of the more general cosmological argument. For our purposes, we shall assume that it requires separate discussion as an argument in its own right. As this argument arose within the Islamic community, rather than the Christian philosophical communities of western Europe, I have decided to treat it as a separate approach.

## The Cosmological Argument

During the Middle Ages, Thomas Aquinas (1225–74) set out a suite of reasons for believing in God, often referred to as the "Five Ways." One of these is known as the "argument from motion." It argues that the observation of change or motion in the world points to the existence of a first cause which is responsible for them. There must be a "prime unmoved mover" which causes change in the world. This "first cause" argument is now often referred to as the "cosmological argument." As Aquinas states it, the argument takes the following form.

1   Motion and change are observed within the world.
2   Everything that moves or changes is changed by something else.
3   Since there cannot be an infinite series of causes for a given event, the chain of causality must terminate at a first cause.
4   There can be no doubt that this first cause or "prime unmoved mover" is none other than God.

In more recent times, this argument has been restated in more explicitly cosmological terms (hence the title now widely used to refer to it). The most commonly encountered statement of the argument runs along the following lines:

1   Everything within the universe depends on something else for its existence;
2   What is true of its individual parts is also true of the universe itself;

3  The universe thus depends on something else for its existence for as long as it has existed or will exist;

4  The universe thus depends on God for its existence.

The argument basically assumes that the existence of the universe is something that requires explanation. It will be clear that this type of argument relates directly to modern cosmological research, particularly the "big bang" theory of the origins of the cosmos. This is also true of the *kalam* version of the cosmological argument, to which we now turn.

## The *Kalam* Argument

The argument which is now generally known as the "*kalam*" argument derives its name from an Arabic school of philosophy which flourished in the early Middle Ages. The basic structure of the argument can be set out as four propositions:

1  Everything which has a beginning must have a cause;
2  The universe began to exist;
3  Therefore the beginning of the existence of the universe must have been caused by something;
4  The only such cause can be God.

Although some scholars regard this as a variant of the cosmological argument, already set out above, others regard it as having distinct features, meriting its treatment in its own right.

The structure of the argument is clear, and its implications need little in the way of further development. If the existence of something can be said to have begun, it follows – so it is argued – that it must have a cause. If this type of argument is linked with the idea of a "big bang" (see pp. 151–2), its relevance for our discussion will be clear. Modern cosmology strongly suggests that the universe had a beginning. If the universe began to exist at a certain time, it must have had a cause. And what cause could there be other than God?

This form of the *kalam* argument has been widely debated in recent years. One of its most significant defenders has been William Lane Craig (born 1949), who sets out its main features as follows:

> Since everything that begins to exist has a cause of its existence, and since the universe began to exist, we conclude, therefore, the universe has a cause of its existence …

Transcending the entire universe there exists a cause which has brought the universe into being. (Craig and Smith, 1993, p. 63)

Debate over the argument has centered on three questions, one of which is scientific and the other two of which are philosophical.

1  Can something have a beginning without being caused? In one of his dialogues, the great Scottish empirical philosopher David Hume (1711–76) argued that it is possible to conceive of something that comes into being, without necessarily pointing to some definite cause of that existence. Nevertheless, this suggestion raises considerable difficulties.
2  Can one speak of the universe having a beginning? At one level, this is a profoundly philosophical question. At another, however, it is a scientific question, which can be considered on the basis of known observations concerning the rate of expansion of the universe, and the background radiation evidence for the "big bang."
3  If the universe can be considered to have been "caused," can this cause be directly identified with God? One line of argument of note here takes the following form. A cause must be prior to the event which it causes. To speak of a cause for the beginning of the existence of the universe is thus to speak of something which existed before the universe. And if this is not God, what is it?

It will be clear that the traditional *kalam* argument has been given a new lease of life by the "big bang" theory of the origins of the universe. The philosophical issues which are raised are likely to remain disputed. A similar debate focuses on the question of whether the universe can be said to be "designed," and we shall consider this issue in what follows.

## The Teleological Argument

The "teleological" argument is often known as the "argument from design" and is among the most widely discussed of the philosophical arguments for the existence of God. Thomas Aquinas frames the argument in terms of apparent design within the natural order. Things do not simply exist; they appear to have been designed with some form of purpose in mind. The term "teleological" (meaning "directed towards a goal") is widely used to indicate this apparently goal-directed aspect of nature. This leads Aquinas to conclude that there exists "an intelligent being by whom all natural things are directed to their end" – in other words, God.

**Figure 8.2** William Paley (© National Portrait Gallery, London)

It is this aspect of nature which has often been discussed in relation to the natural sciences. The orderliness of nature – evident, for example, in the laws of nature – seem to be a sign that nature has been "designed" for some purpose. This line of approach was developed with particular skill in William Paley's *Natural Theology; or Evidences of the Existence and Attributes of the Deity, Collected from the Appearances of Nature* (1802). This book had a profound influence on popular English religious thought in the first half of the nineteenth century, and is known to have been read by Charles Darwin. Paley was deeply impressed by Newton's discovery of the regularity of nature, especially in relation to the area usually known as "celestial mechanics." It was clear that the entire universe could be thought of as a complex mechanism, operating according to regular and understandable principles.

For Paley, the Newtonian image of the world as a mechanism immediately suggested the metaphor of a clock or watch, raising the question of who constructed the intricate mechanism which was so evidently displayed in the functioning of the world. One of Paley's most significant arguments is that mechanism implies "contrivance." Writing against the backdrop of the emerging Industrial Revolution, Paley sought to exploit the apologetic potential of the growing interest in machinery – such as "watches, telescopes, stocking-mills, and steam engines" – within England's literate classes.

The general lines of Paley's approach are well-known (see p. 31). In the early nineteenth century, England was experiencing the Industrial Revolution, in which machinery was coming to play an increasingly important role in industry. Paley argues that it is impossible to take seriously any suggestion that such complex mechanical technology came into being by purposeless chance. Mechanism presupposes contrivance – that is to say, a sense of purpose, and an ability to design and fabricate. Both the human body in particular, and the world in general, could be seen as mechanisms which had been designed and constructed in such a manner as to achieve harmony of both means and ends. It must be stressed that Paley is not suggesting that there exists an analogy between human mechanical devices and nature. The force of his argument rests on an identity: nature *is* a mechanism, and hence was intelligently designed.

Paley argues that nature bears witness to a series of biological structures which are "contrived" – that is, constructed with a clear purpose in mind. Paley is at his best when he deals with the description of mechanical systems within nature, such as the immensely complex structure of the human eye, or the heart. So what does this prove? "Every indication of contrivance, every manifestation of design, which existed in the watch, exists in the works of nature." Indeed, Paley argues, the difference is that nature shows an even greater degree of contrivance than the watch.

The "argument from design" was subjected to criticism on a number of grounds by the Scottish philosopher David Hume. The most significant of Hume's main criticisms can be summarized as follows.

1   The direct extrapolation from the observation of design in the world to a God who created that world is not possible. It is one thing to suggest that the observation of design leads to the inference that there is a design-producing being; it is quite another to insist that this being is none other than God. There is thus a logical weak link in the chain of argument.

2   To suggest that there is a designer of the universe could lead to an infinite regression. Who designed the designer? We noted that Aquinas explicitly rejected the idea of an infinite regression of causes; however, he fails to offer a rigorous justification of this point, apparently assuming that his readers will regard his rejection of this series as being self-evidently correct. Hume's point is that this is not the case.

3   The argument from design works by analogy with machines. The argument gains its plausibility by a comparison with something that has clearly been designed and constructed – such as a watch. But is this analogy valid? Why could the universe not be compared to a plant, or some other living organism? Plants are not designed; they just grow. The importance of this point in relation to Paley's argument will be obvious, especially in the light of the Darwinian view that appearances of design arise naturally.

In recent years, new discussions of the rationality of God's existence have begun to emerge, including those based on fine-tuning and anthropic phenomena. A trend of some importance is a move away from deductive approaches to God's existence, towards those based on abduction or inference. Rather than argue that we can deduce the existence of God from causalities within the natural world, many are arguing that God represents the "best explanation" of the natural world. We considered this point in chapter 7. If you are reading this chapter in isolation, you will find it helpful to read this earlier discussion as well, in that it amplifies the material provided in the present chapter.

This leads us on to our next general theme in science and religion studies, which arises directly from our discussion in this chapter: can scientific or religious beliefs be verified? And if not, can they at least be falsified, if they are incorrect?

## For Further Reading

Craig, William Lane. *The Cosmological Argument from Plato to Leibniz*. London: Macmillan, 1980.

Davidson, Herbert. *Proofs for Eternity, Creation and the Existence of God in Medieval Islamic and Jewish Philosophy*. Oxford: Oxford University Press, 1987.

Manson, Neil A. *God and Design: The Teleological Argument and Modern Science*. London: Routledge, 2003.

McGrath, Alister E. *Dawkins' God: Genes, Memes and the Meaning of Life*. Oxford: Blackwell Publishing, 2004.

Swinburne, Richard. *The Existence of God*, 2nd edn. Oxford: Clarendon Press, 2004.

# Chapter

# 9

## Verification and Falsification in Science and Religion

In chapter 8, we looked briefly at the place of evidence in scientific and religious reasoning. This naturally leads into the question of whether and how beliefs can be confirmed. Two particularly significant approaches emerged during the twentieth century: *verificationism*, which held that the natural sciences were capable of stating their ideas in forms capable of being confirmed from experience; and *falsificationism*, which held that they were able to state their ideas in such a way that defective approaches could easily be shown to be false, even if it was rather more difficult to confirm valid theories than verificationists had once thought. The background to this important debate is to be found within the "Vienna Circle," one of the most significant philosophical movements to arise in the twentieth century, which had its origins in the Austrian capital city of Vienna.

The Vienna Circle is generally regarded as the group of philosophers, physicists, mathematicians, sociologists, and economists who gathered around the philosopher Moritz Schlick (1882–1936) during the period 1924–36. One of the core statements of the group was that *beliefs must be justified on the basis of experience*. This belief is grounded in the writings of David Hume, and is clearly empirical in tone. For this reason, the members of the group tended to hold a particularly high estimation of the methods and norms of the natural sciences (which were seen as the most empirical of human disciplines) and a correspondingly low estimation of metaphysics (which was seen as an attempt to disengage with experience). Indeed, one of the more significant achievements of the Vienna Circle was to cause the word "metaphysics" to have strongly negative connotations.

For the Vienna Circle, statements which did not directly connect up with or relate to the real world were of no value, and simply served to perpetuate fruitless conflicts of the past. The terms in statements or propositions had to be directly related to what we experience. Every proposition must therefore be capable of being stated in a manner which relates directly to the real world of experience.

The Vienna Circle developed this approach by making use of the forms of symbolic logic which had begun to appear in the late nineteenth century, and had been used very effectively by the English philosopher and logician Bertrand Russell (1872–1970) in the early twentieth century. The manner in which terms and sentences relate to each other can be clarified by an appropriate use of logic. As Schlick himself pointed out, the rigorous use of such logical principles could prevent absurd lapses in philosophical rigor. Schlick offered the following as elementary examples of such lapses in reasoning which would be eliminated by this logical rigor:

My friend died the day after tomorrow.
The tower is both 100 and 150 meters high.

The overall program which was proposed by the Vienna Circle thus has two basic parts, as follows:

1   All meaningful statements can be reduced to, or are explicitly defined by, statements which contain only observational terms;
2   All such reductive statements must be capable of being stated in logical terms.

The most significant attempt to carry this program through is to be seen in the works of Rudolph Carnap (1891–1970), particularly his 1928 work *The Logical Structure of the World*. In this work, Carnap set out to show how the world could be derived from experience by logical construction. It was, as he put it, an attempt at the "reduction of 'reality' to the 'given'" by using the methods of logic on statements derived from experience. The only two sources of knowledge are thus sense perception and the analytical principles of logic. Statements are derived from and justified with reference to the former, and related to each other and their constituent terms by the latter.

## The Verification Principle

It was clear from a very early stage that mathematical and logical statements were going to be a problem for the Vienna Circle. In what way was the statement "2 + 2 = 4" related to experience? Some argued that this was a meaningless statement; others (perhaps the majority) held that these were to be regarded as "analytic statements," whose truth was established by definition or convention, so that their validation required no empirical evidence.

To meet this challenge, Carnap set out is what is now generally known as the "principle of verification." In its generally accepted form, this states that only statements which are capable of being verified are meaningful. It will therefore be clear that the natural sciences are being given a position of priority in terms of the theory of knowledge, with philosophy being seen as a tool for clarifying what has been established by empirical analysis. Philosophy, according to Carnap, consists "in the logical analysis of the statements and concepts of empirical science" (Carnap in Ayer, 1959, p. 133).

These views were popularized in the English language world by A. J. Ayer (1910–89), especially in his famous book *Language, Truth and Logic* (1936). Although World War II interfered with the process of its reception and evaluation, this single work is widely regarded as setting the philosophical agenda for at least the two decades which followed that war. Its vigorous and radical application of the verification principle eliminated as "meaningless" virtually everything which had tended to be thought of as metaphysical or religious.

Logical positivism is a philosophical approach which takes its lead from the methods of the natural sciences, and therefore has a particularly significant place in this study. It is therefore important to consider its implications for religion. As might be expected from the above analysis, logical positivism has little time for religious statements, which are dismissed as meaningless due to an inability to verify them. Carnap asserted that religious statements were unscientific. Sentences which make statements about "God," "the transcendent," or "the Absolute" are meaningless, in that there is nothing in experience which can verify them. Ayer allowed that religious statements might provide indirect information concerning the state of mind of the person making such a statement. They could not, however, be considered as making meaningful statements concerning the external world.

So how did theologians respond to this challenge? One favored approach was the notion of "eschatological verification," which enjoyed a degree of popularity during the period 1955–65. This can be regarded as a direct response to the issues raised by the demand for verification as a

**Figure 9.1** A. J. Ayer (Topfoto)

condition for meaningfulness. (The term "eschatological" derives from the Greek phrase *ta eschata*, "the last things"). This approach was developed by the British philosopher of religion John Hick (born 1922), who offers an analogy of two people, traveling the same road and having the same experiences. One believes that the road leads to the New Jerusalem; the other does not. So which is right? And how could this issue be settled? Hick's answer rests on the idea of an "end point verification," which is not (and cannot be) accessible in the present.

> During the course of the journey the issue between them is not an experimental one. They do not entertain different expectations about the coming details of the road, but only about its ultimate destination. And yet when they do turn the last corner it will be apparent that one of them has been right all the time and the other wrong. Thus although the issue between them has been experimental, it has nevertheless from the start been a real issue. They have not merely felt differently about the road; for one was feeling appropriately and the other inappropriately in relation to the actual state of affairs. Their opposed interpretations of the road constituted genuinely rival assertions, though assertions whose assertion-status has the peculiar characteristic of being guaranteed retrospectively by a future crux. (Hick, 1964, pp. 260–1)

However, the issue has receded in importance since the 1960s, not least on account of an awareness of the severe limitations placed upon the verification principle proposed by logical positivism. To illustrate some of these difficulties, we may consider the following statement: "There were six geese sitting on the front lawn of Buckingham Palace at 5.15 p.m. on June 18, 1865." This statement is clearly meaningful, in that it asserts something which could have been verified. But we are not in a position to confirm them. A similar difficulty arises in relation to other statements concerning the past. For someone such as Ayer, these statements must be considered to be neither true nor false, in that they do not relate to the external world. Yet this clearly runs contrary to our basic intuition that such statements *do* make meaningful affirmations.

A further issue concerned unobservable theoretical entities, such as subatomic particles, which cannot strictly be "observed." This raised significant difficulties for logical positivism, and led some of its leading advocates to modify their position on the matter. Thus in a 1938 paper entitled "Procedures of Empirical Science," Victor F. Lenzen (1890–1975) argued that certain entities had to be *inferred* from experimental observation, even thought they could not themselves be observed. For example, the behavior of oil droplets in an electric field leads one to infer the existence of electrons as negatively charged particles of a certain mass. They cannot be seen (and hence cannot be "verified") – yet their existence is a reasonable inference from the observational evidence. This represented a very significant dilution of the original verification principle. What is of especial significance here is that this dilution is partly due to theoretical developments within the natural sciences, so highly esteemed by logical positivism.

Verificationism, then, has serious limits. It is therefore instructive to note a rival which developed in response to some of the perceived difficulties with the approach. This rival approach is generally known as "falsificationism," and will be considered in the following section.

## Falsification: Karl Popper

One of the most significant individual contributions to the philosophy of science during the twentieth century was due to the Austrian philosopher Karl Popper (1902–94). For Popper, the advance of scientific knowledge was to be thought of as an evolutionary process, in which a number of competing conjectures, or tentative theories, are systematically subjected to the most rigorous attempts at falsification possible. This process of error elimination, he suggested, was analogous to the process of natural selection in evolutionary biology. For Popper, scientific knowledge advances through the interplay between tentative theories (conjectures) and error elimination (refutation).

Popper felt that the verification principle associated with the Vienna Circle was too rigid, and ended up excluding many valid scientific statements.

> My criticism of the verifiability criterion has always been this: against the intention of its defenders, it did not exclude obvious metaphysical statements; but it did exclude the most important and interesting of all scientific statements, that is to say, the scientific theories, the universal laws of nature. (Popper, 1963, p. 281)

But he was also convinced that verificationism was misguided for another reason. It ended up by allowing a number of "pseudo-sciences" such as Freudianism and Marxism to pass themselves off as being "scientific" when they were, in reality, nothing of the sort.

Although Popper's original concerns appears to have been the elimination of metaphysics from "meaningful" statements, his attention appears to have shifted to a critique of what he termed "pseudo-sciences" soon afterwards.

**Figure 9.2** Karl Popper (UPP/ Topfoto)

For Popper, pseudo-scientists such as Marxists and Freudians were capable of interpreting virtually anything as supportive of their theories:

> What I found so striking about these theories, and so dangerous, was the claim that they were "verified" or "confirmed" by an incessant stream of observational evidence. And indeed, once your eyes were opened, you could see verifying instances everywhere. A Marxist could not look at a newspaper without finding verifying evidence of the class struggle on every page … A psycho-analyst, whether Freudian or Adlerian, assuredly would tell you that he finds his theories daily, even hourly, verified by his clinical observations … It was precisely this fact – that they always fitted, that they were always "verified" – which impressed their adherents. It began to dawn on me that this apparent strength was in fact a weakness, and that all these "verifications" were too cheap to count as arguments. (Popper, 1983, pp. 163–3)

At some point around 1920, Popper recalls reading a popular scientific account of Einstein's theory of relativity. What impressed him was Einstein's precise statement of what would be required to demonstrate that his theory was incorrect. Einstein declared that "if the red shift of the spectral lines due to the gravitational potential should not exist, then the general theory of relativity will be untenable."

For Popper, this represented a totally different attitude and outlook from that he associated with Marxists and Freudians. Those committed to these ideologies simply looked for evidence which could confirm their ideas. In marked contrast, Einstein was looking for something which might *falsify* his theory! If such evidence was found, he would abandon his theory.

In practice, this turned out to be something of an overstatement. What would happen if the predicted redshift was too small to be observed by the technology then available? Or if it was obscured by interference from another effect? In the case of light emitted from the sun, general relativity predicted that there should be a gravitational redshift due to the reduction of the velocity of light by a very small amount – 2.12 parts in a million. No such redshift was, in fact, observed at the time – a fact which weighed heavily in the deliberations of the Nobel Prize committees in 1917 and 1919. Yet it is now known that the techniques available in the 1920s simply were not good enough to allow the predicted effect to be observed; it was not until the 1960s that final confirmation was forthcoming. By the criterion which Einstein himself had set out, his own theory could not be confirmed.

Yet Popper felt that the principle at stake was important. Theories had to be tested against experience, which would lead to their being verified or falsified.

> I shall certainly admit a system as empirical or scientific only if it is capable of being *tested* by experience. These considerations suggest that not the *verifiability* but the

*falsifiability* of a system is to be taken as the criterion of demarcation … It must be possible for an empirical scientific system to be refuted by experience. (Popper, 1961, pp. 40–1)

From this discussion, it will be clear that Popper has accepted some of the most fundamental themes of logical positivism, above all the foundational role of experience of the real world. A theoretical system must be capable of being tested against observation of the world. But where logical positivism stressed the need for stating the conditions under which a theoretical statement could be verified, Popper held that the emphasis must fall upon being able to state the conditions under which the system could be falsified.

Popper's approach had considerable influence within the philosophy of religion during the 1950s and 1960s, and is especially linked with what has come to be known as the "falsification" debate. In his 1950 paper "Theology and Falsification," the philosopher Anthony Flew (born 1923) argued that religious statements cannot be regarded as meaningful, in that nothing drawn from experience can be regarded as falsifying them. In effect, Flew is following Popper's criticisms of Marxism and Freudianism, which he held to be capable of interpreting observational or experiential evidence in whatever manner they pleased.

Flew sets out his concerns by way of what he calls a parable. Two explorers come across a clearing in the jungle. One of the explorers states his belief that there is an invisible gardener who looks after the clearing. The second explorer denies this, and suggests that they try to confirm this by means of various sensory tests – such as watching for the gardener to visit the clearing, and using bloodhounds and electric fences to detect his presence. None of the tests detects the gardener. The second explorer argues that this demonstrates that there is no gardener. The first, however, meets all these objections with qualifications. "But there is a gardener," he argues, "… who has no scent and makes no sound" (Flew, 1955, p. 96).

In the end, Flew argues that the idea of the gardener meets the "death by a thousand qualifications" (1955, p. 97). The gardener cannot be seen, heard, smelled, or touched. So might one not be forgiven for concluding that there really is no gardener? That, certainly, was Flew's conclusion. It rested upon the fact that religious statements cannot be formulated in a manner in which they can be falsified.

However, the demand for falsification – like the earlier demand for verification – proves to be much more complex than might at first have been thought. For example, Flew's absolute demands cannot be met by the natural sciences, which introduce precisely the modifications or "qualifications" to which Flew objects so strongly in the process of theory development. In reality, anomalous data is generally accommodated within theories by a subtle and complex process of adjustment, modification, and qualification.

Popper's particular concern lay with eliminating metaphysics from science, and he thought that he had found a way of excluding metaphysical statements by demanding that they be falsifiable. Yet Popper's attempt to set up a meaningful falsification criterion turns out to be rather more difficult than he had hoped. An excellent example is provided by what is known as the "tacking paradox." Let us define *T* as a falsifiable theory – for example, "All swans are white." Since *T* is falsifiable, there must be an observation statement *O* which follows from it. On the basis of the example we have given, such an observation statement might take the form "All swans are observed to be white." If we find that this observation does not correspond to the way things really are, then it follows that *T* itself is false.

So far, so good. But the "tacking paradox" now makes this simple scheme rather more complicated. Stated in its simplest form, the paradox involves the "tacking on" of an additional metaphysical statement *M* – for example, "Zeus is hungry" or "The Absolute is blue." Now define theory *T'* as follows:

$$T' = T \& M$$

In other words, the new theory is an amalgam of the original and a new metaphysical statement. Since *T* is falsifiable, it also follows that *T'* is falsifiable, in that the observation of a black swan would show the theory to be false.

Suppose that we have a theory which consists of two parts:

1  All swans are white;
2  The Absolute is blue.

If a black swan were to be observed, the theory which consists of both of these parts would be shown to be incorrect, in that one of its parts would be incorrect. The "tacking paradox" refers to the disconcerting fact that any arbitrary metaphysical hypothesis can be incorporated into a falsifiable theory – which seriously weakens the appeal of Popper's approach. The fact that a totally arbitrary (and, one assumes, unverifiable and unfalsifiable) metaphysical statement has been tacked on makes no difference at this point.

The issues considered in this chapter make it clear that it is much more difficult to confirm a scientific theory or a religious belief than might be expected. An observed anomaly may turn out to be the critical observation that destroys a theory. Or it might turn out to be something that can be accommodated by an expansion of the theory. Sadly, the philosophy of science cannot itself determine which of these possibilities is right. As will be clear from the discussion of theoretical anomalies in chapter 7, only a simplistic positivist philosophy of science holds that an anomaly forces the abandonment of a promising theory.

Our discussion of general issues which arise in any interaction between science and religion has thus far centered on questions about the manner and extent of confirmation of beliefs. We now need to move on to another topic of importance, which concerns what scientific and religious beliefs involve. Are these inventions of the human mind, or are they shaped by an external reality? In the following chapter, we shall explore the place of realism in science and religion, as well as consider some of its alternatives.

## For Further Reading

Ayer, A. J. *Probability & Evidence*. New York: Columbia University Press, 2006.

Baker, Gordon P. *Wittgenstein, Frege, and the Vienna Circle*. Oxford: Blackwell, 1988.

Davis, Stephen T. "Theology, Verification and Falsification." *International Journal for Philosophy of Religion*, 6 (1975): 23–39.

Plantinga, Alvin. *God and Other Minds*. Ithaca, NY: Cornell University Press, 1967, pp. 156–68.

Misak, C. J. *Verificationism: Its History and Prospects*. London: Routledge, 1995.

Sarkar, Sahotra. *The Emergence of Logical Empiricism: From 1900 to the Vienna Circle*. New York: Garland Publishing, 1996.

# Chapter

# 10 Realism and its Alternatives in Science and Religion

The dialogue between science and religion often proceeds on the assumption that there is a shared commitment to an external world, which the human mind is able to discern and represent, to some limited yet significant effect. The term "realism" is generally used to refer to a group of philosophies which affirm that an external reality exists, and that the human mind is able to copy or represent this. So why has realism been so influential in the natural sciences? The best way of approaching this question is to ask: what are the philosophical implications of the explanatory successes of the natural sciences? And what, if any, are the implications for theological statements? We shall be exploring these questions throughout this chapter.

The remarkable explanatory and predictive successes of the natural sciences are widely held to point to the actual existence of the independent reality of what they describe. Airplanes fly, and they fly, at least in part, on account of the relation between pressure and kinetic energy first set out by Daniel Bernoulli in 1738. Television and radio work, at least partly on account of the predictions made by James Clerk Maxwell's theory of electromagnetic radiation, first set out in 1864. A long list of technological developments, widely regarded as essential to modern western existence, can be argued to rest upon the ability of the natural sciences to develop theories which may initially explain the world, but subsequently allow us to transform it.

So what is the best explanation for the success of the natural sciences in this respect? For many, the best explanation of this success is the belief that what scientific theories describe really is present in the world. As the physicist and theologian John Polkinghorne (born 1930) comments:

The naturally convincing explanation of the success of science is that it is gaining a tightening grasp of an actual reality. The true goal of scientific endeavor is understanding the structure of the physical world, an understanding which is never complete but ever capable of further improvement. The terms of that understanding are dictated by the way things are. (Polkinghorne, 1986, p. 22)

The simplest explanation of what makes theories work is that they relate to the way things really are. If the theoretical claims of the natural sciences were not correct, their massive empirical success would appear to be totally coincidental. "If scientific realism, and the theories it draws on, were not correct, there would be no explanation of why the observed world is as if they were correct; that fact would be brute, if not miraculous" (Devitt, 1984, p. 108).

For reasons such as these, natural scientists tend to be realists, at least in the broad sense of that term. It seems to many that the success of the natural sciences show that they have somehow managed to uncover the way things really are, or to lock into something which is fundamental to the structure of the universe. The importance of this point is considerable, not least in that it raises the question of whether theologians wishing to argue for the independent existence of God (rather than as a construct of the human mind) may learn anything from the forms of realism associated with the natural sciences. This present chapter aims to explore this issue, beginning with an examination of the nature of realism itself, before moving on to consider its alternatives.

## Realism

The term "realism" denotes a family of philosophical positions which take the general view that a real world exists, external to the human mind, which the human mind can encounter, understand, and represent, if only in part. The credibility of realism arises directly from the successes of the experimental method, which discloses patterns of observational behavior that seem to be best accounted for on the basis of a realist point of view. As the philosopher of science Michael Redhead notes:

Physicists, in their unreflective and intuitive attitude to their work, the way they talk and think among themselves, tend to be realists about the entities they deal with, and while being tentative as to what they say about these entities and their exact properties and interrelations, they generally feel that what they are trying to do, and to some degree successfully, is to get a "handle on reality." (Redhead, 1995, p. 9)

Scientific realism is thus, at least in part, an *empirical* thesis. Its plausibility and confirmation arise from direct engagement with the real world, through repeated observation and experiment. It should not be thought of primarily as a metaphysical claim about how the world is, or ought to be. Rather, it is a focused and limited claim which attempts to explain why it is that certain scientific methods have worked out so well in practice.

Realism, as the philosopher Hilary Putnam (born 1926) and others have argued, is the only explanation of scientific theories and concepts which does not "make the success of science a miracle" (Putnam, 1975, p. 73). Unless the theoretical entities employed by scientific theories actually existed and the theories themselves were at least approximately true of the world at large, the evident success of science (in terms of its applications and predictions) would surely be a miracle. The argument for realism based upon scientific success can be set out like this:

1   The successes of the natural sciences are far greater than can be accounted for by chance or miracles;
2   The best explanation of this success is that scientific theories offer true, or approximately true, accounts of reality;
3   Scientific realism is justified by its successes.

Realism, as noted earlier, refers to a family of philosophies. One form of realism which has received especial attention in the dialogue between science and religion is generally known as "critical realism." A distinction is often drawn between a "naïve realism" which holds that reality impacts directly upon the human mind, without any reflection on the part of the human knower, and a "critical realism," which recognizes that the human mind attempts to express and accommodate that reality as best it can with the tools at its disposal – such as mathematical formulae or mental models. Both of these can be contrasted with various forms of nonrealism or antirealism, which holds that the human mind freely constructs its ideas without any reference to an alleged external world.

The key feature of a "critical realism" is its recognition that the human mind is active in the process of perception. Far from being a passive recipient of knowledge of the external world, it actively constructs this knowledge using "mental maps," often known as *schema*. This point was made by the psychologist of religion William James (1842–1910) in 1878, and has been widely accepted since.

The knower is an actor, and co-efficient of the truth on the one side, whilst on the other he registers the truth which he helps to create. Mental interests, hypotheses, postulates, so far as they are bases for human action – action which to a great extent transforms the world – help to *make* the truth which they declare. (James, 1976, p. 21)

More recently, the New Testament scholar N. T. Wright (born 1948) offers a helpful account of this approach, which he describes as:

> a way of describing the process of "knowing" that acknowledges the *reality of the thing known, as something other than the knower* (hence "realism"), while also fully acknowledging that the only access we have to this reality lies along the spiralling path of *appropriate dialogue or conversation between the knower and the thing known* (hence "critical"). (Wright, 1992, p. 35)

This insight does not pose a challenge to the notion that there exists a world, independent of the observer. It is to acknowledge that the knower is involved in the process of knowing, and that this involvement must somehow be expressed within a realist perspective on the world.

But what of alternatives to realism? The two most significant are often regarded as idealism and instrumentalism, both of which we shall now consider.

## Idealism

Idealism is an approach to our knowledge of the world which concedes that physical objects exist in the world, but argues that we can have knowledge only of *how things appear to us*, or are experienced by us, not things as they are in themselves. The most familiar version of this approach is that associated with the great German idealist philosopher Immanuel Kant (1724–1804), who argues that we have to deal with appearances or representations, rather than things in themselves. Kant thus draws a distinction between the world of observation (the "phenomena") and "things in themselves," holding that the latter can never be known directly. The idealist will thus hold that we can have knowledge of the manner in which things appear to us through the ordering activity of the human mind. We cannot, however, have knowledge of mind-independent realities.

This view is expressed particularly forcefully in the approach often known as "phenomenalism." This holds that we cannot know extra-mental realities directly, but only through their "appearances" or "representations."

**Figure 10.1** Immanuel Kant. Woodcut by J. L. Raab after a painting by G. Doebler (akg-images)

79

Although this view is relatively uncommon within the natural sciences, it has been defended by a number of significant figures, including the noted physicist Ernst Mach (1838–1916). For Mach, the natural sciences concern what is immediately given by the senses. Science, as Mach said in an 1866 article, concerns only the investigation of the apparent "dependence of phenomena on one another." This led him to take a strongly negative view of the atomic hypothesis, arguing that atoms were merely theoretical constructs which cannot be perceived. Atoms were thus not "real"; they were simply useful fictitious notions which helped observers to understand the relationship between various observed phenomena.

To use the Kantian framework underlying Mach's statements, it is impossible to move from the world of phenomena to the world of "things in themselves." We therefore cannot move beyond the world of experience. Nevertheless, Mach was prepared to allow the use of "auxiliary concepts" which serve as bridges linking one observation with another, provided that it is understood that they have no real existence, and must not be thought of as actual or existing entities. They are thus "products of thought" which "exist only in our imagination and understanding."

The point at issue in Mach's discussion is of considerable importance, and is often discussed in terms of the technical phrases "hypothetical entities," "theoretical terms," or "unobservables." The basic issue is whether something has to be *seen* before it can be held to exist. Mach, who argued that the natural sciences were concerned only with reporting experimental observations, held that science was not committed to defending the real and independent existence of "unobserved" or "theoretical" entities which those observations might suggest – such as atoms.

**Figure 10.2** Bas von Fraassen

A similar approach is adopted by the more recent philosopher of science Bas van Fraassen. He draws a distinction between a realist, who holds that science aims to give a literally true description of what the world is like, and what he calls a "constructive empiricist," who argues that acceptance of a theory does not involve commitment to the *truth* of that theory, but to the belief that it adequately preserves the phenomena to which it relates:

> To be an empiricist is to withhold belief in anything that goes beyond the actual, observable phenomena, and to recognize no objective modality in nature. To develop an empiricist account of science is to depict it as involving a search for truth only about the empirical world, about what is actual and observable … it must invoke throughout a

resolute rejection of the demand for an explanation of the regularities in the observable course of nature, by means of truths concerning a reality beyond what is actual and observable, as a demand which plays no role in the scientific enterprise. (van Fraassen, 1980, pp. 202–3)

To speak of "laws of nature" or theoretical entities such as electrons is to introduce an unwarranted and unnecessary metaphysical element into scientific discourse.

## Instrumentalism

Instrumentalism holds that scientific concepts and theories are merely useful instruments whose worth is measured not by whether the concepts and theories are true or false, or how correctly they depict reality, but by how effective they are in explaining and predicting phenomena. They are not true descriptions of an unobservable reality, but merely useful ways of organizing observations. A scientific theory is best understood as a rule, principle, or calculating device for deriving predictions from sets of observational data.

The distinguishing features of instrumentalism can be studied from Ernest Nagel's comments on the kinetic model of gases. This model proposes that the molecules of a gas can be thought of as analogous to inelastic spherical objects, such as billiard balls. Nagel argues that this approach is nothing more than a useful instrument for making sense of observations.

> The theory that a gas is a system of rapidly moving molecules is not a description of anything that has been or can be observed. The theory is rather a rule which prescribes a way of symbolically representing, for certain purposes, such matters as the observable pressure and temperature of a gas; and the theory shows among other things how, when certain empirical data about a gas are supplied and incorporated into that representation, we can calculate the quantity of heat required for raising the temperature of the gas by some designated number of degrees (i.e., we can calculate the specific heat of the gas.) (Nagel, 1979, p. 129)

Scientific concepts, while being clearly grounded in observations of the natural world, are thus not to be identified with, or reduced to, those observations. Similarly, the English philosopher Stephen Toulmin (born 1922) argues that, instead of speaking about the "existence" or "reality" of such entities as electrons, scientists should recognize that such language is not used to refer to a real entity. The issue has to do with how observations are organized, with a view to stimulating further research.

Yet historically, most instrumentalist understandings of science have often transmuted into realist understandings with the passing of time. The Copernican (and subsequently Keplerian) theory of the solar system is a case in point. Initially, many scientists and nonscientists interpreted the Copernican heliocentric theory instrumentally as a calculating device, believing that there were too many obstacles to viewing it realistically. The German theologian Andreas Osiander (1498–1552), in his famous preface to Copernicus's *On the Revolution of Heavenly Bodies* (1543), suggested that this theory was a fruitful hypothesis which was useful for astronomical calculations, but did not necessarily correspond to the way things were.

> It is the duty of an astronomer to establish the history of the celestial movements through careful and skilful observation, and then to conceive and devise causes of these motions or hypotheses about them. Now since he cannot in any way attain to the true causes, these assumed hypotheses enable those movements to be calculated correctly from the principles of geometry, both for the future and the past. The present author has performed both these duties excellently. For these hypotheses need not be true nor even probable. It is sufficient if they only provide a calculus consistent with these observations.

Yet with growing observational evidence for the heliocentric model of the solar system, an instrumentalist approach subtly changed into its realist counterpart. With the development of Galilean and Newtonian physics and the new observational data that became available through the invention of the telescope, the heliocentric theory began to be interpreted realistically, rather than instrumentally. It was not merely a convenient way of thinking about the solar system, or a convention that enabled certain useful mathematic calculations to be performed. This was the way things were. The solar system really was heliocentric.

## Theology and Realism

So what is the relevance of these debates for theology? Perhaps the most important point to note is that each of these positions in the philosophy of science has its theological counterpart. Nonrealism is well represented by the radical Anglican philosopher of religion Don Cupitt (born 1934), who argues (on his website www. doncupitt.com/realism/aboutnonrealism.html) that we must "abandon ideas of objective and eternal truth, and instead see all truth as a human improvisation." Instead of responding to reality, we create whatever we choose to regard as real. Reality is something which we construct, not something to which we respond. "We constructed all the world-views, we made all the theories … They depend on us, not we on them" (Cupitt, 1985, p. 9).

On the whole, however, theologians who have engaged with the natural sciences tend to be persuaded of the merits of realist approaches to theology. For example,

Thomas F. Torrance (1913–2007) develops a rigorous form of theological realism, insisting that theology gives an account of the reality of things: "Theology and every scientific inquiry operate with the correlation of the intelligible and the intelligent" (Torrance, 1985, p. xii). Ian Barbour (born 1923), Arthur Peacocke (1924–2006), and John Polkinghorne all adopt forms of critical realism, ultimately based on William James's emphasis on the active role of the knower in the process of knowing. Alister McGrath (born 1953) develops a somewhat different form of critical realism, drawing on the insights of Roy Bhaskar concerning the stratification of reality. All intellectual disciplines or sciences are under an intrinsic obligation to give an account of reality according to its distinct nature (*kata physin*).

From this discussion, it will be clear that there is much further exploration to be done on the nature of realism itself, and its potential value for theological discussion. Unfortunately, we cannot consider this here. We must now move on to consider a more theological theme that is often discussed in assessing the relationship between science and religion – the idea of "creation."

## For Further Reading

Alston, William P. "Realism and the Christian Faith." *International Journal for Philosophy of Religion*, 38 (1995): 37–60.

McGrath, Alister E. *A Scientific Theology: 2 – Reality*. London: Continuum, 2002.

Polkinghorne, John. *Reason and Reality*. London: SPCK, 1991.

Torrance, Thomas F. *Reality and Evangelical Theology: The Realism of Christian Revelation*, 2nd edn. Downers Grove, IL: InterVarsity Press, 1999.

Wright, Crispin. *Realism, Meaning and Truth*, 2nd edn. Oxford: Blackwell, 1993.

# 11 The Doctrine of Creation and the Natural Sciences

The idea that the world is created is of fundamental importance to many religions, especially Christianity and Judaism. It is important to draw a distinction between "creation" and "creationism," as these two are often confused, especially in popular debate and media presentations. A belief in creation is found in all major religions. Within Christianity, this can be stated in terms of a general belief that God brings everything into being and sustains it. The British writer John Polkinghorne, for example, in a 2008 article in *The Times*, explains creation as a belief "that the mind and the purpose of a divine Creator lie behind the fruitful history and remarkable order of the universe which science explores." It is thus an ontological, not a chronological, doctrine – in other words, it is concerned with affirming the ultimate dependence of everything upon God, not with providing a detailed account of the mechanisms and timeframes of the origins and development of the universe.

The widespread use of the term "creationism" in a disparaging sense, referring to those who deny any form of biological evolution, has created some difficulties for the legitimate theological concept of creation. The important point is that the term "creation" is open to multiple interpretations, some of which embrace and others of which exclude biological evolution. The movement which is widely known as "creationism" adds specific *timescales* and *processes* to a general belief in creation, often insisting that these are given primary importance, where most Christians regard them as secondary to the more general belief that all things ultimately owe their origins to God. Young Earth Creationism, for example, argues that a general belief in creation must be supplemented by an additional specific belief that creation occurred by

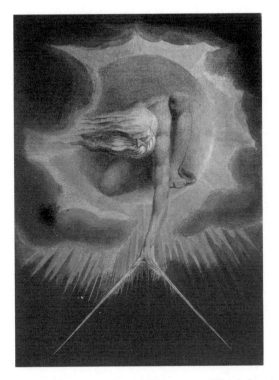

**Figure 11.1** William Blake's "Ancient of Days" (akg-images/ Erich Lessing)

specific, nonnatural divine events over a period of six "days" roughly 6,000 years ago, rather than by God's creative actions through the natural processes of stellar, chemical, and biological evolution.

In chapter 8 we noted the importance of the belief that the world was created in relation to arguments for the existence of God. It is thus clearly of some interest to explore something more of the concept of creation, and its potential relevance to our theme. The present chapter will explore the idea of creation, which is known to have been of major importance to the development of the natural sciences in western culture.

The idea that the world was created is one of the most widely encountered and basic religious ideas, and finds expression in the various religions of the world. Religions of the ancient Near East often take the form of a conflict between a creator deity and the forces of chaos. The dominant form of the doctrine of creation is that associated with Judaism, Christianity, and Islam. In what follows, I shall set out the basic features of this doctrine from a Christian perspective, and explore its implications for the theme of science and religion.

The theme of "God as creator" is of major importance within the Old Testament. Perhaps one of the most significant affirmations which the Old Testament makes is that *nature is not divine*. The Genesis creation account stresses that God created the moon, sun, and stars. The significance of this point is too easily overlooked. Each of these celestial entities was worshiped as divine in the ancient world. By asserting that they were created by God, the Old Testament is insisting that they are subordinate to God, and have no intrinsic divine nature.

Attention has often focused on the creation narratives found in the first two chapters of the book of Genesis, with which the Old Testament canon opens. However, it must be appreciated that the idea of creation is also deeply embedded in the wisdom and prophetic literature in the Old Testament. For example, Job 38: 1–42: 6 sets out what is unquestionably the most comprehensive understanding of God as creator to be found in the Old Testament, stressing the role of God as creator and sustainer of the world. It is possible to discern two distinct, though related, contexts in which the notion of "God as creator" is encountered: first, in contexts which reflect the praise of God within Israel's worship, both individual and corporate; and secondly, in contexts which stress that the God who created the world is also the God who liberated Israel from bondage, and continues to sustain her in the present.

Of particular interest for our purposes is the Old Testament theme of "creation as ordering," and the manner in which the critically important theme of order is established on, and justified with reference to, cosmological foundations. It has often been pointed out how the Old Testament portrays creation in terms of an engagement with and victory over forces of chaos. This divine establishment of order is generally represented in two different ways:

1 Creation is an imposition of order on a formless chaos. This model is especially associated with the image of a potter working clay into a recognizably ordered structure (e.g., Genesis 2: 7).
2 Creation concerns conflict with a series of chaotic forces, often depicted as a dragon or another monster (variously named Behemoth, Leviathan, Nahar, Rahab, Tannim, or Yam) who must be subdued (e.g., Isaiah 27: 1; 51: 9–10).

It is clear that there are parallels between the Old Testament account of God engaging with the forces of chaos and Ugaritic and Canaanite mythology. Nevertheless, there are significant differences at points of importance, not least in the Old Testament's insistence that the forces of chaos are not to be seen as divine. Creation is not be understood in terms of different gods warring against each other for mastery of a (future) universe, but in terms of God's mastery of chaos and ordering of the world.

# Three Views of God's Creative Activity

So how is the idea of creation to be visualized? Three main ways of conceiving the creative action of God have been influential within Christian circles. We shall note them briefly, and identify their relevance to our theme.

1 *Emanation.* This term was widely used by early Christian writers to clarify the relation between God and the world. It is not an idea that is easily grasped by modern readers, as it has philosophical roots in the Platonic tradition. Creation, it is argued, is analogous to light or heat being radiated from the sun, or from a human source such as a fire. This image of creation (hinted at in the Nicene Creed's phrase "light from light") suggests that the creation of the world can be regarded as an overflowing of the creative energy of God. Just as light derives from the sun and reflects its nature, so the created order derives from God, and expresses the divine nature. There is, on the basis of this model, a *natural* or *organic* connection between God and the creation.

However, the model has weaknesses, of which two may be noted. First, the image of a sun radiating light, or a fire radiating heat, implies an involuntary emanation, rather than a conscious decision to create. The Christian tradition has consistently emphasized that the act of creation rests upon a prior decision on the part of God to create, which this model cannot adequately express. This is related to the second weakness – the impersonal nature of the model in question. The idea of a personal God, expressing a personality both in the very act of creation and the subsequent creation itself, is difficult to convey by this image. Nevertheless, the model clearly articulates a close connection between creator and creation, leading us to expect that something of the identity and nature of the creator is to be found in the creation. Thus the beauty of God would be expected to be reflected in the nature of the creation.

2 *Construction.* Many biblical passages portray God as a master builder, deliberately constructing the world (for example, Psalm 127: 1). The imagery is powerful, conveying the ideas of purpose, planning, and a deliberate intention to create. The image is important, in that it draws attention to both the creator and the creation. In addition to bringing out the skill of the creator, it also allows the beauty and ordering of the resulting creation to be appreciated, both for what it is in itself, and for its testimony to the creativity and care of its creator.

However, the image has a deficiency. It portrays creation as involving preexistent matter. Here, creation is understood as giving shape and form to something which is already there – an idea which causes at least a degree of tension with the doctrine of creation out of nothing. The image of God as a builder would seem to imply the assembly of the world from material which is already to hand, which is clearly deficient. Nevertheless, despite this slight difficulty, it can be seen that the model expresses the insight that the character of the creator is, in some manner, expressed in the natural world, just as that of artists is communicated or embodied in their work. In particular, the notion of ordering – that is, the imparting or imposing of a coherence or structure to the material in question – is clearly affirmed by this model. Whatever else the complex notion of creation may mean within a Christian context, it certainly includes the fundamental theme of ordering – a notion which is especially significant in the creation narratives of the Old Testament.

3    *Artistic expression.* Many Christian writers, from various periods in the history of the church, speak of creation as the "handiwork of God," comparing it to a work of art which is beautiful in itself, as well as expressing the personality of its creator. This model of creation as the "artistic expression" of God as creator is particularly well expressed in the writings of the eighteenth-century North American theologian Jonathan Edwards.

The image is helpful, in that it supplements a deficiency of both the two models noted above – namely, their impersonal character. The image of God as artist conveys the idea of personal expression in the creation of something beautiful. Once more, the potential weaknesses need to be noted: for example, the model could easily lead to the idea of creation from preexistent matter, as in the case of a sculptor with a statue carved from an already existing block of stone. However, the model offers us at least the possibility of thinking about creation from nothing, as with the author who writes a novel, or the composer who creates a melody and harmony. It also encourages us to seek for the self-expression of God in the creation, and gives added theological credibility to a natural theology.

The overall impact of these approaches to creation has been summarized by the Scottish theologian Thomas F. Torrance (1913–2007), who points out that the doctrine of God's creation of the world "established the reality of the empirical, contingent world, and thus destroyed the age-old Hellenistic and Oriental assumption that the real is reached only by transcending the contingent" (Torrance, 1985, p. 4). Against any idea that the natural order was chaotic, irrational, or inherently evil (three concepts which were often regarded as interlocking), the early Christian tradition affirmed that the natural order possessed a goodness, rationality, and orderedness which derived directly from its creation by God.

## Creation and the Laws of Nature

The theme of "regularity within nature" is widely regarded as an essential theme of the natural sciences. Indeed, the natural sciences are founded on the *perception of explicable regularity to the world.* In other words, there is something about the world – and the nature of the human mind – which allows us to discern patterns within nature, for which explanations may be advanced and evaluated. One of the most significant parallels between the natural sciences and religion is this fundamental conviction that the world is characterized by regularity and intelligibility. This perception of ordering and intelligibility is of immense significance, both at the scientific and religious levels. As the physicist Paul Davies points out, "in Renaissance Europe, the justification for what we today call the scientific approach to inquiry was the belief in a rational God whose created order could be discerned from a careful study of nature" (Davies, 1992, p. 77).

This insight is directly derived from the Christian doctrine of creation, and reflects the deeply religious worldview of the medieval and Renaissance periods, which ensured that even the most "secular" of activities – whether economic, political, or scientific – were saturated with the themes of Christian theology. This foundational assumption of the natural sciences – that God has created an ordered world, whose ordering could be discerned by humanity, which had in turn been created "in the image and likeness of God" – permeates the writings of the period, whether it is implicitly assumed or explicitly stated.

We have already noted how the theme of order is of major importance within the Old Testament, and noted briefly how it was incorporated into subsequent theological reflection. In view of its importance to our theme, we shall consider it in more detail. One of the most sophisticated explorations of the centrality of the concept of ordering for Christian theology and moral reasoning is to be found in Oliver O'Donovan's *Resurrection and Moral Order*. In this important work, O'Donovan argued for a close connection between the theological notions of "creation" and "order":

> We must understand "creation" not merely as the raw material out of which the world as we know it is composed, but as the order and coherence *in* which it is composed. ... To speak of this world as "created" is already to speak of an order. In the first words of the creed, before we have tried to sketch an outline of created order with the phrase "heaven and earth," simply as we say "I believe in God the Creator," we are stating that the world is an ordered totality. By virtue of the fact that there is a Creator, there is also a creation that is ordered to its Creator, a world which exists as his creation and in no other way, so that by its existence it points to God. (O'Donovan, 1986, pp. 31–2)

Three important points emerge from O'Donovan's analysis.

1   The concept of creation affirms ordering and coherence within the world.
2   This ordering or coherence within the world can be regarded as expressing or reflecting the nature of God himself.

3   The creation can thus be seen as pointing to God, in that the exploration of its ordering or coherence leads to an understanding of the one who ordered it in this manner.

O'Donovan rejects the idea, which is especially associated with the Scottish philosopher David Hume, that such "ordering" as can be discerned is, in fact, a creation of the human mind, rather than an objective reality in itself. For Hume, any perception of "ordering" was the creation of an order-loving human mind, and was not itself objectively present in nature. For O'Donovan, it is something that is discerned, not invented.

A Christian understanding of the concept of creation is, as we have seen, closely linked with the concept of ordering. We have already drawn attention to the notion of the explicable regularity of the world, and linked this with the concept of "creation as ordering." As Stephen Hawking, among many others, has pointed out, the existence of God is easily and naturally correlated with the regularity and ordering of the world. As he said in a letter in *American Scientist* in 1985: "It would be completely consistent with all we know to say that there was a Being who was responsible for the laws of physics." The noted theoretical chemist Charles A. Coulson pointed out the importance of religious convictions in explaining the "unprovable assumption that there is an order and constancy in Nature." In what follows, we shall explore the idea of the "laws of nature," a highly significant way of depicting (and interpreting) the order found within the world.

The theme of cosmic order is of major importance within the writings of Isaac Newton, who argued that the regularity and predictability of the world were a direct consequence of its created origins. Pope's celebrated epitaph for Newton, which we noted earlier, captures aspects of this point well:

> Nature and Nature's Law lay hid in Night
> God said, *let Newton be!*, and all was Light.

The universe is not random, but behaves in a regular manner which is capable of observation and explanation. This led to the widespread belief that systems which satisfied Newton's laws of motion behaved in manners which were predetermined, and which could therefore be predicted with considerable accuracy – a view which is often represented at a popular level in terms of the image of a "clockwork universe."

The phrase "law of nature" appears to have begun to be used systematically during the early eighteenth century. It is generally agreed that the phrase reflects the widely held notion, prevalent within both orthodox Christianity and Deism, that the world was ordered by a divine lawgiver, who laid down the manner in which the creation should behave. A "law of nature" was thus held to be more than a description or summary of observable features of the world; it reflected a divine decision that the world was intended to behave in this manner. With the widespread secularization of western culture, this general belief has been eroded, both inside and outside the scientific community. The phrase "laws of nature" remained, nevertheless, although it has acquired something of the status of a dead metaphor. It remains, however, a concept with profound religious implications.

We may begin by attempting to clarify what a 'law of nature' might be. The general consensus on the nature and scope of the "laws of nature" within the scientific community has been set out by Paul Davies (1992: 72–92). In general terms, the laws of nature can be considered to have the following features:

1  They are *universal*. The laws of physics are assumed to be valid at every place and every time. They are held "to apply unfailingly everywhere in the universe and at all epochs of cosmic history."
2  They are *absolute* – that is to say, they do not depend on the nature of the observer (for example, his or her social status, gender, or sexual orientation). The state of a system may change over time, and be related to a series of contingent and circumstantial considerations; the laws, which provide correlation between those states at various moments, do not change with time.
3  They are *eternal*, in that they are held to be grounded in the mathematical structures which are used to represent the physical world. The remarkable correlation between what we shall loosely term "mathematical reality" and the observed physical world is of considerable significance: all known fundamental laws are mathematical in form.
4  They are *omnipotent*, in that nothing can be held to be outside their scope.

It will be clear that these attributes show remarkable affinities with those which are traditionally applied to God in theistic religious systems, such as Christianity.

David Hume's suggestion that "laws of nature" are imposed on nature is widely regarded as implausible within the scientific community. Regularity, according to this viewpoint, is not to be seen as a feature of the real world, but as a construct of an order-imposing human mind. It is widely held within the scientific community that regularity (including statistical regularity) is an intrinsic feature of the world, uncovered (not imposed) by human investigation. For example, consider the comments of Paul Davies, which would be widely endorsed by natural scientists: "I believe any suggestion that the laws of nature are similar projections of the human mind is absurd. The existence of regularities in nature is an objective mathematical fact. ... In conducting science we are uncovering real regularities and linkages out of nature, not writing them into nature" (Davies, 1992, p. 81).

It will be clear that a religious (and especially a Christian) approach to the debate will focus on the idea of the ordering of the world as something which exists in that world, independent of whether the human mind recognizes it or not, and that this ordering can be understood to be related to the doctrine of creation. While many natural scientists have discarded the original theological framework which led their predecessors of the seventeenth and eighteenth centuries to speak of "laws of nature," there is no reason why such an insight should not be reappropriated by those natural scientists sensitive to the religious aspects of their work.

Yet the doctrine of creation raises some further questions of importance to the dialogue between science and religion. As we noted earlier in this chapter, the notion of creation implies not only a general belief that God brings everything into being, but also the idea that God sustains the world. This naturally raises the question of the nature of God's involvement with the world. In the chapter which follows, we shall consider various approaches to the question of divine action within nature.

## For Further Reading

Fretheim, Terence E. *God and World in the Old Testament: A Relational Theology of Creation.* Nashville, TN: Abingdon Press, 2005.

Gunton, Colin E. *The Triune Creator: A Historical and Systematic Study.* Edinburgh: Edinburgh University Press, 1998.

McGrath, Alister E. *The Open Secret: A New Vision for Natural Theology.* Oxford: Blackwell, 2008.

Polkinghorne, John. *Science and Creation: The Search for Understanding.* London: SPCK, 1988.

Poole, Michael. "Creationism, Intelligent Design, and Science Education." *School Science Review*, 90 (2008): 123–9.

Ward, Keith. *Religion and Creation.* Oxford: Oxford University Press, 1996.

# Chapter

# 12 How Does God Act in the World?

One of the interfaces between scientific and religious thought concerns the manner in which God can be said to act in the world. For example, does God act within the laws of nature? Or can these be violated or transcended in order to serve some special divine purpose? In what follows, we shall explore three broad approaches to this important question which have been influential in the last hundred years, as well as noting some more recent approaches which some consider to have potential value.

## Deism: God Acts Through the Laws of Nature

In chapter 4, we noted how the Newtonian emphasis upon the mechanical regularity of the universe was closely linked with the rise of the movement known as "Deism." The Deist position could be summarized very succinctly as follows. God created the world in a rational and ordered manner, which reflected God's own rational nature, and endowed it with the ability to develop and function without the need for his continuing presence or interference. This viewpoint, which became especially influential in the eighteenth century, regarded the world as a watch, and

God as the watchmaker. God endowed the world with a certain self-sustaining design, such that it could subsequently function without the need for continual intervention. It is thus no accident that William Paley chose to use the image of a watch and watchmaker as part of his celebrated defense of the existence of a creator God.

So how does God act in the world, according to Deism? The simple answer to this question is that God does *not* act in the world. Like a watchmaker, God endowed the universe with its regularity (seen in the "laws of nature"), and set its mechanism in motion. Having provided the impetus to set the system in motion, and establishing the principles which govern that motion, there is nothing left for God to do. The world is to be seen as a large-scale watch, which is completely autonomous and self-sufficient. No action by God is necessary.

Inevitably, this led to the question of whether God could be eliminated completely from the Newtonian worldview. If there was nothing left for God to do, what conceivable need was there for any kind of divine being? If it can be shown that there are self-sustaining principles within the world, there is no need for the traditional idea of "providence" – that is, for the sustaining and regulating hand of God to be present and active throughout the entire existence of the world.

The Newtonian worldview thus encouraged the idea that, although God may well have created the world, there was no further need for divine involvement. The discovery of the laws of conservation (for example, the laws of conservation of momentum) seemed to imply that God had endowed the creation with all the mechanisms which it required in order to continue. It is this point which the astronomer Pierre-Simon Laplace (1749–1827) was making in his famous comment concerning the idea of God as a sustainer of planetary motion: "I have no need of that hypothesis."

A more activist understanding of the manner in which God acts in the world is due to Thomas Aquinas and modern writers influenced by him, which focuses on the use of secondary causes.

## Thomas Aquinas: God Acts Through Secondary Causes

A somewhat different approach to the issue of God's action in the world can be based on the writings of the leading medieval theologian Thomas Aquinas (1225–74). Aquinas's conception of divine action focuses on the distinction between primary and secondary causes. According to Aquinas, God does not work directly in the world, but through secondary causes.

The idea is best explained in terms of an analogy. Suppose we imagine a pianist, who is remarkably gifted. She possesses the ability to play the piano beautifully. Yet the quality of her playing is dependent upon the quality of the piano with which she is provided. An out-of-tune piano will prove disastrous, no matter how expert the player. In our analogy the pianist is the primary cause, and the piano the secondary cause, for a performance of, for example, a Chopin nocturne. Both are required; each has a significantly different role to play. The ability of the primary cause to achieve the desired effect is dependent upon the secondary cause which has to be used.

Aquinas uses this appeal to secondary causes to deal with some of the issues relating to the presence of evil in the world. Suffering and pain are not to be ascribed to the direct action of God, but to the fragility and frailty of the secondary causes through which God works. God, in other words, is to be seen as the primary cause, and various agencies within the world as the associated secondary causes.

For Aristotle (from whom Aquinas draws many of his ideas), secondary causes are able to act in their own right. Natural objects are able to act as secondary causes by virtue

**Figure 12.1** Thomas Aquinas. Painting, c.1476, by Justus van Gent (Paris, Musée du Louvre, akg-images/ Erich Lessing)

of their own nature. This view was unacceptable to theistic philosophers of the Middle Ages, whether Christian or Islamic. For example, the noted Islamic writer al-Ghazali (1058–1111) held that nature is completely subject to God, and it is therefore improper to speak of secondary causes having any independence. God causes things directly. If lightning sets a tree on fire, the fire is not caused by the lightning, but by God. God is thus to be seen as the primary cause who alone is able to move other causes. In the view of many historians of science, this approach to divine causality (often known as "occasionalism") is unhelpful to the development of the natural sciences, as it downplays the regularity of actions and events within nature, and their apparent "lawlike" character.

Thomas Aquinas argues that God is the "unmoved mover," the prime cause of every action, without whom nothing could happen at all. Yet he allows that God can act *indirectly*, through secondary causes. The theistic interpretation of secondary causes thus offers the following account of God's action in the world. God acts indirectly in the world through secondary causes. A great chain of causality can be discerned, leading back to God as the originator and prime mover of all that happens in the world. Yet God does not act *directly* in the world, but through the chain of events which God initiates and guides.

It will thus be clear that Aquinas's approach leads to the idea of God initiating a process which develops under divine guidance. God, so to speak, *delegates* divine action to secondary causes within the natural order. For example, God might move a human will from within so that someone who is ill receives assistance. Here an action which is God's will is carried out *indirectly* by God – yet, according to Aquinas, we can still speak of this action being "caused" by God in some meaningful way.

Aquinas's approach has proved fruitful, and has been adopted and adapted by those wanting to affirm divine involvement in the "big bang" and the process of biological evolution.

A related approach was developed by the British philosophical theologian Austin Farrer (1904–68). This account of divine action is often termed "double agency." According to Farrer, every action which takes place in the world includes a causal role for one or more agents or objects in the world (the "secondary" causes) and a distinct role for God as the "primary" cause of what occurs. We could therefore speak of an ordered nexus of created causes and effects which are ultimately dependent upon divine agency. Two different orders of efficacy can be distinguished: a "horizontal" order of created causes and effects, and a "vertical" order through which God establishes and sustains the former.

An approach which is clearly related to this, but differing radically at points of significance, can be found in the movement known as "process thought," to which we now turn.

## Process Theology: God Acts Through Persuasion

The origins of process thought are generally agreed to lie in the writings of the Anglo-American philosopher Alfred North Whitehead (1861–1947), especially his important work *Process and Reality* (1929). Reacting against the rather static view of the world associated with traditional metaphysics (expressed in ideas such as "substance" and "essence"), Whitehead conceived reality as a process. The world, as an organic whole, is something dynamic, not static; something which *happens*. Reality is made up of building blocks of "actual entities" or "actual occasions," and is thus characterized by becoming, change, and event.

All these "entities" or "occasions" (to use Whitehead's original terms) possess a degree of freedom to develop, and be influenced by their surroundings. It is perhaps at this point that the influence of biological evolutionary theories can be discerned: like Pierre Teilhard de Chardin (1881–1955), Whitehead is concerned to allow for development within creation, subject to some overall direction and guidance. This process of development is thus set against a permanent background of order, which is seen as an organizing principle essential to growth. Whitehead argues that God may be identified with this background of order within the process. Whitehead treats God as an "entity," but distinguishes God from other entities on the grounds of imperishability. Other entities exist for a finite period; God exists permanently. Each entity thus receives influence from two main sources: previous entities and God.

Causation is thus not a matter of an entity being coerced to act in a given manner: it is a matter of *influence* and *persuasion*. Entities influence each other in a "dipolar" manner – mentally and physically. Precisely the same is true of God, as for other entities. God can only act in a persuasive manner, within the limits of the process itself. God "keeps the rules" of the process. Just as God influences other entities, so God is also influenced by them. God, to use Whitehead's famous phrase (in his essay on "God and

**Figure 12.2** Alfred North Whitehead (Topfoto)

the World" in *Process and Reality*) is "a fellow-sufferer who understands." God is thus affected and influenced by the world. This aspect of Whitehead's thought has been developed in the context of the science–religion interaction by a number of writers, especially Ian R. Barbour.

Process thought thus redefines God's omnipotence in terms of persuasion or influence within the overall world-process. This is an important development, as it explains the attraction of this way of understanding God's relation to the world relative to the problem of evil. Where the traditional free-will defense of moral evil argues that human beings are free to disobey or ignore God, process theology argues that the individual components of the world are likewise free to ignore divine attempts to influence or persuade them. They are not bound to respond to God. God is thus absolved of responsibility for both moral and natural evil.

The traditional free-will defense of God in the face of evil is persuasive (although the extent of that persuasion is contested) in the case of moral evil – in other words, evil resulting from human decisions and actions. But what of natural evil? What of earthquakes, famines, and other natural disasters? Process thought argues that God cannot force nature to obey the divine will or purpose for it. God can only attempt to influence the process from within, by persuasion and attraction. Each entity enjoys a degree of freedom and creativity, which God cannot override.

While this understanding of the persuasive nature of God's activity has obvious merits, not least in the way in which it offers a response to the problem of evil (as God is not in control, God cannot be blamed for the way things have turned out) critics of process thought have suggested that too high a price is paid. The traditional idea of the transcendence of God appears to have been abandoned, or radically reinterpreted in terms of the primacy and permanency of God as an entity within the process. In other words, the divine transcendence is understood to mean little more than that God outlives and surpasses other entities.

Whitehead's basic ideas have been developed by a number of writers, most notably Charles Hartshorne (1897–2000), Schubert Ogden (born 1928), and John B. Cobb (born 1925). Hartshorne modified Whitehead's notion of God in a number of directions, perhaps most significantly by suggesting that the God of process thought should be thought of more as a person than an entity. This allows him to meet one of the more significant criticisms of process thought: that it compromises the idea of divine perfection. If God is perfect, how can he change? Is not change tantamount to an admission of imperfection? Hartshorne redefines perfection in terms of a receptivity to change which does not compromise God's superiority. In other words, God's ability to be influenced by other entities does not mean that God is reduced to their level. God surpasses other entities, even though he is affected by them.

One of the most influential early statements of process theology is to be found in Charles Hartshorne's *Man's Vision of God* (1941), which includes a detailed comparison of "classical" and "neoclassical" understandings of God. The former term is used to refer to the understanding of the nature and attributes of God found in the writings of Thomas Aquinas, and the latter to refer to the ideas developed by Hartshorne. Given the importance of Hartshorne to the formulation of process thought, his ideas on the attributes of God will be set out in tabular form, to allow easy comparison with the classical views which he criticizes (see Table 12.1).

While Hartshorne does not use the fully developed vocabulary of process thought, as this would emerge after World War II, it is clear that the basic ideas are firmly in place in this early work.

It will be apparent that process thought has no difficulty in speaking of "God's action within the world," offering a framework within which this action can be described in terms of "influence within the process." Nevertheless, the specific approach adopted causes anxiety to traditional theism, which is critical of the notion of God associated with process theology. For traditional theists, the God of process thought seems to bear little relation to the God described in the Old or New Testaments.

**Table 12.1** Classical and neoclassical understandings of God

| The classical view (Thomas Aquinas) | The neoclassical view (Charles Hartshorne) |
| --- | --- |
| Creation takes place out of nothing by a free act of will. There is no necessary reason for anything other than God existing. Creation depends on God's decision to create; God could have decided not to create anything. | Both God and the creation exist necessarily. The world does not depend on any action of God for its existence, although the fine details of the nature of its existence are a matter of contingency. |
| God has the power to do anything that God wills to do, provided that a logical contradiction is not involved (e.g., God cannot create a square triangle). | God is one agent among many within the world, and has as much power as any such agent. This power is not absolute, but is limited. |
| God is incorporeal, and is radically distinct from the created order. | The world is to be seen as the body of God. |
| God stands outside time, and is not involved in the temporal order. It is therefore inappropriate to think of God "changing" or being affected by any involvement in or experience of the world. | God is involved in the temporal order. God is continually achieving richer syntheses of experience through this involvement. |
| God exists in a state of absolute perfection, and cannot be conceived to exist in a state of higher perfection. | At any point in time, God is more perfect than any other agent in the world. However, God is capable of achieving higher levels of perfection at a later stage of development on account of God's involvement in the world. |

## Other Approaches: Indeterminacy, Downward Causation, and Information

The three approaches just outlined are widely encountered in theological and philosophical discussions of divine agency. In recent years, however, these have been supplemented by other approaches. Although these more recent understandings of divine agency have yet to gain a wide degree of acceptance, they are of sufficient interest and importance to mention here.

One approach, based on the Copenhagen model of quantum mechanics, holds that the idea of *indeterminacy* offers a way of thinking about God's actions in the world. Events which might seem to occur randomly are actually caused by divine agency. The appeal of the approach is obvious. Most philosophers want to affirm that any belief in real freedom in agents, whether human or divine, requires an open future, rather than one which is predetermined. The Copenhagen approach to quantum mechanics incorporates such a notion of indeterminacy, thus suggesting that divine agency can operate without detection, or interference in the autonomy of natural (particularly living) entities. God is thus the "determiner of indeterminacies."

Yet there are problems with this potentially attractive position. The indeterminist Copenhagen interpretation of quantum theory may well be dominant; yet others – such as that developed by David Bohm (1917–92) – are determinist, and seem to offer no such indeterminate quantum nexus as a means of safeguarding the idea of divine agency. Nor is there any indication that quantum fluctuations could have the cumulative force necessary to speaking meaningfully of God "acting" in the world.

Others have turned to the notion of "downward causation." This notion is often stated in slightly vague and imprecise forms. The basic idea is that we can speak of forms of "top-down" or "downward causation" within the natural world, most notably the way in which the human mind operates on various components of the human body. Might the way in which the human mind controls the body be analogous to the manner in which God governs the universe?

It is a fascinating possibility, yet one which at present remains difficult to evaluate. The suggestion that mental causation can elucidate the interaction between divine agency and human free will has an obvious appeal. For example, in initiating processes that are transmitted by neurons, the mind cannot be said to violate or override the nature or properties of neurons. One of the more obvious difficulties, for example, is that the relation between the concept of "mind" and the human brain still remains incompletely understood. Might we eventually have to speak of the brain – rather than the mind – controlling other parts of the body? This would seriously reduce the value of this approach.

A third way of thinking about divine agency is to consider God as a source of information. John Polkinghorne (born 1930) and Arthur Peacocke (1924–2006) have both argued the case for understanding divine action as an "input of pure information." God can be considered as a choreographer, who allows the dancers a degree of freedom in their movements, or a composer, who allows an orchestra to explore possible variations for a yet unfinished symphony. The appeal of this approach lies partly in the fact that, at least at first sight, the transference of information does not seem to require the violation of conservation laws. Yet its critics point out that the input of information into a system implies the reorganization of energy or matter, thus apparently raising more or less the same difficulties encountered by other, more traditional. approaches.

Throughout this chapter, we have used various analogies – such as God as a composer or conductor – in discussing the question of divine action within the world. It is clearly necessary to explore the use of such analogies in more detail. Where do they come from? How are they validated? In the following chapter, we shall consider the use of models in science and religion in some detail.

## For Further Reading

Carroll, William E. "Creation, Evolution, and Thomas Aquinas." *Revue des Questions Scientifiques*, 171 (2000): 319–47.

Clayton, Philip. *Mind and Emergence: From Quantum to Consciousness*. Oxford: Oxford University Press, 2004.

McLain, F. Michael, and W. Mark Richardson (eds). *Human and Divine Agency: Anglican, Catholic, and Lutheran Perspectives*. Lanham, MD: University Press of America, 1999.

Tanner, Kathryn. *God and Creation in Christian Theology: Tyranny or Empowerment?* Oxford: Blackwell, 1988.

Tracy, Thomas F. (ed.). *The God Who Acts: Philosophical and Theological Explorations*. University Park, PA: Pennsylvania State University Press, 1994.

Chapter

# 13 The Use of Models
in Science and Religion

One of the most intriguing aspects of the interface between science and religion is the use of "models" or "analogies" to depict complex entities – whether the entity in question is an atomic nucleus or God. In this chapter, we shall explore the different ways in which these "visual aids" are developed and deployed in science and religion. The theoretical physicist John Polkinghorne notes an important parallel between the two disciplines, which relates specifically to the need to represent entities which cannot presently be seen in a visual manner:

> We habitually speak of entities which are not directly observable. No one has ever seen a gene (though there are X-ray photographs which, suitably interpreted, led Crick and Watson to the helical structure of DNA) or an electron (though there are tracks in bubble chambers which, suitably interpreted, indicate the existence of a particle of negative electric charge of about $4.8 \times 10^{-10}$ esu and mass about $10^{-27}$ gm). No one has ever seen God (though there is the astonishing Christian claim that "the only Son, who is in the bosom of the Father, he has made him known" (John 1:18). (Polkinghorne, 1991, p. 20)

It is a matter of fact that most religions make statements which relate to a series of entities (such as "God," "forgiveness," or "eternal life") which are unobservable in themselves at present. The question of how such theoretical or unobservable entities are to be depicted, and their precise ontological status, is a matter of considerable interest and importance within both science and religion.

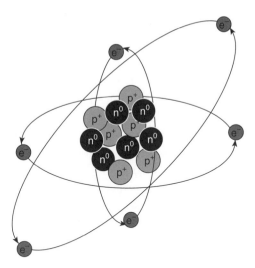

**Figure 13.1** Ernest Rutherford's 1910 "solar system" model of a carbon atom

The natural sciences regularly develop and use "models" to depict at least certain aspects of complex systems. A model is understood to be a simplified way of representing a complex system, which allows its users to gain an increased understanding of at least some of its many aspects. For example, in December 1910 Ernest Rutherford developed a simple model of the atom, based on the solar system. The atom consists of a central body (the nucleus), in which practically the entire mass of the atom is concentrated. Electrons orbit this nucleus, in much the same way as the planets orbit the sun. Whereas the orbits of the planets were determined by the gravitational attraction of the sun, Rutherford argued that the orbits of the electrons were determined by the electrostatic attraction between the negatively charged electrons and the positively charged nucleus. The model was visually simple and easy to understand, and offered a theoretical framework which explained at least some of the known behavior of atoms at this time.

Once a model has been constructed and tested, it can be developed in such a way that it includes some more complicated features of the system which were initially ignored in constructing the model. This same pattern can be seen at work throughout the development of scientific models. The basic features of the pattern that emerges can be set out as follows:

1   The behavior of a system is established, and certain patterns noted.
2   A model is developed, which aims to explain the most important aspects of the system.

3 The model is found to have weaknesses at a number of points, on account of its simplicity.

4 The model can then be made more complex, in order to take account of these weaknesses.

Two serious errors can arise in relation to the use of models in the natural sciences. First, it can be assumed that models are identical with the systems with which they are associated. This is not correct. The atom is not a miniature solar system. Rutherford's model merely points out that we can understand some of their features if we think of them in this way. In each case, we are presented with a visualizable representation of a system, which assists explanation and interpretation. They are to be taken *seriously* (in that they clearly bear some relation to the system that is being modeled); they are not, however, to be taken *literally*.

The second error that can be made is to assume that some aspect of the model is necessarily present in the system being modeled. As we have stressed, models are like analogies: the model and system resemble each other in some ways, and not in others. The fact that there is a parallel in one area does not mean that the same parallel exists in all areas. An excellent example of this problem can be found in late nineteenth-century physics. By this stage, it was widely accepted that light consisted of waves. This had been established by a series of experiments earlier in the century, particularly through studying the phenomenon of diffraction. Light was widely regarded as a wave phenomenon, showing similar behavior to other wave phenomena – such as sound.

One of the most interesting aspects of sound is that it requires a medium through which to travel. If a source of sound is placed in a glass vessel, and the air is pumped out, the intensity of the sound will gradually decrease. Sound has to travel through something, and cannot travel in a vacuum. Noting the many similarities between the behavior of light and sound, many physicists drew the conclusion that an analogy existed at this point as well. If sound needed a medium to travel through, then so did light. The term "luminiferous ether" was used to refer to this medium (the term "luminiferous" literally means "light-bearing").

The 1887 Michelson–Morley experiment was designed to detect "ether drift" – that is, the motion of the ether with respect to the earth. If this "luminiferous ether" really existed, its movement could be detected. Yet all such attempts failed, although it took some time for the implication of this negative result to be fully understood. Either the ether was totally at rest with regard to the movement of the earth, or it did not exist at all. In the end, it had to be accepted that there was no experimental support for the existence of "luminiferous ether." At least in this respect, there was a fundamental distinction between light and sound.

One of the most intriguing ways in which scientific analogies were developed concerns Charles Darwin's concept of "natural selection." It is very clear from Darwin's writings that he believed that some process operated within nature which was analogous to that used by stockbreeders to produce superior or innovative animal breeds – a process often referred to as "artificial selection." By analogy, Darwin argued that some similar process was at work within nature.

Yet the analogy was potentially misleading. Many thought that it implied that nature was active in this process of selection, deliberately and intentionally choosing its preferred outcomes. Darwin himself contributed to this confusion, especially in *The Origin of Species* (1859), in that he often spoke of "natural selection" in strongly anthropomorphic terms. Natural selection, which Darwin often refers to as "nature's power of selection," is regularly described as "acting," implying that it is an agency within nature. "What limit can be put to this power, acting during long ages and rigidly scrutinizing the whole constitution, structure, and habits of each creature, favouring the good and rejecting the bad?" (Darwin, 1859, p. 469). Darwin emphasized the "visual powers" and "skills" of this proposed natural mechanism, arguing that it was vastly superior to anything that human beings had ever managed to devise.

We see here how an analogy can mislead as much as inform. Darwin's language led at least some of his readers to draw the conclusion that his theory of evolution was about nature wisely and actively evaluating each evolutionary development, and choosing which were good enough to be allowed to prosper. It is a classic difficulty with any scientific model or analogy.

From this brief discussion, it will be clear that models play a significant role in the natural sciences. The most important points to note are the following:

1 Models are often seen as significant ways of visualizing complex and abstract concepts. This is especially true in relation to aspects of quantum theory, to which we shall return presently.
2 Models are seen as "intermediates" between complex entities and the human mind.
3 Models do not necessarily "exist," although what they attempt to represent has a real and independent existence.
4 Models are selected or constructed on the basis of the belief that there exist significant points of similarity between the model and what it is meant to represent.
5 Models are therefore not identical with what they model, and must not be treated as if they are.
6 In particular, it must not be assumed that every aspect of the model corresponds to the entity being modeled.

So what of the situation with regard to religion? At first sight, there might be expected to be significant similarities here between the sciences and religion. Both aim to talk about complex entities which cannot be seen in terms of familiar language and images. Theology can be usefully defined as "talk about God." But how can God ever be described or discussed using human language, or objects or images drawn from the everyday world? The Austrian philosopher Ludwig Wittgenstein made this point forcefully: if human words are incapable of describing the distinctive aroma of coffee, how can they cope with something as subtle as God? One of the answers which is given to this question notes the theological importance of analogies and metaphors – ways of thinking and speaking about God which are based on images, such as the biblical images of "God as shepherd" and "God as king." We may begin by considering the way in which analogies and metaphors are used in theology.

Perhaps the most basic idea which underlies the theological reply to such questions is usually referred to as "the principle of analogy." This is particularly associated with the great scholastic theologian Thomas Aquinas (1225–74). According to Aquinas, the fact that God created the world points to a fundamental "analogy of being" between God and the world. For this reason, it is legitimate to use entities within the created order as analogies for God. In doing this, theology does not reduce God to the level of a created object or being. It merely affirms that there is a likeness of correspondence between God and that being, which allows the latter to act as a signpost to God. A created entity can thus be like God, without being identical to God.

An important twentieth-century development of this point was set out by the British philosopher of religion Ian T. Ramsey (1915–72), who argued that religious language uses models or analogies. For Ramsey, these models are not freestanding, but interact with and qualify each other. Ramsey argues that Scripture does not give us one single analogy (or "model") for God or for salvation, but uses a range of analogies. Each of these analogies or models illuminates certain aspects of our understanding of God, or the nature of salvation. However, these analogies also interact with each other. They modify each other. They help us understand the limits of other analogies. No analogy or parable is exhaustive in itself; taken together, however, the range of analogies and parables builds up to give a comprehensive and consistent understanding of God and salvation.

An example of how images interact may make this point clearer. Take the analogies of king, father, and shepherd. Each of these three analogies conveys the idea of authority, suggesting that this is of fundamental importance to our understanding of God. Kings, however, often behave in arbitrary ways, and not always in the best interests of their subjects. The analogy of God as a king might thus be misunderstood to suggest that God is some sort of tyrant. However, the tender compassion of a father towards his children commended by Scripture (Psalm 103: 13–18), and the total dedication of a good shepherd to the welfare of his flock (John 10: 11), show that this is not the intended meaning. Authority is to be exercised tenderly and wisely.

In his influential study of the interaction of science and religion, Ian G. Barbour identified three similarities and a corresponding number of differences between religious models and theoretical models in science. The similarities which he identifies are the following:

1   In both science and religion, models are analogical in their origins, can be extended to cope with new situations, and are comprehensible as individual units.
2   Models, whether scientific or religious, are not to be taken either as literal depictions of reality, nor simply as "useful fictions." "They are symbolic representations, for particular purposes, of aspects of reality which are not directly accessible to us" (Barbour, 1974, p. 69).
3   Models function as organizing images, allowing us to structure and interpret patterns of events in our personal lives and in the world. In the sciences, the models relate to observational data; in the religions, to the experience of individuals and communities.

Significantly, Barbour also identified three areas of difference between the use of models in scientific and religious contexts. At this point, a degree of generalization about the nature of religion may perhaps lead to some incautious conclusions, although there is no doubt that, at least in some cases, the points which Barbour makes are valid.

1   Religious models serve noncognitive functions which have no parallel in science.
2   Religious models evoke more total personal involvement than their scientific counterparts.
3   Religious models appear to be more influential than the formal beliefs and doctrines which are derived from them, whereas scientific models are subservient to theories.

A further point of importance in this comparison concerns the way in which analogies or models are chosen. In the sciences, analogies or models are chosen and validated partly on the basis of whether they offer a good empirical fit. These two themes – selection and validation – are of considerable importance, not least in that they highlight a significant difference between the natural sciences and religion. Analogies are generated within the scientific community; if they prove to be unsatisfactory, they are discarded, and replaced by new ones.

For example, consider the Bohr model (1913) of the hydrogen atom, which postulates that a single electron orbits a central nucleus (a feature derived from the Rutherford model of 1910), with an angular momentum which is confined to certain limited values. On the basis of this model, Bohr was able to explain a growing body of evidence concerning atomic behavior, especially relating to atomic spectra. Yet the model had serious weaknesses (for example, the assumption that the electron orbited the nucleus in a circle) which had to be modified as experimental data built up.

The point here is that a model was *devised*, partly as an analogue of a simple harmonic oscillator and partly as an analogue of the solar system, which was found to have explanatory potential. Bohr's genius lay in devising the model. It was not self-evident, but rested on Bohr's belief that the application of quantum concepts to statistical mechanics by Einstein and Planck could be paralleled in the field of dynamics. Subsequent to its being formulated, the model required validation, both in terms of its ability to explain what was already known, and to predict novel phenomena.

It will also be clear that scientific models may be dispensed with when a superior model has been devised. The Rutherford model of the hydrogen atom, although regularly used at the popular level, was discarded at a relatively early stage within professional circles on account of its obvious deficiencies. There is no commitment within the scientific community to any one model; in principle, the advancement of understanding may – but does not necessarily – lead to the discarding of earlier models.

These key themes of *formulation* and *validation* have no direct parallel in classical Christian thought. For a religion such as Christianity, it has been traditionally understood that the analogies or models in question are "given," not chosen; the two tasks which confront the theologian are those of establishing the limits of the analogy, and correlating it with other such given analogies. Let me make it clear immediately that not all theologians would support this traditional view; some would argue that we are at liberty to develop new models which avoid certain features of traditional models which are deemed to be unsatisfactory. Nevertheless, the traditional view remains influential, as can be seen from works such as Thomas F. Torrance's exploration of "theological science."

There would be no question of abandoning a traditional Christian model of God within orthodox Christian circles – for example, the model of God as "shepherd." Such models are far too deeply embedded in the biblical material and both theological reflection and liturgical practice to be treated in this manner. They have assumed the status of "root metaphors," which are regarded as permanent and essential components of the truth of the Christian tradition.

In chapter 11, we considered the importance of the notion of "creation" in the dialogue between science and religion. It is now appropriate to move on to consider another theological issue that arises from this dialogue: can the creator be known from the creation? This question leads us into a discussion of natural theology, the topic of the chapter which follows.

## For Further Reading

Barbour, Ian G. *Myths, Models and Paradigms: A Comparative Study in Science and Religion.* New York: Harper & Row, 1974.

Hesse, Mary B. *Models and Analogies in Science*. Notre Dame, IN: University of Notre Dame Press, 1966.

Keller, Evelyn Fox. *Making Sense of Life: Explaining Biological Development with Models, Metaphors, and Machines*. Cambridge, MA: Harvard University Press, 2002.

McFague, Sallie. *Metaphorical Theology: Models of God in Religious Language*. Philadelphia: Fortress, 1985.

Ramsey, Ian T. *Models for Divine Activity*. London: SCM Press, 1973.

Young, Robert M. *Darwin's Metaphor: Nature's Place in Victorian Culture*. Cambridge, UK: Cambridge University Press, 1985.

# 14 Natural Science and Natural Theology

Can God be known from nature? If anything of God can be known from a study of the natural world, it will be clear that the religions and the natural sciences will have some significant common features. One of the most important issues here concerns "nature" itself, and whether it is to be regarded as something which has, in some way, been fashioned by God (and thus reflects the nature of God, however indirectly). We explored this theme in chapter 11, noting in particular the way in which doctrine of creation forges a link between God and nature.

In his major study *Perceiving God*, the American philosopher William Alston (born 1921) sets out what he regards as a responsible and realistic approach to natural theology. Alston defines natural theology as "the enterprise of providing support for religious beliefs by starting from premises that neither are nor presuppose any religious beliefs" (Alston, 1991b, p. 289). Conceding that it is impossible to construct a demonstrative proof of the existence of God which avoids religious premises, Alston argues that this is not, in any case, a proper approach to natural theology.

Strictly speaking, natural theology begins from a starting point such as the existence of God or the ordering of the world, and shows that this starting point leads us to recognize the existence of a being which would be accepted as God. There is thus, in Alston's view, a strong degree of convergence between natural theology and traditional arguments for the existence of God, particularly those deriving from Thomas Aquinas. Yet his conception of natural theology goes beyond such narrow proofs, and encourages the engagement with other areas of human life and concern, amongst which he explicitly includes science. Natural theology thus offers "metaphysical reasons for the truth of theism as a general world-view" (Alston, 1991b, p. 270), and allows us to build bridges to other disciplines.

In the present chapter, we shall explore some aspects of what is known as "natural theology" – that is, the religious belief, grounded in a doctrine of creation, which traditionally affirms that at least something of God can be known from the study of nature.

Within Christianity, three general approaches have emerged to the question of whether – and to what extent – God may be known through nature. These are the appeal to reason, to the ordering of the world, and to the beauty of nature. In what follows, we shall give a brief account of each of these three approaches, noting that the second and third have particular importance to the relation of science and religion.

## The Appeal to Reason

One of the most widely encountered approaches to natural knowledge of God is an appeal to human reason. An excellent example of this approach can be found in the writings of Augustine of Hippo (354–430), particularly in his major work *De Trinitate*. The general line of argument developed by Augustine can be summed up as follows. If God is indeed to be discerned within his creation, we ought to expect to find him at the height of that creation. Now the height of God's creation, Augustine reasons (basing his argument on Genesis 1 and 2), is human nature. And, on the basis of the neo-Platonic presuppositions which he inherited from his cultural milieu, Augustine further argued that the height of human nature is the human capacity to reason. Therefore, he concluded, one should expect to find traces of God (or, more accurately, "vestiges of the Trinity") in human processes of reasoning. On the basis of this belief, Augustine develops what have come to be known as "psychological analogies of the Trinity."

For Augustine, God created humanity in his image, thus establishing a correspondence between human reasoning and the deep structures of nature. As a result, the human mind is "fine-tuned" to discern God within the creation, whether by reflection on ideas or on the nature of the world. This "fine-tuning" is the outcome of the doctrine of creation, resting specifically on the idea that God has created humanity in such a way that it bears the image of God. For Augustine, this special characteristic of human nature leads humanity to pursue the quest for the transcendent. According to Augustine:

> The image of the creator is to be found in the rational or intellectual soul of humanity … Although reason and intellect may at times be dormant, or may appear to be weak at some times, and strong at others, the human soul cannot be anything other than rational and intellectual. It has been created according to the image of God in order that it may use reason and intellect in order to apprehend and behold God. (*de Trinitate* XVI. iv. 6)

Augustine's insight was developed by other writers, including the great medieval writer Thomas Aquinas. However, it is not clear that an appeal to human reason has direct relevance to the dialogue between science and religion. Indeed, some would suggest that it actually leads away from an engagement with the natural world, in that it implies that human reason is able to settle the question of the existence of God without reference to the world of nature. The second and third of the three approaches, which are considered below, are therefore of greater interest, in that both are based on reflecting on the natural world itself.

## The Appeal to the Ordering of the World

This is one of the most significant themes for our study, in the light of its close connection with the findings of the natural sciences. Thomas Aquinas's arguments for the existence of God, set out in the thirteenth century, are based on the perception that there is an ordering within nature, which requires to be explained. Equally, the fact that the human mind can discern and investigate this ordering of nature is of considerable significance. There seems to be something about human nature which prompts it to ask questions about the world, just as there seems to be something about the world which allows answers to those questions to be given. This is a recurring theme in the writings of the theoretical physicist and Christian theologian John Polkinghorne:

> We are so familiar with the fact that we can understand the world that most of the time we take it for granted. It is what makes science possible. Yet it could have been otherwise. The universe might have been a disorderly chaos rather than an orderly cosmos. Or it might have had a rationality which was inaccessible to us. … There is a congruence between our minds and the universe, between the rationality experienced within and the rationality observed without. (Polkinghorne, 1988, pp. 20–1)

There is a deep-seated congruence between the rationality present in our minds, and the *orderedness* which we observe as present in the world. One of the most remarkable aspects of this ordering concerns the abstract structures of pure mathematics – a free creation of the human mind – which, as Polkinghorne stresses, nevertheless provides important clues to understanding the world.

An example of this congruence between rationality and the natural order can be seen in the English theoretical physicist Paul Dirac's 1931 explanation of a puzzling aspect of an equation he had derived to explain the behavior of an electron. It had *two* types of solution, one with positive energy and the other with negative energy. The latter class could be interpreted as implying the existence of a particle which was identical to an electron in every respect, save that it was positively charged. This point was brought out clearly by Hermann Weyl's demonstration that such "negative energy solutions" had electron mass.

In 1932, Carl Anderson observed real-life effects which led him to postulate the existence of the positive electron, corresponding to Dirac's postulated particle. The new particle was observed only in cloud chamber experiments; this was accounted for by Patrick Blackett's observation that Dirac's theory indicated that the particle would soon annihilate itself on collision with a (negatively charged) electron, and was therefore not (as some had thought) a constituent element of stable matter. In a sense, the positron can thus be said to have been known to the mathematicians before the physicists discovered it.

So important is this appeal to the ordering of nature that we shall be exploring it in greater detail in a later chapter, as we deal with the concept of a "law of nature," and the relation of such laws to a doctrine of creation. The appeal to the beauty of nature is also of importance in this respect, and we shall consider it in what follows.

## The Appeal to the Beauty of Nature

A number of major Christian theologians have developed natural theologies, based on the sense of beauty which arises from contemplating the world. Hans Urs von Balthasar (1905–88) and Jonathan Edwards (1703–58) offered such an approach in the twentieth and eighteenth centuries respectively, the former from a Roman Catholic and the latter from a Reformed perspective. The English scientist Robert Boyle (1627–91) developed the image of nature as a temple and the natural scientist as a priest, thus drawing attention to the sense of wonder evoked by the study of nature in all its beauty.

Augustine of Hippo argued that there was a natural progression from an admiration of the beautiful things of the world to the worship of the one who had created these things, and whose beauty was reflected in them. The great medieval theologian Thomas Aquinas set out "Five Ways" of inferring from the orderliness of the world to the reality of God; the fourth of those ways is based upon the observation of the existence of perfection in the world. Although Aquinas does not specifically identity "beauty" as one of these perfections at this point, it is clear that this identification can be made without difficulty, and is made elsewhere in Aquinas's work. This general line of argument was developed in the early twentieth century by the noted philosophical theologian F. R. Tennant (1886–1957), who argued that part of the cumulative case for the existence of God was the observation of beauty within the world.

Within the Reformed tradition, a recognition of the importance of "beauty" as a theological theme can be discerned in the writings of John Calvin (1509–64). However, its most powerful exposition within this tradition is generally agreed to be found in the writings of the leading eighteenth-century American theologian Jonathan Edwards. Edwards argues that the beauty of God is to be expected – and duly found – in the derived beauty of the created order.

> It is very fit and becoming of God who is infinitely wise, so to order things that there should be a voice of His in His works, instructing those that behold Him and painting forth and shewing divine mysteries and things more immediately appertaining to Himself and His spiritual kingdom. The works of God are but a kind of voice or language of God to instruct intelligent beings in things pertaining to Himself. (Edwards, 1948, p. 61)

It will therefore be clear that the concept of beauty is of major importance to a religious understanding of the nature of the world. Its importance has long been appreciated in pure mathematics, although the new interest in fractals has opened up the issue in a new and highly exciting manner. In the twentieth century, that interest in beauty also became significant for the natural sciences. While "beauty" can be understood to refer to the natural world itself, it is generally understood to refer to the manner in which that world is to be interpreted, especially at the theoretical level. The beauty of theories is often associated with their symmetry. Steven Weinberg, who received the 1979 Nobel Prize for physics, comments as follows on the beauty of scientific theories:

**Figure 14.1** Portrait of Jonathan Edwards by Joseph Badger (Courtesy of Yale University Art Gallery, bequest of Eugene Phelps Edwards)

> The kind of beauty that we find in physical theories is of a very limited sort. It is, as far as I have been able to capture

it in words, the beauty of simplicity and inevitability – the beauty of perfect structure, the beauty of everything fitting together, of nothing being changeable, of logical rigidity. It is a beauty that is spare and classic, the sort we find in the Greek tragedies. (Weinberg, 1993, p. 119)

This is especially clear from the writings of Paul Dirac, who managed to establish a connection between quantum theory and general relativity at a time when everyone else had failed to do so. Dirac's approach appears to have been based on the concept of "beauty," in that an explicitly aesthetic criterion is laid down as a possible means of evaluating scientific theories:

It is more important to have beauty in one's equations than to have them fit experiment … It seems that if one is working from the point of view of getting beauty in one's equations, and if one has a really good insight, one is on a sure line of progress. (Dirac, 1963, p. 47)

It will be clear that this offers a significant interface between religion and the natural sciences, which points to the importance of natural theology as a means of dialogue between these disciplines.

These, then, are merely some of the ways in which Christian theologians have attempted to describe the manner in which God can be known, however fleetingly, through nature. Within a specifically Christian perspective, these insights which may be obtained into the existence and nature of God are to be seen as pointers to the greater reality of God's self-revelation, rather than as complete in themselves.

## Objections to Natural Theology

Yet if this positive approach to a natural knowledge of God represents the majority report within the Christian tradition, it is important to acknowledge that there have been other views. In what follows, we shall explore two significant (although ultimately not decisive) objections to natural theology, reflecting theological and philosophical concerns respectively.

The leading Swiss Reformed theologian Karl Barth (1886–1968) expressed considerable hostility towards natural theology, believing that it was at best unnecessary, and that at worst it subverted and distorted divine revelation. Why bother looking for God in nature, when God has already revealed himself?

An equally critical approach to natural theology has been developed on other grounds by the noted Scottish theologian Thomas F. Torrance (1913–2007). There

**Figure 14.2** Karl Barth (akg-images/ ullstein bild)

are clear parallels between Torrance and Barth. Thus Torrance sets out what he understands to be Barth's fundamental objection to natural theology – the radical separation which some writers assert between "revealed theology" and a totally autonomous and unconnected "natural theology":

> What Barth objects to in traditional natural theology is not any invalidity in its argumentation, nor even its rational structure, as such, but its *independent* character – i.e., the autonomous rational structure that natural theology develops on the ground of "nature alone," in abstraction from the active self-disclosure of the living and Triune God – for that can only split the knowledge of God into two parts, natural knowledge of the One God and revealed knowledge of the triune God, which is scientifically as well as theologically intolerable. This is not to reject the place of a proper rational structure in knowledge of God, such as natural theology strives for, but to insist that unless that rational structure is intrinsically bound up with the actual content of knowledge of God, it is a distorting abstraction. That is why Barth claims that, properly understood, natural theology is included within revealed theology. (Torrance, 1970, p. 128)

Torrance also stresses that Barth's criticism of natural theology does not rest on any form of dualism – for example, some kind of deistic dualism between God and the world which implies that there is no active relation between God and the world, or with some form of dualism between redemption and creation implying a depreciation of the creature. It is clear that Torrance himself sympathizes with Barth at these junctures.

Torrance also notes a fundamental philosophical difficulty which seems to him to lie behind the forms of natural theology rejected by Barth. This kind of autonomous natural theology, Torrance argues, represents an attempt to find a *logical bridge* between concepts and experience on the one hand, and God and the world on the other. It attempted, by means of establishing a logical bridge between ideas and being, to reach out inferentially towards God, and thus to produce a logical formalization of empirical and theoretical components of the knowledge of God.

For Torrance, this development was assisted considerably by the medieval assumption that "to think scientifically was to think *more geometrico*, that is, on the model of Euclidean geometry, and it was reinforced in later thought as it allowed itself to be restricted within the logico-causal connections of a mechanistic universe" (Torrance, 1985, p. 39). It will thus be clear that Torrance sees the "traditional abstractive form" of natural theology as resting on a "deistic disjunction between God and the world" (p. 39) – a disjunction which we noted in discussing the emergence of the Newtonian worldview, with its associated notion of God as the "clockmaker." It will be clear that Torrance accepts that a natural theology has a significant place within Christian theology, in the light of an understanding of the nature of God and the world which rests on divine revelation, and which cannot itself be ascertained by human inquiry.

Torrance can therefore be thought of as moving natural theology into the domain of systematic theology, in much the same manner as Einstein moved geometry into the formal content of physics. The proper locus for the discussion of natural theology is not debate about the possibility of a hypothetical knowledge of God, but within the context of the positive and revealed knowledge of a creator God. A proper theological perspective on nature allows it to be seen in its proper light:

> So it is with natural theology: brought within the embrace of positive theology and developed as a complex of rational structures arising in our actual knowledge of God it becomes "natural" in a new way, natural to its proper object, God in self-revealing interaction with us in space and time. Natural theology then constitutes the epistemological geometry, as it were, within the fabric of revealed theology. (Torrance, 1985, p. 39)

The Barthian challenge can thus be met, in a manner which Torrance believed had Barth's support.

Other objections, however, have been raised against the idea of a "natural theology" from within Protestantism, particularly those found in the writings of the leading Reformed philosopher of religion Alvin Plantinga. We may turn to consider these before proceeding further.


## Philosophical Objections

In recent years, philosophers of religion working within a Reformed theological perspective have risen to considerable prominence. Alvin Plantinga (born 1932) and Nicholas Wolterstorff (born 1932) are examples of writers belonging to this category of thinkers, who have made highly significant contributions to the philosophy of religion in recent decades. Plantinga understands "natural theology" to be an attempt to prove or demonstrate the existence of God, and vigorously rejects it on the basis of his belief that it depends on a fallacious understanding of the nature of religious belief. The roots of this objection are complex, and can be summarized in terms of two foundational considerations:

1 Natural theology supposes that belief in God must rest upon an evidential basis. Belief in God is thus not, strictly speaking, a basic belief – that is, something which is self-evident, incorrigible or evident to the senses. It is therefore a belief which requires to be itself grounded in some more basic belief. However, to ground a belief in God upon some other belief is, in effect, to depict that latter belief as endowed with a greater epistemic status than belief in God. For Plantinga, a properly Christian approach is to affirm that belief in God is itself basic, and does not require justification with reference to other beliefs.
2 Natural theology is not justified with reference to the Reformed tradition, including Calvin and his later followers.

The latter point is inaccurate historically, and need not detain us. However, the first line of argument has met with growing interest.

Plantinga clearly regards Aquinas as the "natural theologian *par excellence*" (Plantinga, 1998, p. 121) and directs considerable attention to his methods. For Plantinga, Aquinas is a foundationalist in matters of theology and philosophy, in that "*scientia*, properly speaking, consists in a body of propositions deduced syllogistically from self-evident first principles" (1998, p. 122). The *Summa contra Gentiles* shows, according to Plantinga, that Aquinas proceeds from evidential foundations to argue for a belief in God, which clearly makes such belief dependent upon appropriate evidential foundations. Plantinga thus assumes that a natural theology sets out to *prove* the existence of God.

It is clearly not necessary that a natural theology should make any such assumption; indeed, there are excellent reasons for suggesting that, as a matter of historical fact, natural theology is to be understood as a demonstration of the consonance between faith and the structures of the world. In other words, natural theology is not intended to prove the existence of God, but presupposes that existence; it then asks "what should we expect the natural world to be like if it has indeed been created by such a God?" The search for order in nature is therefore not intended to demonstrate that God exists, but to reinforce the plausibility of an already existing belief.

This leads us into a question which was also raised by our earlier discussions about whether God's existence could be proved. What happens if anomalies arise? In other words, what if certain aspects of the natural world seem to be inconsistent with belief in God? In the case of a natural theology, the existence of pain and suffering in the world is often singled out as causing a potential difficulty for belief in God. So how are such inconsistencies or anomalies handled in science and religion? We shall consider this question in the next chapter.

## For Further Reading

Barr, James. *Biblical Faith and Natural Theology*. Oxford: Clarendon Press, 1993.

Brooke, John Hedley. *Science and Religion: Some Historical Perspectives*. Cambridge, UK: Cambridge University Press, 1991.

Kretzmann, Norman. *The Metaphysics of Creation: Aquinas's Natural Theology in Summa contra Gentiles II*. Oxford: Clarendon Press, 1999.

McGrath, Alister E. *The Open Secret: A New Vision for Natural Theology*. Oxford: Blackwell, 2008.

Torrance, Thomas F. "The Problem of Natural Theology in the Thought of Karl Barth." *Religious Studies*, 6 (1970): 121–35.

# Chapter

# 15 Theoretical Anomalies in Science and Religion

What happens when theory and observation seem to be in conflict? This question is important to both science and theology. Suppose something is observed which doesn't fit into existing theories – for example, the orbit of the planet Uranus turns out to be somewhat different than expected. Or suffering exists in the world, when God is meant to be good and all-powerful. Does this misfit between theory and observation force us to abandon a theory? In this chapter, we shall consider the place of "anomalies" – things that don't really fit into existing theories – in both science and theology.

Let's begin with the natural sciences, and consider a classic situation in which an anomaly was observed. The planet Uranus was discovered by Sir William Herschel using a telescope in 1781. Although the planet was actually bright enough to be see with the naked eye, it was assumed to be a dim star until Herschel identified its planetary characteristics. The details of its orbit were soon worked out, and fitted into the general theory of planetary motion developed in the previous century by Isaac Newton. Initially, the behavior of Uranus seemed to be a splendid confirmation of Newton's theory. Yet as more observational evidence accumulated, it became clear that Uranus was not behaving as it ought to. Something was wrong. But what? How was the anomalous behavior of Uranus to be accounted for?

A number of possible explanations had to be considered. To help us consider them, we need to make a distinction between the central assumptions of Newton's theory of planetary motion in the solar system, and minor or "ancillary" assumptions. A core assumption of Newton's model is that the law of gravitation applies throughout the solar system. Perhaps this assumption might have to be revised in the light of Uranus's peculiar orbital motion. Maybe gravitation was a local, not a universal, phenomenon. Yet there was also an ancillary assumption of Newton's view of the solar system that might need to be revised – namely, that there were no planets beyond Uranus. (For Newton, of course, there were no planets known beyond Saturn.)

The question which an anomaly raises for a theory is this. Does the entire theory need to be abandoned? Or is a modification needed for only one hypothesis, which allows the theory as a whole to be saved? In this specific case, it was an auxiliary assumption which proved to be incorrect – namely, the assumption that there was no planet beyond Uranus. When a trans-Uranic planet was postulated, the anomalous orbital parameters of Uranus could be explained by the existence of this planet, which exercised a gravitational pull on Uranus. The planet in question (Neptune) was duly discovered on the basis of calculations carried out independently by John Couch Adams (1819–92) and Urbain Le Verrier (1811–77) in 1846. The anomaly was now explained.

So how do we know when a theory is wrong? The simple answer which might be offered, from a scientific perspective, is to carry out an experiment. A "crucial experiment" could be devised, which will allow the central features of a theory to be tested out. The experiment, provided that it is properly designed, will soon establish whether the theory is right or wrong.

Or will it? The issues which we shall be discussing in the present chapter concern the criticisms of the idea of a "crucial experiment" made by the noted French physicist and philosopher Pierre Duhem (1861–1916). Duhem notes that a theory is made up of a number of hypotheses, some of which may be of central importance, others of which are subsidiary. Duhem's point is that a theory consists of a complex network of crucial and auxiliary hypotheses. So, if something which is predicted by the theory does not correspond with experimentation, which of the assumptions is wrong? A crucial hypothesis? If so, the theory would have to be abandoned. Or one of the auxiliary assumptions? If so, the theory simply needs modification.

According to Duhem, the physicist simply is not in a position to submit an isolated hypothesis to experimental test. A section in chapter VI of Duhem's *The Aim and Structure of Physical Theory* is headed "An Experiment in Physics Can Never Condemn an Isolated Hypothesis but Only a Whole Theoretical Group." The physicist cannot subject an individual hypothesis to an experimental test, in that the experiment can only indicate that one hypothesis within a larger group of hypotheses requires revision.

**Figure 15.1** Pierre Duhem (Science Photo Library)

The experiment does not itself indicate which of the hypotheses requires modification.

So can such a "crucial experiment" be devised? Duhem's argument needs closer examination at this point. In the section of his *Aim and Structure of Physical Theory* entitled "A 'Crucial Experiment' is Impossible in Physics," Duhem argues that we do not have access to the full list of hypotheses which underlie our thinking. It might at first seem that we could enumerate all the hypotheses that can be made to account for a phenomenon, and then eliminate all of these hypotheses except one by experimental contradiction. However, according to Duhem, the physicist is simply never going to be in a position to be sure that all the hypotheses have been identified and checked.

In his seminal essay "Two Dogmas of Empiricism," the Harvard philosopher Willard Van Orman Quine (1908–2000) set out a development of Duhem's argument which has come to be known as the "Duhem–Quine thesis." This asserts that, if incompatible data and theory are seen to be in conflict, one cannot draw the conclusion that any particular theoretical statement is responsible, and is therefore to be rejected. Quine develops this point by noting the complex way in which belief systems or worldviews relate to experience and experimentation:

> The totality of our so-called knowledge or beliefs, from the most casual matters of geography and history to the profoundest laws of atomic physics … is a man-made fabric which impinges on experience only along the edges … A conflict with experience at the periphery occasions adjustments in the interior of the field … But the total field is so underdetermined by its boundary conditions, experience, that there is much latitude of choice as to what statements to reevaluate in the light of any single contrary experience. (Quine, 1953, pp. 42–3)

In other words, experience often has relatively little impact upon worldviews. Where experience or experiment seems to contradict a worldview or system of beliefs, the most likely outcome is an internal readjustment of the system, rather than its rejection. Quine thus points to some of the difficulties in refuting a theory on the basis of experience, which must be addressed by any empirical approach.

Quine's analysis has given rise to what is often referred to as the "underdetermination thesis" – the view, especially associated with sociological approaches to the natural sciences, which holds that there are, in principle, an indefinite number of theories that are capable of fitting observed facts more or less adequately. The choice of theory can thus be explained on the basis of sociological factors, such as interests. According to this view, experimental evidence plays a considerably smaller role in theory generation and confirmation than might be thought. The strongest form of this approach (usually referred to as "maximal underdetermination") would take the following form:

> For any theoretical statement S and acceptable theory T essentially containing S, there is an acceptable theory T′ with the same testable consequences but which contains, essentially, the negation of S.

Two implications of the underdetermination thesis should be noted:

1   That there are a number of possible theories which are consistent with any given experimental result. All are to be regarded as equally valid.
2   That theories cannot be explained purely on the basis of experimental evidence. Additional factors, generally of a sociological nature, need to be taken into account.

It will be clear that the underdetermination thesis has been particularly attractive to sociologists of knowledge, who wish to stress the importance of social conditioning on scientific theory.

Nevertheless, it needs to be noted that underdetermination is a disputed notion. Duhem himself noted that physicists had a pretty good idea as to which theories were workable and which were not. He referred to the idea of "good sense," meaning by this an intuitive perception, based on experience of a laboratory-based scientific culture, as to what constituted a viable theory.

So what of religious theories? How do they cope with anomalies? It is widely agreed that the problem of suffering in the world is a problem for a Christian view of the world. This is often taken to imply a fundamental deficiency in Christian theology, calling into question some essential doctrine, such as the goodness or omnipotence of God. Yet the analysis we find in Duhem and Quine raises a significant question: is suffering an anomaly which necessitates the abandonment or modification of the central teachings of the Christian faith, or merely one of its many subsidiary aspects? And if the latter, which one?

The American philosopher of religion William P. Alston (born 1921) has noted that two fundamentally different approaches to the problem of evil can be discerned in the writings of the twentieth century:

1   A logical approach, which attempts to show that the existence of evil in the world is logically incompatible with the existence of God. Alston reports that it "is now

acknowledged on (almost) all sides" that this particular argument is bankrupt (Alston, 1991a, p. 29).

2   An empirical approach, which asserts that the observable evidence of evil – that is to say, that evil may be observed to exist in the world – is incompatible with the existence of God.

The logical aspects of the problem of evil, as it is traditionally formulated, can be set out as follows. Consider the following three hypotheses:

1   God is omnipotent and omniscient;
2   God is completely good;
3   The world contains instances of suffering and evil.

In the traditional logical formulation of the problem of suffering, the third of these propositions is held to be inconsistent with the first two by critics of theism. If God is both loving and all-powerful, the existence of evil seems to make the postulation of the existence of God as an explanatory device at least problematic, and probably incoherent.

A closer examination of the situation indicates that this judgment is a more than a little premature. At least one further substantial hypothesis needs to be added before the possibility of evil can be regarded as constituting a potential logical difficulty for the theory. An obvious example of such a fourth hypothesis would be:

4   A good omnipotent God would eliminate suffering and evil.

This assumption is actually implicit in the crude analysis just considered, but was not made explicit. If some such assumption is not present, the dilemma loses its force. It might easily be countered, for example, that there is a "greater good" that is somehow brought about by suffering, which therefore blunts the force of the objection.

Yet the issue is not entirely logical. As Alston rightly points out, these four propositions do not all possess the same logical status, making it impossible to set them out in terms of a pure logical syllogism. Whereas three of the propositions could reasonably be defined as "logical ideas" or "propositions," the other – "The world contains instances of suffering and evil" – is actually an observation statement. It takes the form of a report of the way things are, based on experience and observation. Three are logical, concerned with the interconnection of ideas; the fourth is a report on what is to be observed in the external world. The conceptual bridge between experience and logic is fragile at the best of times, and is simply incapable of bearing the epistemic weight that is here being placed upon it.

The fundamental question concerns the relation between theory and observation. A logical riddle, stated or conceived in terms of propositions, can give rise to an inconsistency through the manner in which those propositions are related (as, for example, in the statements "I propose to draw a three-sided square" or "Everything stated in this sentence is false"). The issues involved in the problem of suffering are rather more complex than this, in that they involve the attempted correlation of the world of ideas and empirical observations concerning the external world. The observational component of the problem would have to be stated in a purely logical manner, in order for the deductive objection to have force. Yet this turns out to be intensely problematic.

The problem can therefore be reformulated in a more inductive and empirical manner, as follows. Consider the two following hypotheses:

God is omnipotent.
God is good.

Now add the following observation statement:

The world contains instances of suffering and evil.

The epistemological issues are now not purely logical, but concern the ability of a theory to accommodate observations which appear to be anomalous. The fundamental question which must be addressed in the problem of evil can be formulated, in a Duhemian manner, as follows. Does the observation statement require that these two hypotheses should be abandoned? Or that just one of them should be revised? And if so, which one? Or is there a problem with an as yet unidentified auxiliary hypothesis?

One of the most careful statements of an inductive or empirical approach to the problem of evil can be found in the writings of William Rowe. In his essay "The Problem of Evil and Some Varieties of Atheism," Rowe (1979, p. 336) sets out the following argument.

1 There exist instances of intense suffering which an omnipotent, omniscient being could have prevented without thereby losing some greater good or permitting some evil equally bad or worse.
2 An omniscient, wholly good being would prevent the occurrence of any intense suffering it could, unless it could not do so without thereby losing some greater good or permitting some evil equally bad or worse.
3 There does not exist an omnipotent, omniscient, wholly good being.

Now Rowe believes that this third statement is entailed by the first two. Or, to put this another way, if the first two are true, the third must follow on from them. Yet, on the basis of Duhem's analysis, such a conclusion simply cannot be drawn. There is a problem within the theory as a whole. One or more of its assumptions require revision. But which one? And is this fatal to the theory as a whole? Or is it merely an anomaly, which will be resolved through theoretical or observational advances?

Duhemian objections can easily be raised against each of Rowe's assertions. For example, note how his first assertion combines an observation statement with a hypothesis. We can disentangle them by suggesting that the first statement could more properly be expressed as an empirical observation statement $O$ and a hypothesis $H$:

$O$ = There exist instances of intense suffering;
$H$ = An omnipotent, omniscient being could have prevented instances of intense suffering without thereby losing some greater good or permitting some evil which is equally bad, if not worse.

How, we might reasonably ask, can Rowe know $H$? A number of writers have pointed out that the force of Rowe's objection would seem to be vitiated by an unwarranted confidence in a human ability to determine that God has (or could have) no good reason to allow some of the suffering we experience in the world.

As Alston points out, one of Rowe's difficulties is that he is obliged to rely on inference in establishing his case against God. Arguments from experience must be accompanied by an acceptance of the cognitive limits which are imposed upon us – limits which Rowe seems unwilling to concede. Alston notes three areas of limitation: a lack of data (such as the nature of the universe, the reasons behind divine behavior, and the nature of the afterlife); complexity beyond human capacity (in that the factors involved are too complex and nuanced to permit easy analysis); and difficulty in determining what is metaphysically possible or necessary (in that we are in no position to determine what can and cannot be the case). Alston concludes that we are simply not in a position to justifiably assert that God, if he exists, would have no sufficient reason for permitting suffering.

The kind of considerations that Alston and others bring forward point to the present existence of evil and suffering as being an anomaly within the Christian worldview, rather than constituting its formal disconfirmation. On the basis of a naïve falsificationism, any such apparent contradiction between theory and observation is adequate grounds for the rejection of the theory. The history of science, however, suggests that many alleged contradictions are subsequently accommodated within expanded versions of theories, as the process of scientific advance continues.

On the basis of his survey of the development of the natural sciences, Thomas Kuhn commented that "if any and every failure to fit were ground for theory rejection, all theories ought to be rejected at all times" (Kuhn, 1970, pp. 146–7). A more realistic approach is to recognize that even the best explanations are attended by anomalies and difficulties. The difficulty lies in knowing which anomalies will eventually *be accommodated within* a theory, and which will eventually lead to the *discrediting* of a theory. Only time will tell.

This discussion of how theories cope with anomalies raises some important questions about how theories are developed in the first place. In the following chapter, we shall consider some general issues concerning the development of theory in both the natural sciences and religion.

## For Further Reading

Alston, William P. "The Inductive Argument from Evil and the Human Cognitive Condition." *Philosophical Perspectives*, 5 (1991): 29–67.

Duhem, Pierre. *The Aim and Structure of Physical Theory*. Princeton, NJ: Princeton University Press, 1954.

Greenwood, J. D. "Two Dogmas of Neo-Empiricism: The 'Theory-Informity' of Observation and the Duhem–Quine Thesis." *Philosophy of Science*, 57 (1990): 553–74.

Grosser, Morton. *The Discovery of Neptune*. Cambridge, MA: Harvard University Press, 1962.

Laudan, Larry, and Jarrett Leplin, "Empirical Equivalence and Underdetermination." *Journal of Philosophy*, 88 (1991): 449–72.

Quine, W. V. O. *From a Logical Point of View*. Cambridge, MA: Harvard University Press, 1953.

Rowe, William L. "Evil and the Theistic Hypothesis: A Response to Wykstra." *International Journal for Philosophy of Religion*, 16 (1984): 95–100.

# Chapter

# 16 The Development of Theory in Science and Religion

Both science and religion develop theories, understood as attempts to make sense of what is observed. So how are these theories developed? And how do they change over time? These are important questions for both science and religion, and they will be considered in the present chapter.

First, let us ask why theories arise. Why are scientists not prepared to remain content with merely accumulating data? We saw earlier how the quest for explanation is deeply ingrained in the scientific method. Science is concerned with identifying and representing the deeper patterns underlying the surface appearance of the world. Theories can be seen as proposals to explain observations. They offer "pictures" of reality, within which existing observations may be accommodated, and which lead to the prediction of novel observations. For example, Newton's theory of planetary motion, which we noted earlier, is an attempt to make sense of a vast body of observations – including the way in which an apple falls to the ground. Similarly, Charles Darwin's theory of natural selection was an attempt to discern the deep structure of the biological world, based on a substantial series of observations, including many made while he was the naturalist on HMS *Beagle*.

A good scientific theory is often held to have four characteristics, which we shall summarize as follows:

1   Empirical adequacy. A good theory must be capable of accommodating known observations. This does not prove that a theory is true. As we noted earlier, a set

of observations will be consistent with several theories. Theories are, to use the technical term, "underdetermined" by the evidence. Nor does disagreement with the data necessary invalidate a theory. As we have seen, "anomalies" can often be accommodated by theories. Although some scientists hold that predictive success is a mark of a good theory, others hold that the distinction between accommodation (making sense of what is already known) and prediction is psychological, rather than philosophical.

2  Coherence. A theory should be internally consistent, so that its various elements do not contradict each other. Furthermore, more advanced and sophisticated theories should be consistent with earlier theories that were regarded as good. Thus Albert Einstein's theory of relativity was able to include the earlier theories of Isaac Newton, which came to be seen as a special case of the more general theory.

3  Scope. A good theory has the capacity to bring together hitherto unconnected sets of observations. James Clerk Maxwell's famous demonstration of the unity of electricity and magnetism, which had hitherto been seen as different, is a good example of this. One of the goals of contemporary scientific theorizing is the formulation of "theories of everything" – a theory which is so comprehensive that it is able to unite in a single approach what had hitherto been spread out over a range of theories.

4  Fertility. Many argue that the hallmark of a good theory is its ability to generate research programs and further theoretical development. This may include a theory making predictions which may prove to be verifiable or falsifiable by experiment.

So what of the development of individual scientific theories over time? Scientists today have moved on considerably from the theories of the early modern period. There is no doubt that scientific theories have undergone development, including the displacement of those which were once widely accepted and regarded as the best available explanation of the known evidence. Isaac Newton's theory of mechanics (sometimes known as "kinematics"), for example, was widely accepted in the eighteenth and nineteenth century, and was widely regarded as one of the most firmly established of all scientific theories. Although involving the once counterintuitive notion of "action at a distance" in relation to gravitational forces, Newton's approach achieved such a high degree of explanatory success, both retrodictive and predictive, that it seemed to be the ultimate paradigm of a triumphant scientific theory.

Today, Newton's theories have been displaced by Einstein's general theory of relativity. Newtonian kinematics can now be seen as a limiting case of a more general theory. Where objects are moving with a sufficiently small velocity in comparison with that of light, the relativistic dimensions of the situation are such that the Newtonian account of their motion is a good approximation to the truth. But it is now seen as only an approximation. What was once thought to be an unassailable theory is now seen as a special instance of a more general theory. At one level, Newton is simply wrong. Similarly, Newtonian mechanics offer an excellent approximation to the truth in the case of relatively large (by quantum standards) bodies, now being seen as a limiting case of quantum mechanics. Once more, Newton's approach is seen as a special instance of a more general approach. It is possible to speak of Newtonian mechanics as being "true within its own domain" (meaning "when dealing with large bodies moving at low velocities").

Other examples of apparently firmly established theories which have been subject to radical historical erosion can be drawn from the field of optics. In the eighteenth century, the Newtonian corpuscular theory was widely accepted; by the nineteenth, Fresnel's elastic solid ether theory had largely displaced it. Both attempted to give an account of substantially the same observations; they did so, however, in rather different – and ultimately incommensurable – manners. On the basis of such considerations, the American philosopher of science Larry Laudan (born 1941) argues that the history of science offers a plethora of theories which were once widely accepted but have long since been abandoned or drastically modified. Examples of this category include the crystalline spheres of ancient and medieval astronomy, the humoral theory of medicine, the caloric theory of heat, and the electromagnetic ether. Each of these theories was once judged to be successful by the criteria of their contemporaries; they have now been abandoned.

One of the most widely discussed accounts of the development of the scientific method in general, and theories in particular, was developed by Thomas S. Kuhn (1922–96) in his *Structure of Scientific Revolutions* (first published 1962). Kuhn introduced the idea of "scientific revolutions," which called into question the prevailing view of the nature of scientific progress, which held that radically new theories arise gradually through verification or falsification. A good example of this is the "gradual progress" model set out by Karl Popper in his *Logic of Scientific Discovery*. The transition from one paradigm to another is not gradual, Kuhn argued, but took the form of a rapid transition, with major shifts in understanding. Kuhn introduced a term which has had a profound impact on the history and philosophy of science: the "paradigm shift." "Successive transition from one paradigm to another via revolution is the usual developmental pattern of mature science" (Kuhn, 1970, p. 12).

What did Kuhn mean by this term? Kuhn's use of the term "paradigm" is a little confusing, and has led to serious misunderstandings of what he intended. In general terms, he uses the term in two senses:

1   The word is used in a general sense, to refer to the broad group of common assumptions which unites particular group of scientists. It is an accepted cluster of generalizations, methods, and models.

2   The term is also used in a more specific and restricted sense to refer to a past scientific explanatory success, which seems to offer a framework which can be treated as normative, and is hence treated as exemplary thereafter – until something finally causes that paradigm to be abandoned.

For our purposes in this chapter, we shall use the term to refer to "a strong network of commitments – conceptual, theoretical, instrumental, and methodological" (Kuhn, 1970, p. 42).

On the basis of his studies of the development of the natural sciences, Kuhn argued that a given paradigm is accepted as normative on account of its past explanatory success. Once a given paradigm has been accepted, a period of what Kuhn terms "normal science" follows. During this period, the paradigm which resulted from this earlier success is accepted. Experimental evidence which appears to contradict is treated as anomalous – that is, as items which pose difficulties for the paradigm, but which do not require the paradigm to be abandoned. In effect, the anomaly is regarded as something for which a solution is anticipated within the context of that paradigm, even if at present the precise nature of that solution remains unclear.

**Figure 16.1** Thomas Kuhn (Time & Life Pictures/ Getty Images)

Ad hoc modifications are proposed to the existing paradigm – as in the case of Ptolemaic astronomy, in which growing evidence of discrepancies between theory and observation could be accounted for through the addition of epicycles to the system. The resulting system was cumbersome and inelegant. But people still held on to it, partly because there was no obvious alternative.

So what happens if a series of anomalies build up, and eventually achieve a cumulative force which calls the paradigm into question? Or if a single anomaly becomes of such significance that the challenge which it poses cannot be overlooked? At this point, tinkering becomes impossible. A more radical change is clearly needed. Kuhn argues that, in such situations, a crisis arises within the paradigm which is to be seen as a prelude to a "scientific revolution." Kuhn contrasts this *revolutionary* approach with an essentially *evolutionary* model which sees a steady progression in scientific understanding through a gradual accumulation of data and understanding. Where other historians of science spoke of "scientific progress," Kuhn preferred the imagery of a revolution, in which a major change in assumptions took place over a short period of time.

> The transition between competing paradigms cannot be made one step at a time, forced
> by logic and neutral experience … It must occur all at once (though not necessarily in
> an instant) or not at all. … In these matters neither proof nor error is at issue. The
> transfer of allegiance from paradigm to paradigm is a conversion experience that cannot
> be forced. (Kuhn, 1970, p. 149)

An essential point in Kuhn's argument is that established and future paradigms are incommensurable, so that the old must gave way to the new. There is no way in which part of the older paradigm can be retained; it is displaced by the new. This paradigm shift leads to things being seen, understood, and investigated in a new way.

The critical point to note is that the factors which precipitate this revolution are not necessarily rational in character. Kuhn argues that a complex network of issues lie behind the decision to abandon one paradigm and accept another, and that these cannot be explained solely on the basis of scientific considerations. Highly subjective issues are involved. Kuhn compares a paradigm shift to a religious conversion. His emphasis on the subjective reasons for paradigm shifts has led some of his critics to suggest that his account of scientific development seems to rest too much on "mob psychology."

Kuhn's analysis of the development of scientific understanding has been subjected to considerable criticism on other grounds. In part, this has related to the notion that successive paradigms are incommensurable. For some of his critics, this is simply inaccurate. Stephen Toulmin argues that there is far more continuity across a revolution than Kuhn allows, and that he fails to observe that frequent small changes are far more typical of scientific progress than the more radical "revolutions" which Kuhn proposed. The changeover from, for example, Newtonian to Einsteinian physics does not really require to be described as a "paradigm shift."

Reacting to Kuhn's account of the history of science as a series of paradigm changes, the Hungarian philosopher of science Imre Lakatos (1922–74) described it instead as a series of competing *research programs*. A research program is a vast network of theories, logically related to one another and supported by a variety of data. What unifies this network of theory and data is the "hard core" – a thesis, often metaphysical in character, concerning the nature of the aspect of reality under investigation. The scientists involved in such a program will attempt to shield this theoretical "hard core" behind a protective belt of *auxiliary hypotheses*.

This means that observations that are inconsistent with the theory are understood to apply to this belt of ancillary or auxiliary hypotheses, but not to the core elements of the theory. Thus the philosopher of science Pierre Duhem (1861–1916) argued that one can always protect a cherished belief from hostile evidence by redirecting the criticism toward other things that are believed. Lakatos can be seen as placing this insight on a firmer theoretical foundation, creating a severe difficulty for the naïve falsificationism he discerned in some of Popper's writings.

This discussion is of considerable importance, and cannot be gone into in any further detail here. However, it is important to realize that Kuhn's understanding of how paradigms shift puts considerable emphasis on nonscientific factors, and that this understanding of how paradigms are adopted and abandoned has wider implications for religious belief. Two of Kuhn's central themes may be explored to illustrate his relevance for theology. First, Kuhn's concept of "paradigm shifts" is helpful in attempting to understand the major intellectual shifts which have taken place in the history of religious thought. As we have noted, religious thinking is influenced, at least to some extent, by the cultural and philosophical presuppositions of the day. Radical shifts in these background assumptions can thus be of major importance, as the development of Christian theology has demonstrated. For example, consider the following epochs in modern western Christian thought: the Reformation; the Enlightenment; Postmodernism. Each of these can be seen as representing a "paradigm shift," with radical changes in our understanding of how theology should be done. Existing understandings of background presuppositions, norms, and methods are often radically altered – and occasionally abandoned altogether – in the transition from one paradigm to another.

Our second point of interest concerns the issue of realism. Kuhn rejects realism as an explanation of the successes of scientific research, and thus does not see an increasing convergence between "theory" and "reality" as an explanation of scientific progress. Nothing, he argues is lost in rejecting the realist account of scientific development. Yet how can one meaningfully talk of "progress," unless there is some means of knowing that science is proceeding in the right direction, rather than taking a false turn which will need to be corrected in future?

Kuhn's work has inspired a substantial amount of writing in the field of the sociology of knowledge, arguing that, since theories are always underdetermined by evidence, theory choice takes place on the basis of sociological considerations. In other words, the decision to accept one theory rather than another rests not so much on experimental evidence, as on various social values, vested interests, and institutional concerns. This has raised the very significant question of whether religious doctrines correspond to anything that is "real," or whether they can be seen as determined by social factors. For example, it might be argued that the traditional Christian doctrine of the "two natures" of Christ is not determined by the phenomena this doctrine is required to explain, but by some aspects of the political agenda of the Roman Empire.

So are there any further parallels between the development of scientific theories and theological ideas? An idea that is often discussed in this context is the "development of doctrine." Earlier generations of Christian theologians were reluctant to allow that the teachings of the church can be said to have "developed" or "evolved," preferring to believe that the church's teaching has always been the same. However, by the

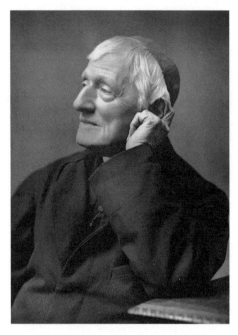

**Figure 16.2** John Henry Newman (© Hulton-Deutsch Collection/CORBIS)

early nineteenth century, the evidence of such development had become so clear that it could no longer be denied. John Henry Newman's classic *Essay on the Development of Doctrine* (1845) established that the development of doctrine had indeed taken place, and suggested that this process could be likened to the growth of a plant.

Yet the publication of Darwin's *Origin of Species* (1859) led to this process being developed in a new way. One of the most remarkable developments within western cultural history of the last century has been the assimilation of the idea of cultural and intellectual change to a Darwinian evolutionary paradigm. So could Darwin's model of evolution be applied to the development of doctrine? Was this also a case of the survival of the fittest? Or simply of the growth of seeds into their intended forms? The debate continues, and lies beyond the scope of this brief introduction. Suffice it to say that the development of Christian doctrine shows how the dialogue between religion and science raises new questions for theology, and may even point to some answers.

As will be clear from these closing comments, this work has chosen to concentrate on Christianity. Rather than talk about "religion" in general, we have considered some specific issues that arise from Christianity in particular. This raises the question of how other religious traditions relate to the natural sciences – a matter to which we shall turn in the following chapter.

## For Further Reading

Kadvany, John. *Imre Lakatos and the Guises of Reason*. Durham. NC: Duke University Press, 2001.

Kuhn, Thomas S. *The Structure of Scientific Revolutions*, 2nd edn. Chicago: University of Chicago Press, 1970.

McGrath, Alister E. *A Scientific Theology: 3 – Theory*. London: T & T Clark, 2003.

Nichols, Aidan. *From Newman to Congar: The Idea of Doctrinal Development from the Victorians to the Second Vatican Council*. Edinburgh: T. & T. Clark, 1990.

Strug, Cordell. "Kuhn's Paradigm Thesis: A Two-Edged Sword for the Philosophy of Religion." *Religious Studies*, 20 (1984): 269–79.

Thagard, Paul. *Conceptual Revolutions*. Princeton, NJ: Princeton University Press, 1992.

# Chapter

# 17

## The Interaction of Science and Religion in Other Faiths

The analysis in the present volume has primarily focused on the relation of the natural sciences to Christianity. The reasons for this emphasis have already been noted. Yet some readers of this work will not unreasonably wonder what issues are associated with the relation between science and religion in other faiths. In this chapter, we shall offer a brief account of the interaction of science and religion in Judaism, Islam, Hinduism, and Buddhism. These necessarily succinct sketches are intended only to highlight some of the themes of these relationships, which are often complex. It is hoped that the bibliographical guidance offered will enable interested readers to take these matters further.

One feature that appears to be common to most religious traditions is a perceived tension between traditional cosmologies and those advocated by the natural sciences. For example, the same kind of antievolutionary attitudes found in some conservative Protestant groups are widespread in more conservative Jewish, Islamic, and Hindu circles. Thus the Turkish Islamist writer Adnan Oktar (born 1956) has published extensively against evolutionary theory using the pseudonym Harun Yahya, including a recent work entitled *The Atlas of Creation* (2006). Oktar often uses arguments against evolution which are very similar to those used by creationists.

In what follows, we shall note some aspects of the interaction of science and religion in these four religious traditions. In each case, we shall consider how these traditions deal with the issues arising from Darwin's theory of evolution, given that this is widely regarded as one of the most important contemporary issues in science and religion.

## Judaism

Even a cursory overview of the history of science shows how Jewish scientists have made a very significant contribution to its development. Albert Einstein (1877–1955), widely credited with some of the greatest theoretical breakthroughs of the twentieth century, is a good example of this phenomenon. Judaism is a very diverse faith, embracing a wide variety of theological perspectives. Furthermore, the complex cultural connotations of being "Jewish" allows for an individual to be ethnically Jewish without necessarily holding any religious beliefs. It is therefore very difficult to generalize about the relationship between Judaism and the natural sciences. Indeed, many of the debates within Judaism concerning the relation of science and religion have their direct counterparts within Christianity, reflecting the fact that both faiths share some common texts, most notably the book of Genesis.

Early Jewish writers generally took a very literal view of the Genesis creation accounts. Typically, these were interpreted to mean that the world originated 6,000 years ago, and that humanity was created directly at that time. Yet many Jewish writers, especially Philo of Alexandria, adopted strongly allegorical interpretations of biblical texts, including the Genesis creation stories. This approach is echoed in the writings of the great medieval Jewish philosopher Maimonides (1135–1204), who went so far as to suggest that if science and biblical interpretation were found to be in tension, this was because the science was not understood properly, or the biblical text was being misinterpreted. If science demanded certain beliefs that did not contradict any fundamentals of faith, then those beliefs should be accepted, and scripture interpreted in their light.

Such approaches allowed most Jewish intellectuals to adopt a relaxed attitude to Darwin's theory of evolution. Most echoed views already associated with Christian

**Figure 17.1** Albert Einstein (© The Print Collector/ Heritage-Images)

writers, which argued that Darwin's theory was best seen as an amplification, not a contradiction, of the biblical creation accounts. Others argued that Darwin's theory clearly indicated that these texts were to be interpreted allegorically or metaphorically, rather than taken as literal historical statements. Yet a minority of voices remain opposed to the notion of biological evolution. For example, Moshe Feinstein (1895–1986), an ultra-Orthodox rabbi, held that belief in evolution amounts to a heresy. Others argue that scientific development offers Judaism the opportunity to revisit and revise some of its key metaphors for God. Rabbi David W. Nelson, for example, argues that theoretical concepts in contemporary physics offer Judaism new metaphors for speaking about God.

## Islam

Islam played a major role in fostering the development of the natural sciences during what is sometimes called the "Golden Age," generally dated from the seventh to the thirteenth centuries. Early Islamic writers preserved and translated many texts of the classical age, particularly Aristotelian works dealing with natural phenomena, such as his *Physics* and *Meteorology*. Yet this emphasis upon Aristotle was ultimately a prescientific intellectual enterprise. The scientific revolution actually involved the abandoning of much of Aristotle as an impediment to scientific progress. The later decline of science in the Islamic world mirrored the rise of science in the West, with the destruction of the astronomical observatory at Istanbul in 1580 often being seen as a symbol of this growing disinterest in science.

Contemporary Islam demonstrates the same tensions that are found in other religious faiths concerning the relation between science and religion, especially with regard to the interpretation of sacred texts in the light of scientific advance. Certain Qur'anic texts call upon their readers to study the natural world as a means of appreciating the wisdom of Allah. This might seem to point to the emergence of an Islamic natural theology, with parallels to its Christian counterpart. However, the situation is not so simple. As has often been pointed out, there is no direct equivalent to the Christian notion of "natural theology" within Islam. In general, Islam recognizes no true knowledge of God outside the Qur'an, thus raising difficulties for any notion of an Islamic natural theology. The term *kalam* is often used to designate the general area of philosophical inquiry which might be taken to include natural theology; yet this does not necessarily involve the notion that knowledge of God may be had through nature. The question has led to some serious disputes within Islam, with the result that shifting patterns of Qur'anic interpretation make generalizations in this area problematic.

Although some schools of Qur'anical interpretation have argued for an appeal to nature as part of a general apologetic for faith, other Muslim theologians, classic and contemporary, have been severely critical of any such development. The most significant of these is the medieval writer Al-Ghazali (1058–1111), who regarded natural philosophy and theology as posing a significant threat to Islamic orthodoxy. In his *Incoherence of the Philosophers*, Al-Ghazali denounced Islamic scholars who made use of Plato, Aristotle, and other non-Islamic sources. While encouraging the development of certain practical sciences, such as astronomy and anatomy, Al-Ghazali did not see such sciences as having any revelatory role. Since about 1500, Al-Ghazali's view has gained the ascendancy, with important implications for Islamic attitudes towards the enterprise of seeking the transcendent within nature. Whereas western Christian theology embraced natural theology in the early modern period, Islam moved with equally great enthusiasm to reject it.

A further issue of importance concerns causality within nature. In what way is God active in nature? As we have seen in chapter 14, Christian theology developed a number of ways of dealing with this. During the Middle Ages, the notion of "secondary causality" came to be of especial importance. This notion allowed the ultimate causality of all things to be located with God, while at the same time allowing for causality within the natural world itself. These natural causalities were open to scientific investigation. Yet some of Islam's most prominent thinkers of this age, including Al-Ghazali, argued for the direct causal influence of God in all things. For example, in his work *Moderation in Faith*, Al-Ghazali argued that all entities and events were directly caused by God, who alone had the power to bring things about.

> You have known from the sum of this that all temporal events, their substances and accidents, those occurring in the entities of the animate and the inanimate, come about through the power of God, may he be exalted. He alone holds the sole prerogative of inventing them. No created thing comes about through another created thing. Rather, all come about through divine power. (Al-Ghazali, 1994, pp. 314–15)

This approach – often known as "occasionalism" – led to the marginalization of the notion of causality within the natural world, which was increasingly becoming the object of study by the natural sciences. It is not possible to attribute "effects" to any direct, necessary "cause" other than God. For example, consider fire burning a flammable substance. Is this action caused by the fire? When fire and cotton are brought together, he argues, the cotton is burned directly by God rather than by the fire. Al-Ghazali is prepared to allow that there might be something inherent in fire that predisposes it to accept from God the act of burning another substance. Yet this only takes place because it is God's will that it should. God can refuse to allow this to happen, as when, according to Islamic tradition, Abraham was not consumed by fire.

Al-Ghazali holds that certain laws of causation generally apply within the observable world, but only because it is God's will that this is the case.

Islam shows the same tensions over Darwin's theory of evolution as those encountered in other religions governed by sacred texts, such as Christianity. Qur'anic texts referring to the creation of humanity can be interpreted in a number of ways. Traditionally, Adam was understood to be created immediately by Allah from clay. This is interpreted by many Islamic scholars to exclude the notion of evolution. Others, however, argue that biological evolution merely clarifies the manner of this act of creation, requiring that it be seen as an extended process, rather than a completed primordial act. Most Islamic writers raise objections to the apparent randomness of the evolutionary process, and therefore either *reject* evolution for this reason, or insist that the will of Allah is to be discerned as lying behind what otherwise appear to be random events. Once more, these debates have direct counterparts to those advocated within Christianity and Judaism.

# Hinduism

Christianity, Judaism, and Islam are faiths which are grounded on sacred texts, which need to be interpreted. The understanding of the relationship of science and religion is thus linked with specific interpretations of these texts. In the case of Hinduism, the situation is more complex. It is certainly correct to speak of the Vedas as "Hindu sacred texts." Yet these are not strictly understood as mediating divine revelation. Hinduism considers these texts to be *sruti* ("things that were heard") by *rishis* (holy men who are the mythical founders of Hinduism) during deep meditation. These texts are thus understood to originate neither from divine revelation nor human wisdom, but from the fundamental nature of the cosmos itself.

Hinduism is a complex religious tradition, bringing together a wide variety of ideas which originated over time across a wide geographical area. The diversity of Hindu religious texts has often been noted, such as the six major schools of thought concerning the nature of divine reality. This has particular significance in relation to Hindu views on creation. Hinduism does not accept that the world was created in the biblical sense of the term, familiar to Christians, in that God and the universe are essentially the same. Rather, Hinduism speaks of the cosmic being "manifesting" himself as the universe. A wide variety of mutually inconsistent creation narratives are encountered in exploring this idea. For example, the Rig Veda recounts how the universe was created from the cosmic being, Purusha, who is described as having a thousand heads, a thousand eyes, and a thousand feet. The four classes of Hindu society emerged from Purusha's mouth, arms, thighs, and feet. Other creation narratives speak of the creation of the universe using a wide variety of imagery. The Rig Veda says, "Who really knows, and who can swear, how, when, or where the creation took place?"

As a result, many Hindu scholars believe that Hinduism has little relevance to the natural sciences. There is no regnant creation narrative or cosmogony that is challenged by modern scientific development. The development of Indian astronomy does not appear to have been significantly impeded by religious concerns. The diversity of Hindu creation stories is such that at least some of them are open to the possibility of incorporating at least some aspects of evolutionary theory. Some Hindus thus find explicit support for, and others a foreshadowing of, evolutionary ideas in the Vedas. Despite this, however, a school of "Vedic creationism" has emerged, which holds that that all species, including humans, have "devolved," or come down, from a highly evolved pure consciousness. Different species of plants and animals are simply material forms adopted by this pure consciousness as it transmigrates in endless cycles of births and rebirths over vast periods of time.

# Buddhism

It is generally considered that Buddhism offers a particularly constructive relationship with the natural sciences. In part, this has to be seen as the result of a historical accident. Throughout most of Buddhism's history, it had no contact with the natural sciences. As with Hinduism, the Buddhist encounter with the natural sciences really began during the sixteenth century, when western colonial expansion in Asia led to scientific ideas being exported to this region. There were thus no deeply ingrained suspicions about the sciences to threaten their consideration. Furthermore, most of the constructive thinking concerning the relation of Buddhism and science has been undertaken in the United States of America by western scientists who have adopted or affirmed some form of Buddhist outlook. As a result, the dialogue between science and Buddhism has been encouraged through a matrix of positive cultural associations, which are not always present in Buddhism's original homelands.

Yet the generally benign attitude of Buddhism to science is due to more than the accidents of history. There are other factors of a more theological nature involved. For example, Buddhism is nontheistic. This has led some recent Buddhist writers to point to parallels between Buddhism's "nontheistic" worldview and current scientific cosmology as evidence that Buddhism is more in harmony with the sciences than Christian theism. Like the scientific method itself, it is argued, Buddhism is nontheistic. Some have argued that early Theravada Buddhism employs empirical and experimental methods which are broadly equivalent to those of modern science. One could therefore argue that Buddhism is a "scientific" religion, in the sense that Buddhist doctrines harmonize with current scientific models of physical reality in a way that other religions do not.

Furthermore, Buddhism does not acknowledge a definitive divine revelation which is challenged by scientific advance. Also, the question of the time and manner of the creation of the universe is seen as meaningless, since traditional Buddhist cosmology describes the universe as an eternally changing system of interdependent interrelationships without beginning or end. The absence of what many westerners would regard as distinctively religious elements has led them to wonder whether they are actually dealing with a philosophy or a type of applied psychology, rather than a religion. This comment is not without merit, as it raises questions about how a "religion" is to be defined (see pp. 4–5, 185).

Yet this does not necessarily mean that Buddhism is more sympathetic to the natural sciences than other religions, or that its intrinsic structures are somehow more open to the scientific method. Most recent Buddhist writings on the natural sciences create the impression that the structure of Buddhist tradition remains untouched by the sciences, either positively or negatively. The avoidance of tension is often secured by the avoidance of interaction. In contrast, Victor Mansfield, Professor of Physics and Astronomy at Colgate University, has argued that Buddhism has spiritual resources that can fill in the "gaps" of western science relative to mental and emotional experiences, which allow the psychology to develop coherent theories of cognition, while informing other sciences. Mansfield thus suggests that the Buddhist dialogue with science is more likely to lead to the creative transformation of science than of Buddhism itself.

Yet there are areas of science in which Buddhism clearly has a particular interest. Perhaps the most important of these is psychology. Buddhist teachings and concerns about the inner self and the practice of meditation have led many Buddhists to explore contemporary psychology, and develop their traditional doctrines of suffering and its causes, the notion of "enlightenment," and the practice of meditation into a more contemporary context. Carl Jung, for example, noted the potential importance of Buddhism for psychotherapy. The growing interest in this field is evident from the recent formation of Buddhist sections in many professional psychological associations.

In this chapter, we have looked very briefly at science and religion issues in religions other than Christianity. There is clearly much more that needs to be said, if an overall understanding of the complex relationship between science and religion is to be understood. It is hoped that this necessarily short overview will encourage those with interests in these fields to take their reading and thinking further.

## For Further Reading

Cantor, Geoffrey, and Marc Swetlitz (eds). *Jewish Tradition and the Challenge of Darwinism.* Chicago: University of Chicago Press, 2006.

Efron, Noah J. *Judaism and Science: A Historical Introduction.* Westport, CT: Greenwood Press, 2007.

Giacaman, George, and Raja Bahlul. "Al-Ghazali on Miracles and Necessary Connection." *Medieval Philosophy and Theology*, 9 (2000): 39–50.

Kak, Subhash C. "Birth and Early Development of Indian Astronomy." In Helaine Selin (ed.), *Astronomy across Cultures: The History of Non-Western Astronomy*, pp. 303–40. Dordrecht: Kluwer, 2000.

Mansfield, Victor. *Tibetan Buddhism and Modern Physics: Toward a Union of Love and Knowledge.* Philadelphia: Templeton Foundation Press, 2008.

Nelson, David W. *Judaism, Physics, and God: Searching for Sacred Metaphors in a Post-Einstein World.* Woodstock, VT: Jewish Lights Publications, 2005.

Ragep, F. Jamil. "Freeing Astronomy from Philosophy: An Aspect of Islamic Influence on Science." *Osiris*, 16 (2001): 49–71.

Ricard, Matthieu, and Xuan Thuan Trinh. *The Quantum and the Lotus: A Journey to the Frontiers Where Science and Buddhism Meet.* New York: Crown Publishers, 2001.

Saliba, George. *A History of Arabic Astronomy: Planetary Theories during the Golden Age of Islam.* New York: New York University Press, 1994.

Zajonc, Arthur, and Zara Houshmand. *The New Physics and Cosmology: Dialogues with the Dalai Lama.* New York: Oxford University Press, 2004.

# PART

# III Science and Religion
*Contemporary Debates*

In Part II, we considered some general themes relating to the dialogue between science and religion. As we noted earlier, however, one of the most significant difficulties in developing this dialogue is that the terms "science" and "religion" can refer to a wide variety of disciplines and practices. It is therefore important to be more specific. In Part III, we shall focus on religious or theological issues which arise from specific scientific disciplines.

We shall begin by considering whether the scientific method itself is intrinsically atheistic, interacting particularly with the atheist propagandist and scientific popularizer Richard Dawkins. Our attention then turns to the significant debates in contemporary cosmology concerning the origins of the universe, and especially the critical value of the fundamental constants of nature in shaping the process of cosmic development. What is the religious significance of what are now widely known as "anthropic" phenomena? We then turn to quantum theory, and ask whether the notion of "complementarity" has any theological significance and value. What can be learned theologically from the difficulties quantum theory has encountered in trying to make sense of the complex data of experience?

The next chapter deals with the biological sciences, beginning with the theologically significant question of whether contemporary evolutionary biology permits us to speak of there being "purpose" within nature. This leads us on to consider evolutionary psychology, looking especially at its accounts of the origins of religion. This is followed by a brief exploration of the psychology of religion, including Sigmund Freud's famous psychoanalytical explanation of the origins of belief in God. Finally, we consider the relatively new discipline of the cognitive science of religion, and ask whether it forces us to speak of religious belief as being a "natural" phenomenon.

Limitations on space means that our discussion of each of these major areas is limited. However, the suggestions for further reading will enable readers to develop their thinking on these important topics.

# Chapter

# 18 Richard Dawkins and Scientific Atheism

*Does Science Deny God?*

One of the most important questions which arises from the interaction of science and religion is whether the natural sciences either deny the existence of God, or render God's existence totally unnecessary in order to explain things. This debate has rumbled on since the seventeenth century. It was given a new injection of life and intellectual energy through the publication of a series of works in the period 2006–7, often referred to as the "new atheism." Two of these works defended the idea that the natural sciences endorsed an atheist perspective. We shall consider Daniel Dennett's approach, as set out in his influential work *Darwin's Dangerous Idea* (1995), later (see chapter 22). In this chapter, we shall consider some of the arguments put forward by Richard Dawkins in his *The God Delusion* (2006), and some of the works leading up to this.

Richard Dawkins (born 1941) is perhaps the best-known representative of "scientific atheism." He held the position of Professor of the Public Understanding of Science at Oxford University until his retirement in 2008. He is best known for a series of works popularizing scientific themes. Of these, the most famous is his first – *The Selfish Gene* (first published 1976). In this work, Dawkins argued for a "gene's-eye" view of evolution. This "gene's-eye view of the world" regards an individual organism as a "survival machine," a "passive receptacle for genes," or a "colony of genes."

[Genes] swarm in huge colonies, safe inside gigantic lumbering robots, sealed off from the outside world, communicating with it by tortuous indirect routes, manipulating it by remote control. They are in you and me; they created us, body and mind; and their preservation is the ultimate rationale for our existence. (Dawkins, 1989, p. 21)

For Dawkins, evolutionary biology in general, and the "gene's-eye" view of evolution in particular, eliminates the plausibility of belief in God. This point is made with particular force in *The Blind Watchmaker* (1986), which demonstrates how a neo-Darwinian account of evolution eliminates any need to believe in God as an alleged "designer" or "creator" of the natural order. Dawkins focuses on the approach of William Paley (see pp. 31, 64–5), who held that the complexity of the biological realm – such as the intricate structure of the human eye – pointed to a divine creator. Dawkins notes with appreciation Paley's "beautiful and reverent descriptions of the dissected machinery of life." Yet Paley's case for God – though made with "passionate sincerity" and "informed by the best biological scholarship of his day" – is "gloriously and utterly wrong." The "only watchmaker in nature is the blind forces of physics" (Dawkins, 1986, p. 5).

**Figure 18.1** Richard Dawkins (PA Photos)

This, Dawkins argues, leaves the "argument from design" in tatters. Dawkins argues that one can only speak of "apparent design" in nature, and that this delusion of design arises through the blind forces of nature. What an earlier generation saw as proof of God's existence is now seen simply as the outcome of entirely natural processes, which need not involve or invoke God. This point is developed further by Dawkins in *Climbing Mount Improbable* (1996), which argues that statistically highly improbable events can happen over the vast periods of time envisaged by the evolutionary process, through the accumulation of small, incremental changes.

Dawkins makes some good points. Yet he seems to assume that the intellectual case for Christianity rests largely, if not totally, upon an "argument for design," such as that proposed by Paley. However, this kind of argument is actually quite a recent development, having emerged in England in the late seventeenth and early eighteenth centuries, especially through the work of John Ray (1627–1705), such as his *Wisdom of God Manifested in the Works of Creation* (1691). Dawkins makes an excellent case for abandoning Paley. Sadly, he seems to think this also entails abandoning God. Paley's arguments were being openly criticized as intellectually and aesthetically inadequate a decade before the publication of Darwin's *Origin of Species*. John Henry

Newman, one of the religious luminaries of that age, expressed the view that Paley's approach simply made Christianity intellectually vulnerable, and was more likely to lead to atheism than religious faith as its outcome.

Yet Dawkins's arguments are not limited to the sphere of evolutionary biology. The natural sciences, he argues, taken as a whole, are supportive of atheism. In particular, Dawkins is severely critical of those who invoke God as any kind of scientific explanation. Dawkins is particularly critical of theologians who allow themselves "the dubious luxury of arbitrarily conjuring up a terminator to an infinite regress" (Dawkins, 2006, p. 77). Anything that explains something itself has to be explained – and *that* explanation in turn needs to be explained, and so on. There is no justifiable way of ending this infinite regression of explanations. What explains the explanation? Or, to change the metaphor slightly: Who designed the designer?

However, it needs to be pointed out here that the holy grail of the natural sciences is the quest for the "grand unified theory" – the "theory of everything." Why is such a theory regarded as being so important? Because it can explain everything, without itself requiring or demanding an explanation. The explanatory buck stops right there. There is no infinite regress in the quest for explanation. If Dawkins's brash and simplistic arguments carried weight, this great scientific quest could be dismissed with a seemingly profound, yet in fact trivial, question: "what explains the explainer"?

Furthermore, Dawkins seems to assume that scientific explanation is purely causal in nature. This is certainly one approach, which has a distinguished history, and remains an important part of scientific theorizing. However, more recent work on scientific explanation has emphasized the importance of two alternative approaches, neither of which appeals to causality. The approach known as "inference to the best explanation" (see chapter 7) asks what explanatory framework or theory offers the best fit to what is actually observed in the world. The issue is the degree of fit between theory and observation. Many Christian theologians would argue that a Trinitarian view of God offers an excellent explanation of what is observed, without becoming embroiled in complex discussions about divine causality.

A second alternative approach is the "unificationist" approach to scientific explanation, which explores how well a new theory can account for existing theories. For example, the great British physicist and mathematician James Clerk Maxwell (1831–79) was able to offer a single theory which accounted for both electricity and magnetism, which had earlier been thought of as two quite separate phenomena. Once more, the question of causality is not of critical importance, although causal issues can easily be incorporated into this approach.

Perhaps a more important issue to consider is whether the scientific method is capable of adjudicating whether there is a God or not. Dawkins, who is a strident advocate of the "warfare" model of the relation of science and religion, holds that science is poised to conquer the territory once falsely claimed by religion. What science cannot explain today, it will be able to explain tomorrow.

This raises the critically important question of the scope and limits of the scientific method. Dawkins's approach to this question represents a significant school of thought, which holds that the only secure and valid forms of knowledge are those deriving from the sciences. A similar view is taken by the Oxford chemist Peter Atkins (born 1940). Others, however, argue that the scope of the scientific method is restricted, and that there exist valid and significant areas of human knowledge which cannot be established on the basis of the scientific method.

One leading exponent of this view is Peter Medawar (1915–87), an Oxford immunologist who won the Nobel Prize for medicine for the discovery of acquired immunological tolerance. In *The Limits of Science* (1985), Medawar affirmed that "science is incomparably the most successful enterprise human beings have ever engaged upon" (p. 66). Nevertheless, he insisted on the need to distinguish between "transcendent" questions, which are better left to religion and metaphysics, and questions about the organization and structure of the material universe. With regard to the latter, he argues, there are no limits to the possibilities of scientific achievement. He thus agrees with Dawkins – but only by defining and limiting the domain within which the sciences possess such competency. So what of other questions, such as whether there is a God? Or whether there is purpose within the universe? Though a self-confessed rationalist, Medawar is clear on this matter: there are "questions that science cannot answer, and that no conceivable advance of science would empower it to answer" (1985, p. 66).

The question is also addressed by the evolutionary biologist Stephen Jay Gould (1941–2002). In a 1992 critique of an antievolutionary work which posited that Darwinism was *necessarily* atheistic, Stephen Jay Gould invoked the memory of Mrs. McInerney, his third grade teacher, who was in the habit of rapping young knuckles when their owners said or did particularly stupid things:

> To say it for all my colleagues and for the umpteenth millionth time (from college bull sessions to learned treatises): science simply cannot (by its legitimate methods) adjudicate the issue of God's possible superintendence of nature. We neither affirm nor deny it; we simply can't comment on it as scientists. If some of our crowd have made untoward statements claiming that Darwinism disproves God, then I will find Mrs. McInerney and have their knuckles rapped for it (as long as she can equally treat those members of our crowd who have argued that Darwinism must be God's method of action). (Gould, 1992, p. 119)

Gould rightly insists that science can work only with naturalistic explanations; it can neither affirm nor deny the existence of God. The bottom line for Gould is that Darwinism actually has no bearing on the existence or nature of God. Either a conclusion cannot be reached at all on such matters, or it is to be reached on other grounds.

A final question of importance is the relationship between faith and proof in science and religion. Dawkins is noted for his vigorous argument that religious faith is simply blind trust, involving ignoring evidence and argument. As the core belief that faith is "blind trust" permeates Dawkins's many criticisms of religion, it clearly needs careful examination. Let's examine one of his statements on the nature of faith in a little more detail. In *The Selfish Gene*, Dawkins proposes an absolute dichotomy between "blind faith" and "overwhelming, publicly available evidence":

But what, after all, is faith? It is a state of mind that leads people to believe something – it doesn't matter what – in the total absence of supporting evidence. If there were good supporting evidence, then faith would be superfluous, for the evidence would compel us to believe it anyway. (Dawkins, 1989, p. 330)

This, I must stress, is Dawkins's definition of faith, and it bears no recognizable resemblance to what Christians believe.

Yet Dawkins seems also to have misunderstood or misrepresented the scientific method here, presenting it as if the evidence invariably led to a single, reliable theoretical outcome. The scientific evidence is usually open to multiple interpretations, leaving open the question of which is true (an idea often expressed in terms of the "underdetermination of theory by evidence"). For example, consider this question: is there a single universe, or are there many universes (a multiverse)? The scientific evidence is ambivalent, and a case can be made for each. The evidence does not compel us to believe either. Major scientists can be found on each side of the debate, each taking their position as a matter of faith (in that this cannot be proved). In his *God Delusion*, Dawkins himself advocates the multiverse. Yet he takes that position as a matter of faith – something that he appears to believe that the scientific method excludes.

This brief engagement with "scientific atheism" indicates both the importance of the issues which it raises for the dialogue between science and religion, and the inadequacy of the answers which this form of atheism provides. Yet it seems to be a debate that is certain to continue in the future, not least on account of the importance of the issues which it raises.

One of those debates concerns whether the growing body of evidence suggesting that there is "fine-tuning" in nature points to the existence of a creator. In the following chapter, we shall look at this intriguing debate in greater detail.

## For Further Reading

Dawkins, Richard. *The God Delusion*. Boston: Houghton Mifflin, 2006.

Grafen, Alan, and Mark Ridley (eds). *Richard Dawkins: How a Scientist Changed the Way We Think*. New York: Oxford University Press, 2006.

Lustig, Abigail. "Natural Atheology." In Abigail Lustig, Robert J. Richards, and Michael Ruse (eds), *Darwinian Heresies*, pp. 69–83. Cambridge, UK: Cambridge University Press, 2004.

McGrath, Alister E. *Dawkins' God: Genes, Memes and the Meaning of Life*. Oxford: Blackwell Publishing, 2004.

Medawar, Peter B. *The Limits of Science*. Oxford: Oxford University Press, 1985.

Shanahan, Timothy. "Methodological and Contextual Factors in the Dawkins/Gould Dispute over Evolutionary Progress." *Studies in History and Philosophy of Science*, 31 (2001): 127–51.

Sterelny, Kim. *Dawkins vs. Gould: Survival of the Fittest*. Cambridge, UK: Icon Books, 2001.

# Chapter

# 19 Cosmology

## *Does the Anthropic Principle Mean Anything?*

It is generally thought that modern physics and cosmology offer some of the most important and fruitful possibilities for dialogue between the sciences and religion. In this chapter, we shall focus on two issues of relevance: the "big bang" and the so-called "anthropic principle."

## The "Big Bang"

The question of the origin of the universe is without doubt one of the most fascinating areas of modern scientific analysis and debate. That there are religious dimensions to this debate will be clear. Sir Bernard Lovell (born 1913), the distinguished British pioneer of radio astronomy, is one of many to note that discussion of the origins of the universe inevitably raises fundamentally religious questions. More recently, the physicist Paul Davies has drawn attention to the implications of the "new physics" for thinking about God, especially in his widely read book *God and the New Physics*.

The origins of the "big bang" theory may be argued to lie in the general theory of relativity proposed by Albert Einstein (1879–1955). Einstein's theory was proposed at a time when the scientific consensus favored the notion of a static universe. The equations which Einstein derived to describe the effects of relativity were interpreted by him in terms of a gravitational and levitational equilibrium. However, the Russian meteorologist Alexander Friedman (1888–1925) noticed that the solutions to the equations which he himself derived pointed to a rather different model. If the universe was perfectly homogenous and expanding, then it must have expanded from a singular initial state at some point in the past characterized by zero radius, and infinite density, temperature, and curvature. Other solutions to the equations suggested a cycle of expansion and contraction. The analysis was disregarded, probably because it did not conform to the consensus viewpoint within the scientific community. All that began to change with the astronomical observations of Edwin Hubble (1889–1953), which led him to interpret the redshifts of galactic spectra in terms of an expanding universe.

A further major development took place (largely by accident, it has to be said) in 1964. Arno Penzias and Robert Wilson were working on an experimental microwave antenna at the Bell Laboratories in New Jersey. They were experiencing some difficulties: irrespective of the direction in which they pointed the antenna, they found that they picked up a background hissing noise which could not be eliminated. Their initial explanation of this phenomenon was that the pigeons roosting on the antenna were interfering with it. Yet even after the enforced removal of the offending birds, the hiss remained.

It was only a matter of time before the full significance of this irritating background hiss was appreciated. It could be understood as the afterglow of a primal explosion – a "big bang" – which had been proposed in 1948 by George Gamow, Ralph Alpher, and Robert Herman. This thermal radiation corresponded to photons moving about randomly in space, without discernible source, at a temperature of 2.7 K. Taken alongside other pieces of evidence, this background radiation served as significant evidence that the universe had a beginning (and caused severe difficulties for the rival "steady state" theory advocated by Thomas Gold and Hermann Bondi, with theoretical support from Fred Hoyle).

It is now widely agreed that the universe had a beginning. This immediately points to at least some level of affinity or consonance with the Christian idea that the universe was created. Yet the belief that the universe had a "beginning" does not necessarily imply that it was "created." However, a number of writers, such as Stanley L. Jaki (born 1924), have argued that this is the most obvious implication of the notion of origination. One of the factors which has been of particular importance in focusing this debate has been the "anthropic principle," to which we now turn.

# The Anthropic Principle

The term "anthropic principle" is used in a variety of ways by different writers; nevertheless, the term is generally used to refer to the remarkable degree of "fine-tuning" observed within the natural order. Paul Davies argues that the remarkable convergence of certain fundamental constants is laden with religious significance. "The seemingly miraculous concurrence of numerical values that nature has assigned to her fundamental constants must remain the most compelling evidence for an element of cosmic design" (Davies, 1983, p. 189).

The most accessible introduction to the principle is widely agreed to be the 1986 study of John D. Barrow and Frank J. Tipler, entitled *The Anthropic Cosmological Principle*. The basic observation which underlies the principle may be stated as follows:

> One of the most important results of twentieth-century physics has been the gradual realization that there exist invariant properties of the natural world and its elementary components which render the gross size and structure of virtually all its constituents quite inevitable. The size of stars and planets, and even people, are neither random nor the result of any Darwinian selection process from a myriad of possibilities. These, and other gross features of the Universe are the consequences of necessity; they are manifestations of the possible equilibrium states between competing forces of attraction and compulsion. The intrinsic strengths of these controlling forces of Nature are determined by a mysterious collection of pure numbers that we call the *constants of Nature*. (Barrow and Tipler, 1986, p. 5).

The importance of this point was brought out in an important review article by B. J. Carr and M. J. Rees published in 1979. Carr and Rees pointed out how most natural scales – in particular, the mass and length scales – are determined by a few physical constants. They concluded that "the possibility of life as we know it evolving in the Universe depends on the values of a few physical constants – and is in some respects remarkably sensitive to their numerical values" (Carr and Rees, 1979, p. 612). The constants which assumed a particularly significant role were the electromagnetic fine structure constant, the gravitational fine structure constant, and the electron-to-proton mass ratio.

Examples of the "fine-tuning" of fundamental cosmological constants include the following:

**Figure 19.1** John Barrow

If the strong coupling constant was slightly smaller, hydrogen would be the only element in the universe. Since the evolution of life as we know it is fundamentally dependent on the chemical properties of carbon, that life could not have come into being without some hydrogen being converted to carbon by fusion. On the other hand, if the strong coupling constant were slightly larger (even by as much as 2%), the hydrogen would have been converted to helium, with the result that no long-lived stars would have been formed. In that such stars are regarded as essential to the emergence of life, such a conversion would have led to life as we know it failing to emerge.

If the weak fine constant was slightly smaller, no hydrogen would have formed during the early history of the universe. Consequently, no stars would have been formed. On the other hand, if it was slightly larger, supernovae would have been unable to eject the heavier elements necessary for life. In either case, life as we know it could not have emerged.

If the electromagnetic fine structure constant was slightly larger, the stars would not be hot enough to warm planets to a temperature sufficient to maintain life in the form in which we know it. If smaller, the stars would have burned out too quickly to allow life to evolve on these planets.

If the gravitational fine structure constant were slightly smaller, stars and planets would not have been able to form, on account of the gravitational constraints necessary for coalescence of their constituent material. If stronger, the stars thus formed would have burned out too quickly to allow the evolution of life (as with the electromagnetic fine structure constant).

This evidence of "fine-tuning" has been the subject of considerable discussion among scientists, philosophers, and theologians. It will be clear that the considerations are actually quite anthropocentric, in that the observations derive their significance partly on account of their assumption that life is carbon-based.

So what is the religious significance of this? There is no doubt that these coincidences are immensely interesting and thought-provoking, leading at least some natural scientists to posit a possible religious explanation for these observations. The physicist Freeman Dyson said: "As we look out into the Universe and identify the many accidents of physics and astronomy that have worked together to our benefit, it almost seems as it the Universe must in some sense have known that we were coming" (Dyson, 1979, p. 250). It must be stressed, however, that this does not command general assent within the scientific community, despite its obvious attractions to a significant subset of that community which endorses the notion of a creator God.

The anthropic principle, whether stated in a weak or strong form, is strongly consistent with a theistic perspective. A theist (for example, a Christian) with a firm commitment to a doctrine of creation will find the "fine-tuning" of the universe to be an anticipated and pleasant confirmation of his or her religious beliefs. This would not constitute a proof of the existence of God, but would be a further element in a cumulative series of considerations which is at the very least consistent with the existence of a creator God. This is the kind of argument set forth by F. R. Tennant (1886–1957) in his important study *Philosophical Theology* (1930), which many believe used the term "anthropic" for the first time to designate this specific type of teleological argument:

> The forcibleness of Nature's suggestion that she is the outcome of intelligent design lies not in particular cases of adaptedness in the world, nor even in the multiplicity of them … [but] consists rather in the conspiration of innumerable causes to produce, either by united and reciprocal action, and to maintain, a general order of Nature. Narrower kinds of teleological arguments, based on surveys of restricted spheres of fact, are much more precarious than that for which the name of "the wider teleology" may be appropriated in that the comprehensive design-argument is the outcome of synopsis or conspection of the knowable world. (Tennant, 1930, vol. 2, p. 79)

This does not mean that the factors noted above constitute irrefutable evidence for the existence or character of a creator God; few religious thinkers would suggest that this is the case. What would be affirmed, however, is that they are consistent with a theistic worldview; that they can be accommodated with the greatest of ease within such a worldview; that they reinforce the plausibility of such a worldview for those who are already committed to them; and that they offer apologetic possibilities for those who do not yet hold a theistic position.

But what of those who do not hold a religious viewpoint? What status might the "anthropic principle" have in relation to the long-standing debate about the existence and nature of God, or the divine design of the universe? Peter Atkins, a physical chemist with stridently antireligious views, notes that the "fine-tuning" of the world may appear to be miraculous; however, he argues that on closer inspection a purely naturalist explanation may be offered.

And what of the notion of the "multiverse"? This debate continues, with no obvious sign of resolution. The crux of the debate is whether there exists a singular universe, or a multiplicity of universes. The possibility of multiple universes arises from the idea of an inflationary universe, first proposed by Alan Guth in 1981. One way of making theoretical sense of the observed properties of the universe is to suggest that it underwent massive inflation in the first instant – less than a trillionth of a second – of its existence. This involved the emergence of a multiplicity of universes.

On this approach, we happen to live in a universe with biologically friendly properties. We do not inhabit or observe other universes, where these conditions do not pertain. Our insights are restricted by observation selection effects, which means that our location within a biophilic universe inclines us to propose that the entire cosmos possesses such properties, when in fact other universes will exist which are inimical to life. Indeed, some argue that such biophobic universes are predicted to be the norm. We happen to exist in an exceptional universe, and we have generalized from its properties. Our universe may possess anthropic properties. But others do not. The debate will continue, and its outcome is uncertain.

Our attention now shifts to a debate in theoretical physics, which has often been seen as having important theological implications. The development of quantum mechanics involved the recognition of the limits of classical models for dealing with quantum phenomena. One of the results of this recognition was the notion of "complementarity" – the idea that two classical models of light are necessary to do justice to the observational evidence, despite the fact that these were mutually inconsistent. In the following chapter, we shall explore the importance of this development.

## For Further Reading

Barrow, John, and Frank J. Tipler. *The Anthropic Cosmological Principle*. Oxford: Oxford University Press, 1986.

Carr, Bernard (ed.). *Universe or Multiverse?* Cambridge, UK: Cambridge University Press, 2007.

Gribbin, John R., and Martin J. Rees. *Cosmic Coincidences: Dark Matter, Mankind, and Anthropic Cosmology*. New York: Bantam Books, 1991.

Holder, Rodney D. *God, the Multiverse, and Everything: Modern Cosmology and the Argument from Design*. Aldershot, UK: Ashgate, 2004.

McGrath, Alister E. *A Fine-Tuned Universe: Science, Theology and the Quest for God*. Louisville, KY: Westminster John Knox Press, 2009.

Rees, Martin J. *Just Six Numbers: The Deep Forces That Shape the Universe*. London: Phoenix, 2000.

# Chapter

## 20 Quantum Theory

### *Complementarity in Science and Religion*

In an earlier chapter, we considered how models or analogies served an important role in both science and religion. The present chapter considers a particular situation which arises through the use of models. What happens if the behavior of a system is such that it appears to need more than one model to represent it? In religion, this situation is well known. The Old and New Testaments, for example, use a wide variety of models or analogies to refer to God, such as "father," "king," "shepherd," and "rock." Each of these is regarded as illustrating one aspect of the divine nature. Taken together, they provide a cumulative and more comprehensive depiction of the divine nature and character than any one such analogy might allow on its own.

But what happens if two apparently contradictory analogies seem to be required, on the basis of the evidence available? For example, let us define two models, $A$ and $A'$, which are linked by the logical condition that the two are mutually exclusive. This immediately raises the question of the ontological status of the thing which is being modeled. Can we say that it "is" $A$, when the associated suggestion that it is also $A'$ would lead to a blatant logical contradiction?

In the present section, we shall explore the issue of complementarity in science and religion, focusing on the work of Niels Bohr (1885–1962) in quantum theory, and the identity of Jesus Christ in theology. We begin by exploring the way in which the issue of complementarity arose in quantum theory.

Niels Bohr's theory of complementarity emerged during the 1920s, during the early period of the development of quantum theory. A major question was under active

**Figure 20.1** Niels Bohr (Time & Life Pictures/ Getty Images)

discussion at that time: is light composed of waves or particles? From the standpoint of classical physics, these are two completely different and mutually incompatible entities. Waves cannot be particles, nor can particles be waves. By the beginning of the final decade of the nineteenth century, it was widely agreed that light consisted of waves.

One of the questions which this raised was whether light waves required a medium for their propagation. The nearest analogy seemed to be sound, which consisted of waves which required a medium if they were to be propagated. The analogy seemed to suggest that light also seemed to require a medium. As we noted earlier, this led many to postulate the existence of a so-called "luminiferous ether" – a light-bearing medium. The quest for this ether became of major importance during the final decade of the century. Particles, of course, did not require a medium in order to travel.

Yet evidence was beginning to accumulate which called the wave model of light into question. One of the most important pieces of evidence relates to black-body radiation – that is, the way in which a perfect body radiates energy. Classical physics found it impossible to explain why something known as the "ultraviolet catastrophe" did not occur – that is, why a black body did not emit radiation at an infinite density at very high frequencies. This phenomenon was explained in 1900 by the great German physicist Max Planck (1858–1947), who suggested the "quantization" of energy. Plank argued that energy was not infinitely continuous, but was made up of "packets" of fixed size. The word *quantum* was used to refer to these small packets of energy. Planck introduced a fundamental constant $h$ (now universally known as "Planck's constant") to refer to this basic unit of energy. For an oscillator of frequency $\nu$, the energy of the oscillator can be defined as $h\nu$. The basic point is that energy turns out not to be continuous but is actually discrete.

An analogy may be helpful to explain this very difficult idea. It is like looking at a great sand dune in the African desert. From a distance, it seems smooth; on closer examination, it is made up of millions of small grains of sand. Energy may seem to be continuous; on closer examination, it is made up of tiny grains. At very high energy levels, these packets of energy are so small that they have little or no discernible impact on anything. But at very low energy levels, the effect is pronounced.

A further development of importance was Albert Einstein's explanation of the photoelectric effect in 1905. It had been known for some time that electrons were emitted by some metals when they were exposed to light. Yet the experimental observations were proving very difficult to interpret. Traditional understandings of the nature of light, such as those developed by James Clerk Maxwell, suggested that the energy of these emitted electrons should be related to the brightness of the light. But it turned out that this was not the case. In fact, their energy was actually related to the frequency of the light, not its intensity. Furthermore, electrons were not emitted if the light used was below a certain frequency, no matter how bright it was. How could these observations be explained?

Einstein argued that the photoelectric effect was best understood as a collision between an incoming particle-like bundle of energy and an electron close to the surface of the metal. The electron could only be ejected from the metal if the incoming packets of light (or particle-like bundles of energy) possessed sufficient energy to eject this electron. Einstein's theory (which need not be explored in greater detail for our purposes) allowed the following facts to be explained.

1  The critical factor which determines whether an electron is ejected is not the intensity of the light, but its frequency. Planck had shown that the energy of an oscillator was directly proportional to its frequency.
2  The observed features of the photoelectric effect can be accounted for by assuming that the collision between the incoming photon and the metallic electron obeys the principle of the conservation of energy. If the energy of the incoming photon is less than a certain quantity (the "work function" of the metal in question), no electrons will be emitted, no matter how intense the bombardment with photons. Above this threshold, the kinetic energy of the emitted photons is directly proportional to the frequency of the radiation.

Einstein's brilliant theoretical account for the photoelectric effect suggested that electromagnetic radiation had to be considered as behaving as particles under certain conditions. The incoming light can be treated as if it consists of packets of energy (now referred to as "photons") with a definite energy or momentum. Einstein's theory met with intense opposition, not least because it appeared to involve the abandonment of the prevailing classical understanding of the total exclusivity of waves and particles: something could be one, or the other – but not both. Even those who subsequently verified Einstein's analysis of the photoelectric effect were intensely suspicious of his postulation of "photons." Einstein himself was careful to refer to the light-quantum hypothesis as a "heuristic point of view" – that is, as something which was helpful as a model to understanding, but without any necessary existence on its part. (In other words, Einstein adopted an instrumentalist, not a realist, approach to the photon: see chapter 10.)

By the 1920s, it was clear that the behavior of light was such that it required to be explained on the basis of a wave model in some respects, and a particle model in others. The work of Louis de Broglie (1892–1987) suggested that even matter had to be regarded as behaving as a wave in some respect. These theories led Niels Bohr to develop his concept of "complementarity."

For Bohr, the classical models of "waves" and "particles" were both required to explain the behavior of light and matter. This does not mean that electrons "are" particles or that they "are" waves. Rather, it means that the *behavior* of electrons may be described on the basis of both wave or particle models, and that a complete description of that behavior rests upon the bringing together of what are, in effect, mutually exclusive ways of representing them.

This is not an intellectually shallow and lazy expedient of affirming two mutually exclusive options, rather than attempting to determine which is superior. For Bohr, this was the inevitable outcome of a series of critical theories and experiments which demonstrated the impossibility of representing the situation in any other manner. In other words, Bohr held that the experimental data at his disposal forced him to the conclusion that a complex situation (the behavior of light and matter) had to be represented by using two apparently contradictory and incompatible models.

It is this principle of holding together two apparently irreconcilable models of a complex phenomenon in order to account for the behavior of that phenomenon which is known as the "principle of complementarity." So what is the religious relevance of this point? We shall explore this issue by focusing on one specific area of Christian theology which is widely regarded as illustrating the religious significance of complementarity – Christology. Before this, however, it is appropriate to note some important general convergences in this field, focusing on the convergences between Niels Bohr on the scientific side, and the theologians Karl Barth (1886–1968) and Thomas F. Torrance (1913–2007) on the theological side.

Some scholars have noted parallels between Bohr's "principle of complementarity" and Karl Barth's "dialectical method." For example, the American writers James Loder and Jim Neidhardt suggested that a number of significant points of convergence can be noted between the two writers. In the case of Bohr, the "phenomenon" to be accounted for is the behavior of quantum events; for Barth, it is the relation between time and eternity on the one hand, and humanity and divinity in the person of Jesus Christ on the other. For both Bohr and Barth, they argue, classical forms of reason are pushed to their limits to explain the phenomena in question. The outcome is thus theoretical models which seem deeply counterintuitive. Both writers vigorously maintain the principle that the phenomenon should be allowed to disclose how it can be known, and avoid reducing the phenomenon to known forms – for example, by reducing it to classical forms. A similar approach is found in the writings of Thomas F.

Torrance, widely respected both as an interpreter of Barth and an advocate of dialogue between theology and the natural sciences.

Limits on space allow us to consider in more detail only one of the parallels noted by Loder and Neidhardt between Bohr and Barth. Bohr's reflections on complementarity were forced upon him by the experimental evidence which accumulated during the period 1905–25. Much simpler ways of visualizing the situation could have been put forward (and, as the development of quantum theory over this period indicates, were indeed adduced). Yet the simplicity of these models foundered against the experimental evidence, which ineluctably led Bohr to the conclusion that two apparently mutually exclusive ways of conceiving quantum phenomena were required.

The area of Christian theology which shows the greatest similarity to this way of thinking is Christology, which addresses how best to conceptualize the identity of Jesus Christ. The development of Christology during the period 100–451 shows this same pattern of concern to have been of overwhelming importance. Patristic writers insisted that the phenomenon (if we may be allowed to use this term to refer to the complex amalgam of "historical testimony and religious experience") had to be allowed to determine its own interpretation. Simplistic reductionist modes of representing the identity and significance of Jesus of Nazareth foundered on the phenomena which they were required to represent. In particular, the model of Jesus of Nazareth as a purely human figure (generally held to be found in the Ebionite heresy) or as a purely divine figure (generally held to be found in the Docetic heresy) were regarded as quite inadequate. Both the representation of Jesus in the New Testament and the manner in which the Christian church incorporated Jesus into its life of prayer and worship required a more complex understanding of his identity and significance than either of these simpler models were able to offer.

The patristic period witnessed a decisive rejection of any attempt to explain Jesus in terms which involved the construction of a mediating or hybrid concept between divinity and humanity. There is a direct Christological parallel with Bohr's insistence on the completeness of the principle of complementarity. As with Bohr's complementary accounts of waves and particles, the approach to Christology established by the Council of Chalcedon in 451 affirmed that the approach offered by the "two natures" doctrine was *complete* (in that only two such models or natures are needed) and *complementary* (in that only one of these mutually exclusive models or natures can apply at any one time).

These points could be developed in greater detail. What really matters here, however, is to note that both science and religion have had to confront the problems raised when a phenomenon is encountered which cannot be represented adequately by any analogy from the everyday world. The development of Bohr's "principle of complementarity" and the classic theological notion of the "two natures" of Christ both illuminate this concern, and point to the continuing importance of maintaining a dialogue in science and religion.

Our discussion of specific issues in science and religion has thus far concentrated on the physical sciences. Yet many would argue that some of the most important (and difficult) questions for the religions arise from the biological sciences. In the following chapter, we shall begin to explore these, beginning with assessing the implications of evolutionary biology for religion.

## For Further Reading

Bauckham, Richard. *God Crucified: Monotheism and Christology in the New Testament.* Grand Rapids, MI: Eerdmans, 1998.

Kaiser, Christopher B. "Christology and Complementarity." *Religious Studies*, 12 (1976): 37–48.

Loder, James E., and W. Jim Neidhardt. "Barth, Bohr and Dialectic." In W. Mark Richardson and Wesley J. Wildman (eds), *Religion and Science: History, Method, Dialogue*, pp. 271–89. New York: Routledge, 1996.

Pais, Abraham. *Niels Bohr's Times, in Physics, Philosophy and Polity.* Oxford: Clarendon Press, 1991.

Petruccioli, Sandro. *Atoms, Metaphors and Paradoxes: Niels Bohr and the Construction of a New Physics.* Cambridge, UK: Cambridge University Press, 1993.

# Chapter

# 21 Evolutionary Biology

## *Can One Speak of "Design" in Nature?*

One of the most interesting debates in contemporary evolutionary biology concerns the notion of "teleology." This word, which derives from the Greek word *telos* ("a goal"), is usually interpreted to mean something like "the theory that a process is directed towards a specific goal or outcome." It is an idea that underlies William Paley's celebrated *Natural Theology* (1802), which argues that nature demonstrates certain features which indicate that it has been designed by God in the light of certain very specific ends or goals. Nature is "contrived" – that is to say, designed and constructed with a specific purpose and intention in mind.

It is an idea that remains attractive. Henri Bergson (1859–1941) and Pierre Teilhard de Chardin (1881–1955) both developed philosophies of life which were founded on the acceptance of biological evolution, yet interpreted this as having some kind of purpose or goal. Yet this is now seen as very controversial. In this chapter, we shall consider why the idea of teleology in biology has become so controversial, and why it has significant religious implications.

Earlier in this work, we considered the basic features of the neo-Darwinian understanding of evolution, which combines Charles Darwin's emphasis upon the role of natural selection, and Gregor Mendel's theory of genetics (p. 55). One of the most discussed aspects of this approach to evolution is its implicit rejection of any "purpose" to the evolutionary process. It may have direction; it does not, however, have a goal. This clearly raises a number of significant issues.

In his influential and widely discussed book *The Blind Watchmaker* (1986), the atheist zoologist Richard Dawkins deals with the appearance of design within the world, which has led many to draw religious conclusions. For Dawkins, while these conclusions may be understandable, they remain mistaken and unfounded.

> This [appearance of design] is probably the most important reason for the belief, held by the vast majority of people that have ever lived, in some kind of supernatural deity. It took a very great leap of the imagination for Darwin and Wallace to see that, contrary to all intuition, there is another way and, once you have understood it, a far more plausible way, for complex "design" to arise out of primeval simplicity. (Dawkins, 1986, p. xii)

As we saw earlier, the title of Dawkins's work is inspired by an analogy used by William Paley, one of the more noted advocates of the "argument from design." Paley argues that the world is like a watch, which shows evidence of design and construction (see p. 31). Just as the existence of a watch points to a watchmaker, so the appearance of design in nature (evident, for example, in the human eye) points to a designer. Dawkins, while appreciating Paley's imagery, regards it as fatally flawed. The whole idea of "design" or "purpose" is out of place.

> Paley drives his point home with beautiful and reverent descriptions of the dissected machinery of life, beginning with the human eye … Paley's argument is made with passionate sincerity and is informed by the best biological scholarship of his day, but it is wrong, gloriously and utterly wrong … Natural selection, the blind, unconscious, automatic process which Darwin discovered, and which we now know is the explanation for the existence and apparently purposeful form of all life, has no purpose in mind. It has no mind and no mind's eye. It does not plan for the future. It has no vision, no foresight, no sight at all. If it can be said to play the role of watchmaker in nature, it is the *blind* watchmaker. (Dawkins, 1986, p. 5)

The process of natural selection is thus seen as unguided and undirected, "selecting" only in the sense that certain natural forces tend to lead to the failure of certain species to establish themselves in the face of intense competition with other species, fighting for existence in the same environment.

This strongly antiteleological tone can be found in a number of earlier works by noted molecular biologists, perhaps most significantly Jacques Monod (1910–76) in his book *Chance and Necessity* (1971). Monod here argued that evolutionary change took place by chance and was perpetuated by necessity. The term "teleonomy" was introduced into biological use in 1958 by the Princeton biologist C. S. Pittendrigh (1918–96) in order to emphasize that "recognition and description of end-directedness" does not carry any commitment to a teleology (Pittendrigh, 1958, p. 394). This idea was developed further by Jacques Monod, who argued that *teleonomy* had displaced *teleology* in evolutionary biology. In using this term, Monod wished to highlight that evolutionary biology was concerned with identifying and clarifying the mechanisms underlying the evolutionary process. While the mechanisms which governed evolution were of interest, they had no goal. It is thus not possible to speak meaningfully of "purpose" within evolution.

Or is it? The biologist and philosopher Francisco Ayala (born 1934) argues that some notion of teleological explanation is actually fundamental to modern biology. It is required to account for the familiar functional roles played by parts of living organisms, and to describe the goal of reproductive fitness which plays such a central role in accounts of natural selection.

> A teleological explanation implies that the system under consideration is directively organized. For that reason, teleological explanations are appropriate in biology and in the domain of cybernetics but make no sense when used in the physical sciences to describe phenomena like the fall of a stone. Moreover, and most importantly, teleological explanations imply that the end result is the explanatory reason for the *existence* of the object or process which serves or leads to it. A teleological account of the gills of fish implies that gills came to existence precisely because they serve for respiration. If the above reasoning is correct, the use of teleological explanations in biology is not only acceptable but indeed indispensable. (Ayala, 1970, p. 12)

Natural selection itself, the ultimate source of explanation in biology, is thus for Ayala a teleological process for two reasons. First, because it is directed to the goal of increasing reproductive efficiency; and second, because it produces the goal-directed organs and processes required for this.

Ernst Mayr (1904–2005), widely credited with inventing the modern philosophy of biology, especially of evolutionary biology, sets out four traditional objections to the use of teleological language in biology:

1 Teleological statements or explanations imply the endorsement of unverifiable theological or metaphysical doctrines in the sciences. Mayr has in mind Bergson's *élan vital* or the notion of "entelechy," formulated by Hans Driesch (1867–1941).
2 A belief that acceptance of explanations for biological phenomena that are not equally applicable to inanimate nature constitutes rejection of a physicochemical explanation.
3 The assumption that future goals were the cause of current events seemed incompatible with accepted notions of causality.

4   Teleological language seemed to amount to an objectionable anthropomorphism. The use of terms such as "purposive" or "goal-directed" appears to represent that transfer of human qualities – such as purpose and planning – to organic structures.

As Mayr points out, as a result of these and other objections, teleological explanations in biology were widely believed to be "a form of obscurantism" (Mayr, 1988, p. 41). Yet paradoxically, biologists continue to use teleological language, insisting that it is methodologically and heuristically appropriate and helpful.

Yet, as Mayr rightly observes, nature abounds in processes and activities that lead to an end or goal. However we choose to interpret them, examples of goal-directed behavior are widespread in the natural world; indeed, "the occurrence of goal-directed processes is perhaps the most characteristic feature of the world of living systems" (Mayr, 1997, p. 389). The evasion of teleological statements through their restatement in nonteleological forms invariably leads to "meaningless platitudes." Although surrounding his conclusion with a thicket of qualifications, Mayr insists that it is appropriate to conclude that "the use of so-called 'teleological' language by biologists is legitimate; it neither implies a rejection of physicochemical explanation nor does it imply noncausal explanation" (Mayr, 1997, p. 402).

There is no doubt that serious objections may be, and have been, raised about the notion of evolution as a conscious agent, actively planning its goals and outcomes, or drawn to a preordained goal by some mysterious force. Yet it must be pointed out that such anthropomorphic ways of speaking (and thinking) are evident in some sections of contemporary biology. An excellent example is provided by the "gene's-eye" view of evolution, popularized by Richard Dawkins, which entails envisaging the gene as an active agent. While rightly cautioning that "we must not think of genes as conscious, purposeful agents," Dawkins goes on to argue that the process of natural selection "makes them behave rather as if they were purposeful" (Dawkins, 1989, p. 196). This anthropomorphic way of speaking involves the attribution of both agency and intentionality to an entity which is ultimately a passive participant in the process of replication, rather than its active director.

The question of directionality in the evolutionary process was reopened in 2003 by the Cambridge evolutionary biologist Simon Conway Morris (born 1951). In his book *Life's Solution*, Conway Morris argues that the number of evolutionary endpoints is limited. "Rerun the tape of life as often as you like, and the end result will be much the same" (Conway Morris, 2003, p. 282). *Life's Solution* builds a forceful case for the predictability of evolutionary outcomes. Conway Morris's case is based on the phenomenon of convergent evolution, in which two or more lineages have independently evolved similar structures and functions. His examples range from the aerodynamics of hovering moths and hummingbirds to the use of silk by spiders and some insects to capture prey.

Evolution regularly appears to "converge" on a relatively small number of possible outcomes. Convergence is widespread, despite the infinitude of genetic possibilities, because "the evolutionary routes are many, but the destinations are limited." Certain destinations are precluded by "the howling wildernesses of the maladaptive." Biological history shows a marked tendency to repeat itself, with life demonstrating an almost eerie ability to find its way to the correct solution, repeatedly. "Life has a peculiar propensity to 'navigate' to rather precise solutions in response to adaptive challenges" (Conway Morris, 2003, p. 308).

In making this important point, Conway Morris offers a nonbiological analogy to help his readers grasp his point. He appeals to the discovery of Easter Island by the Polynesians, perhaps 1,200 years ago. Easter Island is one of the most remote places on earth, about 1,865 miles from the nearest population centers, Tahiti and Chile. Yet though surrounded by the vast, empty wastes of the Pacific Ocean, it was nevertheless discovered by Polynesians. Is this, asks Morris, to be put down to chance and happenstance? Possibly. But probably not. Morris points to the "sophisticated search strategy of the Polynesians" which made its discovery inevitable. The same, he argues, happens in the evolutionary process: "Isolated 'islands' provide

**Figure 21.1** Simon Conway Morris (Simon Conway Morris/ Dudley Simons: © University of Cambridge)

havens of biological possibility in an ocean of maladaptedness" (2003, p. 19). These "islands of stability" give rise to the phenomenon of convergent evolution.

So what is the theological significance of these reflections? Most of the traditional objections to the appeal to the notion of teleology in biology noted by Mayr reflect a belief that an *a priori* metaphysical system, often theistic, is imposed upon the process of scientific observation and reflection, thus prejudicing its scientific character. From the standpoint of the scientific method, one may indeed protest against the imposition of *a priori* notions of goals and causes, such as those associated with many traditional approaches to teleology. The natural sciences rightly protest about the smuggling of preconceived teleological schemes into scientific analysis. But what if they arise from the process of reflection on observation? What if they are *a posteriori* inferences, rather than dogmatic *a priori* assumptions? Conway Morris's analysis suggests that a form of teleology may indeed be inferred *a posteriori*, as the "best explanation" of what is observed. This may not directly map onto a traditional Christian doctrine of providence; nevertheless, there is a significant degree of overlap.

This is not necessarily, it should be noted, a matter of discerning "purpose" – a heavily metaphysically freighted notion – within the evolutionary sequence, and inferring from this to a divine ordainer of purpose. Rather, we are reverting to the approach that is summarized in John Henry Newman's enlightening, yet curiously understudied, remark: "I believe in design because I believe in God; not in God because I see design." Furthermore, the notion of "create" need not be interpreted as a single, once-for-all event, but can equally – and many would now say rightly – be understood as a directed process. This is the view of creation that was set out by Augustine of Hippo (354–430), who spoke of God creating a world with an inbuilt capacity to develop and evolve. A similar point was made by the English churchman Charles Kingsley (1819–75) in a letter to Darwin in 1871: "We knew of old that God was so wise that He could make all things: but behold, He is so much wiser than even that, that He can make all things make themselves." Once more, it is clear that we are dealing with a debate that has a long way still to run.

One of the issues that arises from an evolutionary account of nature is whether certain aspects of human behavior can be seen as reflecting our evolutionary past. Are some of our central ethical assumptions – such as altruism – ultimately grounded in the biological need to survive? And what about religious belief itself? Does this confer survival value on communities? In the next chapter, we will explore these contemporary debates.

## For Further Reading

Ayala, Francisco J. "Teleological Explanations in Evolutionary Biology." *Philosophy of Science*, 37 (1970): 1–15.

Conway Morris, Simon. *Life's Solution: Inevitable Humans in a Lonely Universe.* Cambridge, UK: Cambridge University Press, 2003.

Dawkins, Richard. *The Blind Watchmaker: Why the Evidence of Evolution Reveals a Universe Without Design.* New York: W. W. Norton, 1986.

Mayr, Ernst. *Toward a New Philosophy of Biology: Observations of an Evolutionist.* Cambridge, MA: Harvard University Press, 1988.

Monod, Jacques. *Chance and Necessity: An Essay on the Natural Philosophy of Modern Biology.* New York: Alfred A. Knopf, 1971.

# 22 Evolutionary Psychology

## *The Origins of Religious Belief*

Earlier in this volume (particularly in chapters 5 and 21) we explored the develop-ment of evolutionary theory, and considered some of its implications for religious belief in general, and Christian theology in particular. These questions include whether one can speak of God having "designed" the world, and whether neo-Darwinian evolutionary theory is inconsistent with belief in God. Yet the questions raised by evolutionary theory go much deeper than this.

During the 1990s, the philosopher Daniel Dennett set out to explore a series of issues from an evolutionary standpoint, including the question of what distinguishes human minds from animal minds, how human free will may be reconciled with a naturalist view of the world, and how the origins and successes of religion may be accounted for. Dennett argued that evolutionary theory allows naturalist accounts to be given of human belief in the transcendent in general, and the concept of God in particular.

In *Darwin's Dangerous Idea* (1995), Dennett set out to show "why Darwin's idea is so powerful, and why it promises – not threatens – to put our most cherished visions of life on a new foundation" (Dennett, 1995, p. 11). Darwinism, for Dennett, is a "universal acid" that erodes outdated, superfluous metaphysical notions, from the idea of God downwards. Darwinism, he asserts, achieves a correlation of "the realm of life, meaning, and purpose with the realm of space and time, cause and effect, mechanism and physical law" (p. 21). The Darwinian world is devoid of purpose and transcendence, in that all can and should be explained by the "standard scientific epistemology and metaphysics" (Dennett, 1993, p. 234). The Darwinian worldview demystifies and unifies our experience of the world, and places it on more secure foundations.

Dennett argues that Darwinism allows us to eliminate transcendent causes and presences within the natural realm in general, and from scientific explanation in particular. This is the essential point of his ingenious distinction between "cranes" and "skyhooks." Cranes are natural, yet complex, intermediary mechanisms that arise in the course of the process of evolution itself, and contribute to that process by enabling the emergence of still more complex structures. "Skyhooks" are arbitrary, imaginary inventions, devised to evade purely naturalist explanations and accounts of the natural world and its processes. God is perhaps the most obvious example of such a "skyhook." For Dennett, "good reductionism," which is fundamentally a "commitment to non-question-begging science" holds that "everything in nature can all be explained without skyhooks" (Dennett, 1995, p. 82).

One of the most interesting developments of the twentieth century has been the growing trend to regard it as transcending the category of provisional scientific theories, and constituting a "worldview." Darwinism is here regarded as establishing a coherent worldview through its evolutionary narrative, which embraces such issues as the fundamental nature of reality, the physical universe, human origins, human nature, society, psychology, values, and destinies. This extension of the scope of Darwinism beyond the realm of biological origins and development has led to the opening up of many new fields of investigation among philosophers of science. While being welcomed by some, others have expressed alarm at this apparent failure to distinguish between good, sober, and restrained science on the one hand, and nonempirical metaphysics, fantasy, myth, and ideology on the other.

One of these new areas of exploration is the discipline now known as "evolutionary psychology." This holds that the cognitive programs of the human brain are adaptations, which arose because they produced behavior in our ancestors that enabled them to survive and reproduce. Charles Darwin (1809–82) himself suggested in *The Descent of Man* (1871) that ethics represented a human response to biological needs. Although this idea was explored by a number of writers after Darwin, such as Herbert Spencer (1820–1903), it is generally agreed that serious discussion of the point began in 1975, with the publication of Edward O. Wilson's *Sociobiology: The New Synthesis*. For Wilson, all ethics emerges from biological necessity, and can be explained on the basis of humanity's biological and social evolution. Wilson introduced the term "sociobiology" to refer to "the systematic study of the biological basis of all social behavior" (1975: 4). In this approach, human ethics evolved through natural selection. Moral characteristics such as altruism, cooperation, mutual concern, and so on, could therefore be explained in terms of the biological roots of human social behavior.

The suggestion that altruism can be accounted for using the Darwinian paradigm will strike some readers as strange. If evolution is about a struggle for survival, how can altruism help in this process? This concern was famously expressed by Thomas H. Huxley in his 1893 Romanes Lecture at Oxford University, in which he disavowed Darwinism as a basis for ethics. If what Huxley called the "cosmic process" is characterized by "relentless combat," how could anyone construct a social ethic on its basis? The only way that Huxley could see was to allow humans the capacity to transcend the process by which they came into existence: "Social progress means a checking of the cosmic process at every step and the substitution for it of another, which may be called the ethical process." The future survival of humanity would depend on replacing the "State of Nature" with the "State of Art," allowing for the survival of those who were best *ethically*.

Huxley's anxieties were not without foundation. Herbert Spencer's "social Darwinism" can be seen as the construction of a set of social and political values based on evolutionary paradigms. Spencer elevated alleged biological facts (such as the struggle for existence, natural selection, and survival of the fittest) to prescriptions for human moral conduct. Human beings are engaged in the struggle for survival. In order for the best to survive, the weak must be prevented from breeding. In his 1874 *The Study of Sociology*, Spencer wrote: "To aid the bad in multiplying, is, in effect, the same as maliciously providing for our descendants a multitude of enemies." Spencer's philosophy gave rise to a new interest in eugenics, by which the human gene pool would be strengthened.

Yet this is only one approach, and bears little relation to the evolutionary account of ethics developed by Wilson in his *Sociobiology*. Wilson made it clear that his concern was not to develop a system of ethics, but to account for the origin of ethics in the first place. In particular, Wilson was interested in how a competitive evolutionary process could give rise to apparently noncompetitive, or even anticompetitive, values. He argued that the answer lay in the emergence of values that favored the survival of certain groups. According to Wilson, the prevalence of selfish or egoistic individuals will make a community vulnerable and ultimately lead to the extinction of the whole group. The evolutionary process thus favors the emergence of groups which were characterized by their altruistic behavior.

Given its importance, it may be helpful to set this argument out more fully. Wilson's argument is that altruistic behavior will evolve if the benefits it brings to the com-

**Figure 22.1** Herbert Spencer (© Hulton-Deutsch Collection/ CORBIS)

171

**Figure 22.2** Edward O. Wilson (Justin Ide/ Harvard News Office)

munity's survival exceed the costs. From this perspective, unselfish behavior can be the upshot of "selfish" genetic strategies. For example, suppose a father decides to deprive himself of food so that his children can eat, and hence survive. On the face of it, his action appears to be altruistic and selfless. Yet on the genetic level it is quite self-serving, and it ensures that his genes are passed on to later generations.

It will be clear that the word "altruism," used in this context, is a biological concept, which cannot be equated with the moral notion of "goodness." Indeed, there is no reason to assume that a biologically altruistic behavior is morally good. Nevertheless, this analysis clearly raises questions for morality. Why should we be moral? Because, Wilson argues, we are genetically inclined to be moral. It is a heritage of earlier times in our history. Hence we do not need divine revelation to be good; we are simply genetically wired to do certain things that have proven to possess a survival advantage.

The general method just noted for altruism can be extended to other values. The central argument of evolutionary psychology is that certain inherited behavioral mechanisms are deeply embedded in human nature in that they proved to be adaptive, leading to the survival of those groups which adopted them. Human beings act in ways that have proven to be evolutionarily successful over an extended period of time, which led to the emergence of complex social processes that have proven to be conducive to evolutionary fitness. Selfishness is bad for a group's survival prospects. "A consistently egoistic species would be either solitary or extinct" (Midgley, 1980, p. 94). These ways of thinking and acting thus come to be presumed to have some intrinsic "moral" quality, when in fact they are simply biologically effective. In his *Darwin's Cathedral* (2002), David Sloan Wilson offers a group selection perspective on the evolution of religious beliefs and values. Wilson argues that religious systems encourage prosocial behavior, and groups that exhibit such prosocial behavior are more likely to survive, prosper, and reproduce than groups which do not exhibit these traits.

And what of belief in God? David Sloan Wilson has argued that religion evolved through natural selection, in that religion conferred some sort of evolutionary advantage. Others, such as Stephen Jay Gould, have suggested that religion is essentially an evolutionary by-product, a neurological accident. According to Gould, religion evolved as a by-product of psychological mechanisms that conferred other evolutionary benefits. Religion itself thus did not confer any advantages on humanity, but was linked with other adaptive developments. To use Gould's distinctive language, religion is thus to be seen as a "spandrel."

So how are we to evaluate such suggestions? Does evolutionary psychology offer a viable account of the origins of ethical values, or religious belief? Two points are regularly made in academic evaluations of the approaches adopted by evolutionary psychology.

First, critics assert that many hypotheses put forward to explain the adaptive nature of human behavioral traits are often little more than *ad hoc* explanations for the evolution of given traits that do not rest on any evidence beyond their own internal logic. Such explanations can be constructed to fit any behavior. Yet these often appear as contrived and forced, being accommodationist rather than predictive in nature. For this reason, they are virtually impossible to assess empirically. The term "Just So Story" is often used in this context, referring to a collection of stories published in 1901 by the English poet and novelist Rudyard Kipling (1865–1936). The titles of these stories include "How the Camel got his hump" and "How the Leopard got his spots." The stories, though entertaining, bear no relation to established scientific findings.

Second, evolutionary psychology locates the origins of certain patterns of thinking and acting in the distant evolutionary past. Yet surely, critics argue, human beings have moved beyond their biological roots and transcended their evolutionary origins? In which case, they would be able to formulate goals in the pursuit of goodness, beauty, and truth that have nothing directly to do with survival, and which may at times even militate against survival? The final words of Richard Dawkins's book *The Selfish Gene* are often quoted in this respect:

> We have the power to defy the selfish genes of our birth and, if necessary, the selfish memes of our indoctrination. We can even discuss ways of deliberately cultivating and nurturing pure, disinterested altruism – something that has no place in nature, something that has never existed before in the whole history of the world. We are built as gene machines and cultured as meme machines, but we have the power to turn against our creators. We, alone on earth, can rebel against the tyranny of the selfish replicators. (Dawkins, 1989, pp. 200–1)

And finally, there is the question of whether such evolutionary explanations exclude the idea that religious beliefs refer to something real. This assumption is often implicit in the evolutionary psychology literature, yet is open to challenge and revision. For example, it is generally assumed that selective evolutionary pressures will produce reliable intuitive and ontological categories in humans, so that they generate mostly true beliefs about their environment. Why should religious beliefs be the exception to that rule? Selection pressures, whether operating on groups or individuals, may well have led to various dispositions or propensities in human minds that naturally give rise to the holding of religious beliefs. Yet whether any particular religious belief is warranted is an entirely different matter. The debate continues.

We now move from the realm of biology to that of the cognitive sciences. Since the nineteenth century, there has been considerable discussion of whether religious belief can be accounted for on psychological grounds. In the next chapter, we shall consider two classic accounts of this question, before moving on to consider more recent discussion of the issue.

## For Further Reading

Buller, David J. *Adapting Minds: Evolutionary Psychology and the Persistent Quest for Human Nature*. Cambridge, MA: MIT Press, 2005.

Dennett, Daniel C. *Darwin's Dangerous Idea: Evolution and the Meaning of Life*. New York: Simon & Schuster, 1995.

Dugatkin, Lee Alan (ed.). *The Altruism Equation: Seven Scientists Search for the Origins of Goodness*. Princeton, NJ: Princeton University Press, 2006.

Hagen, Edward H. "Controversial Issues in Evolutionary Psychology." In David M. Buss (ed.), *The Handbook of Evolutionary Psychology*, pp. 145–74. Hoboken, NJ: John Wiley & Sons, 2005.

Richerson, Peter J., and Robert Boyd. *Not by Genes Alone: How Culture Transformed Human Evolution*. Chicago: University of Chicago Press, 2005.

Segerstråle, Ullica. *Defenders of the Truth: The Battle for Science in the Sociobiology Debate and Beyond*. Oxford: Oxford University Press, 2000.

Wilson, Edward O. *Sociobiology: The New Synthesis*. Cambridge, MA: Belknap Press, 1975.

# Chapter

# 23 The Psychology of Religion

*Exploring Religious Experience*

The psychology of religion is becoming an increasingly important field, not least because of a series of recent empirical studies suggesting that religious belief might play a significant positive role in relation to well-being. The discipline traditionally explores such questions as how religious faith develops and matures, ways in which religious faith can be benevolent or harmful, the different religious responses associated with various personality types, and the brain mechanisms underlying religious experience.

The psychological study of religion has encountered some resistance within religious communities, mainly on account of a concern that psychology aims for explanatory reductionism – in other words, that religious beliefs will be reduced to, or explained away as, psychology. There is no doubt that some such agenda can be seen in some strongly reductionist approaches to religion – such as that of Sigmund Freud (1856–1939), which we shall consider below. However, this is not necessarily the case. Many psychologists, including William James (1842–1910), treat religion as a phenomenon with its own integrity and distinctive features, which are to be acknowledged and respected. Where Freud was convinced that the origins of religious belief lay in certain deep-rooted delusions, James offered a more appreciative and positive approach to religion.

It may also be noted that psychology and religion can be seen as offering different levels of explanation. It is certainly possible to argue that some aspects of human

**Figure 23.1** William James (The Granger Collection / Topfoto)

cognitive processes may help explain how religious ideas are generated or sustained. Yet, as the psychologist Fraser Watts points out, it is necessary to recognize a multiplicity of causes in such areas. Some scientists have fallen into the habit of asking: "What caused A? Was it X or Y?" But in the human sciences, multiple causes are the norm. For example, consider the question "Is depression caused by physical or social factors?" The answer is that it is caused by both. As Watts says, the history of such research "ought to make us wary of asking whether an apparent revelation of God really is such, or whether is has some other natural explanation, in terms of people's thought processes or brain processes." To put it crudely, God, human brain processes, the cultural context, and psychological processes may all be causal factors in human religious experience.

In what follows, we shall explore some psychological approaches to religion, and note their importance for our theme. We shall focus on two of the most important writers in this field – William James and Sigmund Freud.

## William James

William James studied at Harvard University, where he subsequently became professor of psychology (1887–97) and then philosophy (1897–1907). His most influential work was based on his Gifford Lectures at Edinburgh University, which were published under the title *The Varieties of Religious Experience* (first published 1902). In this landmark study, James drew extensively on a wide range of published works and personal testimonies, engaging with religious experience on its own terms, and taking accounts of such experiences at face value. James's discussion of mysticism identifies four characteristics of these religious experiences:

*Ineffability:* The experience "defies expression"; it cannot be described adequately in words. "Its quality must be directly experienced; it cannot be imparted or transferred to others" (James, 1917, p. 380).
*Noetic quality:* Such an experience is seen to possess authority, giving insight and knowledge into deep truths, which are sustained over time. These "states of insight into depths of truth unplumbed by the discursive intellect" are understood to be

"illuminations, revelations, full of significance and importance, all inarticulate though they remain" (p. 380).

*Transiency:* "Mystical states cannot be sustained for long." Usually they last from a few seconds to minutes and their quality cannot be accurately remembered, though the experience is recognized if it recurs. "When faded, their quality can but imperfectly be reproduced in memory" (p. 381).

*Passivity:* "Although the oncoming of mystical states may be facilitated by preliminary voluntary operations," once they have begun, the mystic feels out of control as if he or she "were grasped and held by a superior power" (p. 381).

While James notes that the second two characteristics are "less marked" than the others, he considers them to be integral to any phenomenology of religious experience.

Although other writers, such as F. D. E. Schleiermacher (1768–1834), had addressed the issue of religious experience before him, James brought to his task a more rigorously empirical and analytical way of thinking. Yet James is aware that experience is a private matter, which is not easily open to public description. James's pioneering effort to construct an empirical study of the phenomenon of religious experience is still widely regarded as authoritative, balanced, and finely observed.

James makes it clear that his primary interest is personal religious experience, rather than the type of religious experiences which are associated with institutions. "In critically judging of the value of religious phenomena, it is very important to insist on the distinction between religion as an individual personal function, and religion as an institutional, corporate or tribal product" (James, 1917, p. 334). So what is it about "experiences" which determine whether they are religious or not? James answers this critically important question by asserting that religious experience is distinguished qualitatively from other modes of experience: "The essence of religious experiences, the thing by which we finally must judge them, must be that element or quality in them which we can meet nowhere else" (p. 45). James regards religious experience as imparting a new quality to life. He speaks of religious experience raising "our centre of personal energy" (p. 196), and giving rise to "regenerative effects unattainable in other ways" (p. 523). In his 1897 essay, "The Will to Believe," James claimed that God is to be conceived of as "the deepest power in the universe" who can be "conceived under the form of a mental personality" (James, 1956, p. 122).

*The Varieties of Religious Experience* is often seen as establishing the science of the psychology of religion. While clearly lacking the analytical rigor which some might now expect, James's masterpiece is based on two fundamental principles. First, that an experience of "God" or "the divine" is existentially transformative, leading to the renewal or regeneration of individuals. Second, that any attempt to codify or formulate these experiences will fail to do justice to them. A number of intellectual responses are possible; none of them, however, is adequate.

So what is the significance of James to our study? One major theme to emerge from his study is that organized religion has relatively little to offer those interested in religious experience. It trades in "second hand" experience, where what needs to be studied is fresh and vital, often being perceived as a threat to the settled ways of organized religion:

> A genuine first hand religious experience … is bound to be a heterodoxy to its witnesses, the prophet appearing as a lonely madman. If his doctrine proves contagious enough to spread to any others, it becomes a definite and labelled heresy. But, if it still proves contagious enough to triumph over persecution, it becomes itself an orthodoxy; and when religion has become an orthodoxy, its way of inwardness is over; the spring is dry; the faithful live at second hand exclusively, and stone prophets in their turn. ( James, 1917, p. 337)

This suggests that empirical study of religious experience is best carried on outside the sphere of organized religion – an assertion which has had considerable impact on the scientific study of the phenomenon of religious experience. Subsequent empirical studies have not provided substantiation of this suggestion; nevertheless, it is impor-

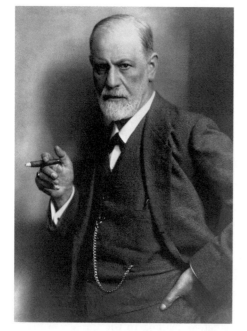

tant to appreciate that James's approach was an important stimulus to work in this area.

One of the most significant aspects of James's work is that it does not attempt to reduce religious experience to social or psychological categories, but attempts to describe the phenomena in a manner which respects their integrity. This heightens the contrast between James and Freud, to whom we now turn.

## Sigmund Freud

It is widely agreed that Freud's discussion of religion is one of his most significant contributions to the debate on science and religion. As we noted earlier (chapter 3), Freud spoke of three great "narcissistic wounds" inflicted on human self-esteem by scientific advance. The Copernican revolution demolished the notion that human beings stood

**Figure 23.2** Sigmund Freud (© CORBIS)

at the center of the universe. Charles Darwin demonstrated

that humanity did not even have a unique place on the planet earth, being the outcome of a natural process. The third wound, Freud declared, was his own demonstration that human beings were not even the master of their own destiny. They were imprisoned and molded by hidden psychological forces, located in the human unconscious.

Freud developed the idea of humanity being the prisoner of its own inner demons by arguing that religion could be accounted for psychoanalytically. Religion is a human creation, the result of an obsession with ritual and veneration of a father figure. Freud's account of the "psychogenesis of religion" is totally unsympathetic in tone, lacking rigorous empirical evidential foundations, and strongly reductionist in approach. *Totem and Taboo* (1913) considers how religion has its origins in society in general; *The Future of an Illusion* (1927) deals with the psychological origins (Freud often uses the term "psychogenesis" here) of religion in the individual. For Freud, religious ideas are "illusions, fulfilments of the oldest, strongest and most urgent wishes of mankind" (1961, p. 30). Similar ideas were developed in a later work *Moses and Monotheism* (1939), published at the end of his life.

To understand Freud at this point, we need to examine his theory of repression. These views were first made known in *The Interpretation of Dreams* (1900), a book which was largely ignored by the critics and the general reading public. Freud's thesis here is that dreams are wish-fulfillments. They are disguised fulfillments of wishes that are repressed by the consciousness (the ego), and are thus displaced into the unconsciousness. In *The Psychopathology of Everyday Life* (1904), Freud argued that these repressed wishes intrude into everyday life at a number of points. Certain neurotic symptoms, dreams, or even small slips of the tongue or pen – so-called "Freudian slips" – reveal unconscious processes.

The task of the psychotherapist is to expose these repressions which have such a negative effect on life. Psychoanalysis (a term coined by Freud) aims to lay bare the unconscious and untreated traumatic experiences, by assisting the patient to raise them up into consciousness. Through persistent questioning, the analyst can identify repressed traumas which are having so negative an effect upon the patient, and enable the patient to deal with them by bringing them into the open.

As we noted earlier, Freud's views on the origin of religion need to be considered in two stages: first, its origins in the development of human history in general, and second, its origins in the case of the individual person. We may begin by dealing with his account of the psychogenesis of religion in the human species in general, as it is presented in *Totem and Taboo*.

Developing his earlier observation that religious rites are similar to the obsessive actions of his neurotic patients, Freud declared that religion was basically a distorted form of an obsessional neurosis. His studies of obsessional patients (such as the "Wolf Man") led him to argue that such disorders were the consequence of unresolved developmental issues, such as the association of "guilt" and "being unclean" which he associated with the "anal" phase in childhood development. He suggested that aspects of religious behavior (such as the ritual cleansing ceremonies of Judaism) could arise through similar obsessions.

Freud argued that the key elements in all religions included the veneration of a father figure and a concern for proper rituals. He traces the origins of religion to the Oedipus complex. At some point in the history of the human race, Freud argues (without substantiation), the father figure had exclusive sexual rights over females in his tribe. The sons, unhappy at this state of affairs, overthrew the father figure and killed him. Thereafter, they are haunted by the secret of parricide, and its associated sense of guilt. Religion, according to Freud, has its origins in this prehistorical parricidal event, and for this reason has guilt as a major motivating factor. This guilt requires purging or expiation, for which various rituals were devised.

The emphasis within Christianity upon the death of Christ and the veneration of the risen Christ seemed to Freud to be a superb illustration of this general principle. "Christianity, having arisen out of a father-religion, became a son-religion. It has not escaped the fate of having to get rid of the father" (Freud, 1964, p. 136). The "totem meal," Freud argued, had its direct counterpart in the Christian celebration of communion.

Freud's account of the social origins of religion is not taken with great seriousness, and is often regarded as a "period piece," bearing witness to the highly optimistic and somewhat simplistic theories which were emerging in the aftermath of the general acceptance of the Darwinian theory of evolution. His account of the origins of religion in the individual is, however, more significant. Once more, the theme of the veneration of a "father figure" emerges as significant. Interestingly, Freud's account of the development of religion in individuals seems not to rest upon careful study of the actual development of such views in children, but an observance of similarities (often rather superficial ones, it has to be said) between some adult neuroses and some religious beliefs and practices, particularly those of Judaism and Roman Catholicism.

In an essay on a childhood memory of Leonardo da Vinci (1910), Freud sets out his explanation of individual religion.

> Psychoanalysis has made us familiar with the intimate connection between the father-complex and belief in God; it has shown us that a personal God is, psychologically, nothing other than an exalted father, and it brings us evidence every day of how young people lose their religious beliefs as soon as their father's authority breaks down. Thus we recognize that the roots of the need for religion are in the parental complex. (Freud, 1957, p. 123)

The veneration of the father figure has its origins in childhood. When going through its oedipal phase, Freud argues, the child has to deal with anxiety over the possibility of being punished by the father. The child's response to this threat is to venerate the father, identify with him, and to project what it knows of the father's will in the form of the superego.

Freud explored the origins of this projection of an ideal father figure in *The Future of an Illusion*. Religion represents the perpetuation of a piece of infantile behavior in adult life. Religion is simply an immature response to the awareness of helplessness, by going back to one's childhood experiences of paternal care: "my father will protect me; he is in control." Belief in a personal God is thus little more than an infantile delusion, the projection of an idealized father figure.

Yet Freud's highly negative approach to religion was not the only view on the matter to emerge from early psychoanalytic circles. Carl Gustav Jung (1875–1961) was the son of a Swiss pastor, who was closely associated with Freud from 1907. In 1914, Jung resigned as president of the International Psychoanalytical Society, an action which signaled his growing distance from Freud on a number of matters, particularly the latter's emphasis upon the libido. As we remarked earlier, Freud is noted for a hostile and reductionist approach to religion. Jung is generally regarded as being more sympathetic to religion than Freud, and clearly wished to distance himself from Freud's reductionism. While Jung remained sympathetic to Freud's belief that the "image of God" is essentially a human projection, he located its origins increasingly in the "collective unconscious." Humans are naturally religious; it is not something which they "invent." Perhaps more significantly, Jung stressed the positive aspects of religion, particularly in relation to an individual's progress towards wholeness and fulfillment.

# The Present State of Affairs

In the previous sections, we considered two landmark contributions to the psychology of religion. It is appropriate to end this chapter with a brief overview of present trends within the discipline. We shall here draw on the analysis of Ralph W. Hood, widely regarded as a major figure in American psychology of religion. Hood distinguishes six psychological schools of thought regarding religion. We shall identify each of these below, and offer some comments.

1  *Psychoanalytical* schools draw upon the work of Freud, noted above, and attempt to reveal and identify unconscious motives for religious belief. Although Freud reduced religious belief to a natural, if ultimately misguided, attempt to cope with life's stresses, contemporary psychoanalytic interpretations are not necessarily hostile to religious faith. For example, it is increasingly recognized that the obser-

vation that illusional processes may be involved in religious belief does not sustain the much deeper ontological claim that religion is a delusion.

2 *Analytical* schools are rooted in Carl Jung's description of the spiritual life, noted above. Although analytical approaches to religious belief generally lack rigorous empirical support, they have been found useful by those who are concerned with pastoral counseling. These approaches tend to be interpretative, rather than causal, aiming to illuminate the religious situation rather than account for its origins.

3 *Object relations* schools also draw from psychoanalysis, but focus their efforts on maternal influences on the child. As a result, many feminist writers have found this a particularly productive area to explore. Like the psychoanalytical and analytical approaches, this school tends to rely on clinical case studies and other descriptive methods based on small samples.

4 *Transpersonal* schools attempt to confront spiritual or transcendent experiences in a nonreductive manner, making use of a variety of methods, scientific and religious. Most work on the assumption that such experiences reflect an ontological reality. Some scholars suggest that this approach is perhaps better regarded as "religious psychology" rather than as "psychology of religion."

5 *Phenomenological* schools focus on the assumptions underlying religious experience and on the commonalities of that experience. They place an emphasis upon description and critical reflection over experimentation and measurement. This contrasts with the more empirical approach of measurement schools.

6 *Measurement* schools use mainstream psychological methods in order to study religious experience. Significant areas of research include the development of appropriate scales to allow the measurement of religious phenomena. This approach often involves the correlation of phenomena, rather than their explanation.

This discussion of possible psychological accounts of religious belief raises some important questions, one of which is whether human beings are naturally inclined to believe in God. This question has been considered in some detail by the relatively new discipline of the cognitive science of religion, and we shall consider these discussions in more detail in the concluding chapter of this part of the book.

## For Further Reading

Hood, Ralph W. "Psychology of Religion." In W. H. Swatos and P. Kvisto (eds), *Encyclopedia of Religion and Society*, pp. 388–91. Walnut Creek, CA: Altamira, 1998.

Spilka, Bernard, Ralph W. Hood, Bruce Hunsberger, and Richard Gorsuch. *The Psychology of Religion: An Empirical Approach*, 3rd edn. New York: The Guilford Press, 2003.

Vanden Burgt, R. J. *The Religious Philosophy of William James*. Chicago: Nelson-Hall, 1981.

Watts, Fraser. "Cognitive Neuroscience and Religious Consciousness." In R. J. Russell, N. Murphy, T. Meyering, and M. Arbib (eds), *Neuroscience and the Person*, pp. 327–46. Vatican City: Vatican Observatory, 1999.

Wulff, David W. "Rethinking the Rise and Fall of the Psychology of Religion." In A. L. Molendijk and P. Pels (eds), *Religion in the Making: The Emergence of the Sciences of Religion*, pp. 181–202. Leiden: Brill, 1998.

# Chapter

# 24 The Cognitive Science of Religion

*Is Religion "Natural"?*

In recent years, a new kid has appeared on the science and religion block. The term "cognitive science of religion," introduced by the Oxford scholar Justin Barrett (born 1971), has come to designate approaches to the study of religion that are derived from the cognitive sciences. This approach brings theories from the cognitive sciences to bear on the question of why religious thought and action is so common in humans, and why religious phenomena have their observed forms. Setting the metaphysical claims of religion to one side, what is observed as "religion" can be regarded as a complex amalgam of essentially human phenomena, which are communicated and regulated by natural human perception and cognition.

Religion is here treated as a natural phenomenon, which arises through – not in spite of – natural human ways of thinking. This represents a significant challenge to some ways of evaluating religion, often inspired by the agenda of Enlightenment rationalism, which held that religion arose through the "sleep of reason" – in other words, through the suspension of normal human critical and rational faculties. The anthropologist Pascal Boyer (2003) set out the differences between these approaches in a tabular form, which is reproduced in Table 24.1.

Further exploration of this "naturalness-of-religion" thesis currently focuses on three main issues:

1   How human beings represent concepts of supernatural agents;
2   How people acquire these religious concepts; and

3  How they respond to these religious concepts through religious actions, such as rituals.

The cognitive science of religion thus does not require a rigorous definition of "religion" in order to proceed. Indeed, some would argue that the emergence of this new cognitive approach to religion was motivated by dissatisfaction with the vagueness of previous theories of religion, and their inability to be empirically tested. As Justin Barrett notes:

**Figure 24.1** Pascal Boyer

> Rather than specify what religion is and try to explain it in whole, scholars in this field have generally chosen to approach "religion" in an incremental, piecemeal fashion, identifying human thought or behavioral patterns that might count as "religious" and then trying to explain why those patterns are cross-culturally recurrent. If the explanations turn out to be part of a grander explanation of "religion," so be it. If not, meaningful human phenomena have still been rigorously addressed. (Barrett, 2007, p. 1)

A further element of importance is the recognition that religion is not primarily about what might be termed "theological" notions – such as the omnipotence of God, or the doctrine of the Trinity. Religious perceptions tend to be much simpler and more "natural" than their theological counterparts. Whereas some have argued that religious beliefs are impositions upon human beings, the cognitive science of religion suggests that there are natural predispositions towards believing in God. Two themes of particular importance in developing this stance are the notion of "minimally counterintuitive concepts" and the "Hyperactive Agency Detection Device (HADD)," both of which we shall discuss further.

Pascal Boyer has argued that religious beliefs belong to a class of ideas which could be called "minimally counterintuitive concepts." By this, he means that, on the one hand, they fulfill certain intuitive assumptions about any given class of things (such as persons or objects), yet on the other hand violate some of those assumptions in ways which make the resulting concepts particularly exciting or memorable. In other words, religious notions are both plausible and memorable. They both belong to the everyday world, yet stand out from it. They are easily represented, and highly memorable. It is not quite clear, however, whether Boyer is arguing that counterintuitiveness is a universal characteristic of all religion, or whether it is simply a sufficient criterion for religion.

**Table 24.1** Do's and don't's in the study of religion (from Boyer, 2003, p. 120)

| *Do not say …* | *But say …* |
| --- | --- |
| Religion answers people's metaphysical questions | Religious thoughts are typically activated when people deal with concrete situations (this crop, that disease, this new birth, this dead body, etc.) |
| Religion is about a transcendent God | It is about a variety of agents: ghouls, ghosts, spirits, ancestors, gods, etc., in direct interaction with people |
| Religion allays anxiety | It generates as much anxiety as it allays: vengeful ghosts, nasty spirits and aggressive gods are as common as protective deities |
| Religion was created at time $t$ in human history | There is no reason to think that the various kinds of thoughts we call "religious" all appeared in human cultures at the same time |
| Religion is about explaining natural phenomena | Most religious explanations of natural phenomena actually explain little but produce salient mysteries |
| Religion is about explaining mental phenomena (dreams, visions) | In places where religion is not invoked to explain them, such phenomena are not seen as intrinsically mystical or supernatural |
| Religion is about morality and the salvation of the soul | The notion of salvation is particular to a few doctrines (Christianity and doctrinal religions of Asia and the Middle East) and unheard of in most other traditions |
| Religion creates social cohesion | Religious commitment can (under some conditions) be used as signal of coalitional affiliation, but coalitions create social fission (secession) as often as group integration |
| Religious claims are irrefutable; that is why people believe them | There are many irrefutable statements that no one believes; what makes some of them plausible to some people is what we need to explain |
| Religion is irrational/superstitious (therefore not worthy of study) | Commitment to imagined agents does not really relax or suspend ordinary mechanisms of belief formation; indeed it can provide important evidence for their functioning (and therefore should be studied attentively) |

A number of workers in the field of the cognitive science of religion have proposed that humanity is generally characterized by possessing a "Hyperactive Agency Detection Device" (or HADD"). An early statement of this idea can be found in Stewart Guthrie's *Faces in the Clouds* (1993), which set out the idea of "agency detection" as a human perceptual function. The idea, however, is developed in cognitive terms by writers such as Justin Barrett:

> Part of the reason people believe in gods, ghosts and, goblins also comes from the way in which our minds, particularly our agency detection device (ADD) functions. Our ADD suffers from some hyperactivity, making it prone to find agents around us, including supernatural ones, given fairly modest evidence of their presence. This tendency encourages the generation and spread of god concepts. (Barrett, 2004, p. 31)

**Figure 24.2** Justin Barrett (Photo Sherry Barrett)

The argument here, deriving from evolutionary psychology, is that human beings have a naturally selected agency-detection system, which is wired to respond to fragmentary information in the environment which might point to a looming threat from an agent – such as a predatory mammal, or hostile human being. The original evolutionary function of the HADD was thus to detect and evade predators; the evolutionary by-product is a susceptibility to infer superhuman beings from noises and movements in the environment.

So where do these reflections take us? One obvious question concerns whether the "minimal counterintuitiveness" approach to religious beliefs implies or entails the nonexistence of the referents of these concepts and beliefs. While most cognitive scientists of religion state that this is not to be regarded as an implication of the theory, it is clear that some scholars in the field (such as Scott Atran and Pascal Boyer) tend to imply that this "minimal counterintuitiveness" theory of religion excludes or precludes a supernatural interpretation of the data, whereas others (such as Justin Barrett) hold that they do not. This raises a question that goes back to Sigmund Freud, whose precommitment to atheism famously led to his "explanations" of religion: are cognitive scientists of religion allowing their worldviews to shape their interpretation of the data?

So how might Christian theology respond to the suggestion that we are predisposed to believe in God? For many theologians, this is simply a scientific description of what has long been held to be theologically true. The idea that humanity is inclined to quest for God is deeply embedded in many theological traditions. The biblical maxim that that God has placed eternity within the human heart (Ecclesiastes 3:11) is one way of expressing this. Others might point to the famous prayer from Augustine of Hippo's *Confessions*: "You have made us for yourself, and our hearts are restless until they finds their rest in you." There are clearly some intriguing possibilities for further exploration here.

So does the cognitive science of religion cast any light on the dialogue between science and religion? There are good reasons for thinking that this new discipline may help clarify this relationship. In an important recent study, Robert N. McCauley (2000) has argued that religious belief is natural. McCauley argues that a belief or action is to be thought of as "natural" when it is "familiar, obvious, self-evident, intuitive, or held or done without reflection" – in other words, when it "seems part of the normal course of events."

Belief in God or supernatural agents therefore seems, McCauley argues, entirely natural. Yet he makes the important point that, when it comes to offering detailed explanations of *what* is believed about such supernatural agents, ways of thinking rapidly emerge which seem very unnatural. Although McCauley does not phrase it in precisely this way, his argument is essentially that a basic belief in God or divine agency is much more natural than the theological descriptions which arise from this belief. In other words, the enterprise traditionally known as "systematic theology" seems relatively unnatural, in that it involves a number of apparently counterintuitive steps. The doctrine of the Trinity would be a good example of a counterintuitive or "unnatural" belief, which stands in contrast to a very natural belief in divine agency.

So what of the natural sciences? McCauley argues that, in certain ways, the natural sciences are experienced as unnatural, in that they involve methods, assumptions, and outcomes which often – though by no means invariably – seem to be natural, in the sense of that which is "familiar, obvious, self-evident, intuitive, or held or done without reflection." McCauley illustrates this point in a number of ways, particularly by noting the counterintuitive character of innovative scientific theories.

> Science challenges our intuitions and common-sense *repeatedly*. With the triumph of new theories, scientists and sometimes even the public must readjust their thinking. *When first advanced*, the suggestions that the earth moves, that microscopic organisms can kill human beings, and that solid objects are mostly empty space were no less contrary to intuition and common sense than the most counterintuitive consequences of quantum mechanics have proved for us in the twentieth century. (McCauley, 2000, p. 69)

As McCauley suggests, the point will be familiar to any who have wrestled with the deeply counterintuitive notions of quantum mechanics. Yet even classical physical notions – such as the idea of "action at a distance," which so troubled Isaac Newton – seem to contradict common sense.

Yet there is another level at which science appears to be unnatural. McCauley argues that the scientific enterprise demands extensive training and preparation, which often involves habits of thought and practice which seem some distance removed from the ordinary world.

In addition to the persistent unnaturalness of scientific proposals, institutionalized science also involves forms of thought and types of practice that human beings find extremely difficult to master. The acquisition of scientific knowledge is a painstaking and laborious process. To become a professional scientist requires at least a decade of focussed education and training, and even then the scientist typically gains command of only one sub-field within a single scientific discipline. Not only is scientific knowledge not something that human beings acquire naturally, its mastery does not even guarantee that someone will know how to *do* science. After four centuries of astonishing accomplishment, science remains an overwhelmingly *unfamiliar activity*, even to most of the learned public and even in those cultures where its influence is substantial. (McCauley, 2000, p. 71)

In suggesting that, in some respects, the natural sciences are "unnatural," McCauley is not suggesting that they are wrong. He is simply making the point that they require developing certain ways of thinking which are not self-evidently true, and often seem to fly in the face of everyday experience or common sense.

So what are the implications of these ideas for the dialogue between science and religion? McCauley's analysis suggests that the dialogue is not really between science and *religion*, but between science and *theology*. Both science and theology represent ways of thinking which are at least one step removed from the everyday and natural habits of thought which are typical of religion. This point would also be defended, although on slightly different grounds, by Thomas F. Torrance (see pp. 115–17, 197–200), who wished to emphasize the specificity of the Christian vision of reality by stressing its Trinitarian and incarnational roots, rather than the "religious" character of the Christian faith.

The field of the cognitive science of religion is relatively new, and this short chapter must be taken as a summary of work in progress. However, it seems very likely that the importance of this field will increase in coming decades, opening up some potentially important new discussions in the field of science and religion – or, perhaps we should say, in science and *theology*.

## For Further Reading

Atran, Scott. *In Gods We Trust: The Evolutionary Landscape of Religion*. Oxford: Oxford University Press, 2002.

Barrett, Justin L. *Why Would Anyone Believe in God?* Lanham, MD: AltaMira Press, 2004.

Boyer, Pascal. *Religion Explained: The Evolutionary Origins of Religious Thought.* New York: Basic Books, 2001.

Guthrie, Stewart. *Faces in the Clouds: A New Theory of Religion.* New York: Oxford University Press, 1993.

McCauley, Robert N. "The Naturalness of Religion and the Unnaturalness of Science." In F. Keil and R. Wilson (eds), *Explanation and Cognition*, pp. 61–85. Cambridge, MA: MIT Press, 2000.

# IV

## Case Studies in Science and Religion

One of the most fascinating aspects of the dialogue between science and religion is the way in which it has brought together a rich diversity of writers from different fields. Some of the most significant writers to contribute to our understanding of this area began their scholarly careers in the natural sciences, and then found themselves being drawn to explore the religious implications of their work. Others began as specialists in the field of religious thought, and found themselves drawn to study the natural sciences on account of a growing awareness of the importance of the distinctive contributions of the sciences to religion.

In what follows, we shall explore some of the ideas and approaches found in 10 contributors to the dialogue between science and religion, offering brief sketches of their careers, and focusing on some aspects of their thought which may be said to have advanced or influenced the dialogue between these two disciplines. The 10 writers chosen could easily have been extended to include others – such as the noted Danish Lutheran theologian Niels Henrik Gregersen (born 1956), or the veteran philosopher of science Ernan McMullin (born 1924), to name only two of the many active and important writers in this field. The purpose of Part IV is simply to gain an idea of some representative contributions to the field, and how these came to be developed.

Furthermore, most of the writers discussed here are noted for multiple contributions to the field of science and religion. Limits of space mean that generally only one such contribution can be considered, which is to be taken as representative of their work, and is not intended to be an exhaustive account of their significance. These short chapters are to be seen as a "taster," intended to encourage and facilitate engagement not merely with these writers, but with others working in the field.

We begin our reflections by considering a French writer who is often regarded as a pioneer in developing an engagement between paleontology and Christian theology – Pierre Teilhard de Chardin.

# Chapter

# 25 Pierre Teilhard de Chardin (1881–1955)

One of the most remarkable contributions to the twentieth-century debate over the relation of science and religion was made by the distinguished French paleontologist Pierre Teilhard de Chardin. Teilhard de Chardin joined the Society of Jesus (also known as the "Jesuits") in 1899. He initially studied theology, but found himself increasingly attracted to the natural sciences, particularly geology and paleontology. He was part of a team which worked in China, and uncovered the fossilized remains which are often referred to as "Peking man." After his work in China, he settled in the United States, where he remained to his death. During his lifetime, Teilhard de Chardin published a number of scientific papers. Despite having given considerable thought to the relation of science and religion, he was not able to gain permission from his religious superiors to publish his writings in this field, partly because they were regarded as being of dubious orthodoxy.

Teilhard de Chardin's death in 1955 opened the way to the publication of these writings. Within months of his death, the first major work appeared. *Le phénomène humaine* ("The human phenomenon") was written during the years 1938–40. It finally appeared in French in 1955, and in English translation in 1959. This was followed by *Le milieu divin*, which was originally written in 1927, and appeared in French in 1957. The title is notoriously difficult to translate into English, on account of the rich connotations of the French word *milieu*. (The English word "medium" conveys at least some of these senses, but not all.) This difficulty led to the work appearing under two different titles in translation. It was published in English under its original French

**Figure 25.1** Pierre Teilhard de Chardin (© Philippe Halsman/Magnum Photos)

title in London in 1960, and under the title *The Divine Milieu* in New York. These two works, taken together, set out a remarkable fusion of evolutionary biology, philosophical theology, and spirituality, which captured the imagination of many working in the field of science and religion.

Teilhard de Chardin viewed the universe as an evolutionary process which was constantly moving towards a state of greater complexity and higher levels of consciousness. Within this process of evolution, a number of critically important transitions (generally referred to as "critical points") can be discerned. For Teilhard, the origination of life on earth and the emergence of human consciousness are two particularly important thresholds in this process. These "critical points" are like rungs on a ladder, leading to new stages in a continuous process of development. The world is to be seen as a single continuous process – a "universal interweaving" of various levels of organization. Each of these levels has its roots in earlier levels, and its emergence is to be seen as the actualization of what was potentially present in earlier levels. Teilhard de Chardin thus does not consider that there is a radical dividing line between consciousness and matter, or between humanity and other animals. The world is a single evolving entity, linked together as a web of mutually interconnected events, in which there is a natural progression from matter to life to human existence to human society.

For some of his critics, this seems to suggest that there is some way in which matter can be thought of as "rational." Teilhard de Chardin's stress on the potential of lower levels flowering or becoming actualized in later levels leads him to the conclusion that, since matter has the potential to become "conscious," it can therefore be thought of as being "conscious" in some manner. There must therefore have been a "rudimentary consciousness" which "precedes the emergence of life" in the physical matter of the universe. Teilhard de Chardin, in *Le phénomène humaine*, expresses this idea in the following manner: "there is a 'Within' to things." In other words, there is some form of biological layer lying within the fabric of the universe. This biological layer may be "attenuated to the uttermost" in the early stages of the evolutionary process, but its existence is necessary to explain the emergence of consciousness in later periods. It is important to note how this conclusion arises from his insistence that there are no radical discontinuities or innovations within the evolutionary process, which proceeds in a constantly progressive manner. New phases are to be thought of in terms of crossing thresholds, not breaking with earlier stages.

This clearly raises the question of how God is involved in evolution. It is clear that Teilhard de Chardin places considerable emphasis on the theme of the consummation of the world in Jesus Christ, an idea which is clearly stated in the New Testament (especially the letters to the Colossians and Ephesians: see Colossians 1: 15–20; Ephesians 1: 9–10, 22–3), and which was developed with particular enthusiasm by some Greek patristic writers, including Origen. Teilhard de Chardin develops this theme with particular reference to a concept which he calls "Omega" (after the final letter of the Greek alphabet). In his earlier writings, he tends to think of Omega primarily as the point towards which the evolutionary process is heading. The process clearly represents an upward ascent; Omega defines, so to speak, its final destination. It will be clear that Teilhard de Chardin regards evolution as a teleological and directional process. As his thinking developed, however, he began to integrate his Christian understanding of God into his thinking about Omega, with the result that both the directionality of evolution and its final goal are explained in terms of a final union with God.

Teilhard de Chardin is not as lucid in his discussion of this issue as might be hoped, and there are some difficulties in understanding him at points. However, the main points in his later thinking appear to be the following. Omega is to be seen as a force which attracts the evolutionary process towards it. It is "the Prime Mover ahead," the principle which "moves and collects" the process. Unlike gravity, which attracts downwards, Omega is "an inverse process of gravitation" which attracts the evolutionary process upwards, so that it may finally ascend into union with God. The entire direction of the evolutionary process is thus not defined by its point of departure, by where it started from, but by its goal, by its final objective, which is Omega.

Teilhard de Chardin argues that the existence of Omega is suggested, but not proved, by scientific analysis. It is reached only by extrapolation, rather than observation, and is best regarded as an "assumption and conjecture" rather than an established scientific fact. Yet it is confirmed and given substance by the Christian revelation. It is argued that the New Testament theme of all things finding their goal in Christ (which, as we noted, is clearly stated in the letters to the Colossians and Ephesians) provides a theological underpinning for this religious interpretation of evolution. While some might consider scientific accounts of the universe to pose a threat to Christ, de Chardin argues that Christ is in fact "the guarantee of its stability." Jesus Christ, as God incarnate, is therefore understood as the ground and goal of the entire process of cosmic evolution. The terminus or goal of the evolutionary process is thus understood to be the "well-defined personal reality of the Incarnate Word," in whom all things find their ultimate unity. If all things are to be "summed up in Christ" (Ephesians 1: 9–10), then Christ is to be seen as the final goal of the evolving cosmos.

The overall vision that Teilhard de Chardin sets out is thus that of a universe in the process of evolution – a massive organism which is slowly progressing towards its fulfillment through a forward and upward movement. God is at work within this process, directing it from inside – yet also at work *ahead* of the process, drawing it towards himself and its final fulfillment. In a paper entitled "What I Believe," Teilhard de Chardin set out his cosmic vision in four terse statements:

I believe that the universe is in evolution.
I believe that evolution proceeds towards the spiritual.
I believe that the spiritual is fully realized in a form of personality.
I believe that the supremely personal is the universal Christ.

Teilhard de Chardin has evoked admiration and irritation in about equal measure. Many have found themselves fascinated by the vision which he offers of a universe converging towards its final goal. Others have found his ideas lacking in intellectual rigor, and hopelessly optimistic in terms of the final outcome of cosmic evolution. Nevertheless, he remains a fascinating example of a twentieth-century writer who found points of connection between his scientific and religious thinking.

## For Further Reading

### Primary Sources

Teilhard de Chardin, Pierre. *The Phenomenon of Man*. New York: Harper, 1959.
Teilhard de Chardin, Pierre. *The Divine Milieu: An Essay on the Interior Life*. New York: Harper, 1960.

### Significant Secondary Studies

Grumett, David. "Teilhard de Chardin's Evolutionary Natural Theology." *Zygon*, 42 (2007): 519–34.
King, Ursula. Spirit of Fire: The Life and Vision of Teilhard de Chardin. Maryknoll, NY: Orbis Books, 1996.
Lane, David. *The Phenomenon of Teilhard: Prophet for a New Age*. Macon, GA: Mercer University Press, 1996.

# Chapter

# 26 Thomas F. Torrance (1913–2007)

Thomas Forsyth Torrance was born on August 30, 1913, at Chengdu, in the Szechuan region of China, to Scottish missionary parents. He was initially educated at the Chengdu Canadian Mission School (1920–7), before returning to Scotland to continue his education at Bellshill Academy (1927–31). He then entered the University of Edinburgh, gaining his MA in Classical Languages and Philosophy in 1934, and his BD (with specialization in systematic theology) in 1937. He subsequently undertook further research work at Oxford and Basle, and was awarded a doctorate from Basle for a study of the doctrine of grace in the writings of some early Christian theologians. After a year spent as Professor of Systematic Theology at Auburn Theological Seminary in New York State (1938–9), he was ordained as a Presbyterian minister, and served as Parish Minister at Alyth in Perthshire 1940–7, including a period spent on chaplaincy service with the British Army during World War II. After a second period of ministry at Beechgrove Parish Church, Aberdeen (1947–50), Torrance was appointed Professor of Church History, at Edinburgh University and New College. In 1952, he was appointed Professor of Christian Dogmatics at Edinburgh, and remained in this position until his retirement in 1979. Some of Torrance's best books – most notably, *The Trinitarian Faith* – were written during this later period.

Torrance is widely regarded as the most significant British theologian of the twentieth century, and it is therefore particularly important to note his interest in the relation of the natural sciences and Christian theology. Among his major writings to

**Figure 26.1** Thomas F. Torrance

deal with the theme, two may be singled out as being of particular significance. *Theological Science* (1969), based on the Hewett Lectures delivered in 1959 at Union Theological Seminary, New York, can be seen as an early landmark statement of Torrance's views on the relation of the natural sciences and Christian theology. These views were developed in subsequent works, especially in *Reality and Scientific Theology: Theology and Science at the Frontiers of Knowledge* (1985), which was based on the Harris Lectures at the University of Dundee in 1970. Torrance was awarded the Templeton Prize for Progress in Religion in 1978 in recognition of his major contribution to the dialogue between the two disciplines.

At the heart of Torrance's approach is his firm belief that there is a "hidden traffic between theological and scientific ideas of the most far-reaching significance for both theology and science" which shows that they have "deep mutual relations" (Torrance, 1985, pp. x–xi). Of the various convergences which Torrance identifies, the most important is that both are *a posteriori* reflections on an independent reality which they attempt to describe in their respective manners.

Torrance draws a careful and critical distinction between "religion" and "theology." The distinction is important, as many discussions of the interaction of religious and scientific ways of thinking often treat the issues of "science and religion" and "science and theology" as synonymous – different ways of speaking about the same thing. Drawing partly on a Barthian perspective, Torrance insists that this is unacceptable. "Religion" is to be understood as concerning human consciousness and behavior. Religion is essentially a human creation. Theology, on the other hand, has to do with our knowledge of God.

> Theology is the unique science devoted to knowledge of God, differing from other sciences by the uniqueness of its object which can be apprehended only on its own terms and from within the actual situation it has created in our existence in making itself known … As a science theology is only a human endeavour in quest of the truth, in which we seek to apprehend God as far as we may, to understand what we apprehend, and to speak clearly and carefully about what we understand. (Torrance, 1969, p. 281)

It follows from this that both theology and the natural sciences are determined by the reality of the object which is to be apprehended. They cannot set out from preconceptions of their own devising, but must allow their inquiry to be guided by the independent reality which they are seeking to understand. Torrance therefore argues that Christian theology arises out of the actual knowledge of God given in and with concrete happenings in space and time. It concerns knowledge of the God who actively meets us and gives himself to be known in Jesus Christ. We do not therefore begin with ourselves or our questions, nor indeed can we choose where to begin; we can only begin with the facts prescribed for us by the actuality of the subject positively known.

Torrance is thus critical of the use of *a priori* notions in both science and theology, believing that both should respond to the objective reality with which they are confronted, and which they are required to describe. Theology and the natural sciences are to be seen as *a posteriori* activities, conditioned by what is given. Developing this line of thought further, Torrance goes on to argue that both theology and the natural sciences are committed to some form of realism, in that they deal with a reality whose existence and nature exist prior to their attempts to comprehend or represent it. Both disciplines thus need to be open to the way things are, and adjust their modes of inquiry to accommodate the nature of the reality which they encounter. As Torrance puts this important point:

> We are concerned in the development of scientific theories to penetrate into the comprehensibility of reality and grasp it in its mathematical harmonies or symmetries or its invariant structures, which hold good independently of our perceiving: we apprehend the real world as it forces itself upon us through the theories it calls forth from us. Theories take shape in our minds under the pressure of the real world upon us … This is the inescapable "dogmatic realism" or a science pursued and elaborated under the compelling claims and constraints of reality. (Torrance, 1985, pp. 54–5)

In the case of the natural sciences, the "reality" is the natural order; in the case of theology, it is the Christian revelation.

> The basic convictions and fundamental ideas with which our knowledge of God is built up arise on the ground of evangelical and liturgical experience in the life of the Church, in response to the way God has actually taken in making himself known to mankind through historical dialogue with Israel and the Incarnation of his Son in Jesus Christ and continues to reveal himself to us through the Holy Scriptures. Scientific theology or theological science, strictly speaking, can never be more than a refinement and extension of the knowledge informed by those basic convictions and fundamental ideas, and it would be both empty of material content and empirically irrelevant if it were cut adrift from them. (Torrance, 1985, p. 85)

It will be clear that Torrance's view is grounded in an approach which stresses the priority of God's self-revelation. This is seen as an objective reality, independent of human rational activity. Although Torrance is no uncritical supporter of Barth, this would unquestionably be one area in which he identifies with Barth's agenda. This means that the approach adopted by Torrance would not find favor with religious thinkers who regard theology as reflection on human experience, or who adopt a postmodern stance, according to which there is no such objective reality in the first place.

Yet Torrance must be seen as developing Barth's theological program in a manner which is fundamentally more friendly and receptive toward the natural sciences. Where Barth tended to be dismissive of any dialogue between theology and the natural sciences, Torrance noted that such a dialogue had considerable potential. His argument that natural theology had a role within systematic theology which paralleled the use made by Einstein of geometry is particularly important in this respect.

## For Further Reading

### Primary Sources

Torrance, Thomas F. *Theological Science*. London: Oxford University Press, 1969.

Torrance, Thomas F. *Divine and Contingent Order*. Oxford: Oxford University Press, 1981.

Torrance, Thomas F. *Reality and Scientific Theology: Theology and Science at the Frontiers of Knowledge*. Edinburgh: Scottish Academic Press, 1985.

### Significant Secondary Studies

Colyer, Elmer M. *How to Read T. F. Torrance: Understanding His Trinitarian & Scientific Theology*. Downers Grove, IL: InterVarsity Press, 2001.

Luoma, Tapio. *Incarnation and Physics: Natural Science in the Theology of Thomas F. Torrance*. Oxford: Oxford University Press, 2002.

McGrath, Alister E. *Thomas F. Torrance: An Intellectual Biography*. Edinburgh: T. & T. Clark, 1999.

# Chapter

# 27    Charles A. Coulson
(1910–74)

Charles Alfred Coulson was born on December 13, 1910 in the English West Midlands town of Dudley. His father, who was principal of the local technical college, had earlier been a science teacher at the School of Science, Norwich. He was instrumental in cultivating the deep religious faith that was to become so characteristic of Coulson himself. In the dedication to the work on science and religion for which he is best remembered – *Science and Christian Belief* – Coulson referred to his father as the one who "first showed me the unity of science and faith."

In 1928, at the age of 17, Coulson went up to Trinity College, Cambridge, to study mathematics and physics. During his time at Cambridge University, he became heavily involved in student Christian activities, especially through a group organized by the local Methodist church. He once wrote that he experienced God for the first time in a personal manner during his first weeks at Cambridge. His deep interest in Christianity developed further during his time as an undergraduate, and caused his father to worry that he was neglecting his academic work.

In the event, that anxiety proved to be misplaced. Coulson gained first class honors in each of the three parts of the Cambridge tripos – Mathematics Part I (1929), Mathematics Part II (1930), and Physics Part II (1931). He developed a particular interest in quantum theory, and its application to chemistry. He was appointed Professor of Theoretical Physics at King's College, London in 1947, and went on to become Rouse Ball Professor of Mathematics at Oxford University in 1952. At King's College, he built up a new department and greatly expanded his research into the

**Figure 27.1** Charles A. Coulson (Oxfam GB)

application of molecular orbital theory to problems in organic chemistry, particularly to large condensed ring systems. In 1972, he became the first Professor of Theoretical Chemistry at Oxford. It was already known that he was suffering from cancer at the time of his appointment to the new Oxford chair, but it was thought that an operation in 1970 to remove cancerous growth had been successful. Sadly, it turned out that the tumor had not been fully removed. Coulson died in his sleep on January 7, 1974.

Among Coulson's most significant scientific works, we may note *Valence* (1952) and *The Shape and Structure of Molecules* (1973). In addition to a substantial corpus of writings dealing with aspects of physics, chemistry, and mathematics, Coulson wrote a number of works specifically dealing with the relation of the sciences and Christian belief. The two most important such writings are the Riddell Memorial Lectures, published as *Christianity in an Age of Science* (1953) and the John Calvin McNair lectures, published as *Science and Christian Belief* (1955).

Coulson's major contribution to the discussion of the relation of science and religion lies in his vigorous and insistent rejection of the notion of a "God of the gaps." The "gaps" in question could be described as explanatory lacunae – in other words, gaps in our understanding. Coulson was alarmed at the tendency of some religious writers to propose that what could not at present be explained was to be put down to the action or influence of God.

For Coulson, this was a vulnerable and unjustified strategy. It was vulnerable on account of scientific progress. What might be unexplained today might find an explanation tomorrow. "When we come to the scientifically unknown, our correct policy is not to rejoice because we have found God: it is to become better scientists" (Coulson, 1958, p. 16). Coulson was fond of quoting the Scottish theologian and scientist Henry Drummond (1851–97) on the pointlessness of an appeal to such gaps: "There are reverent minds who ceaselessly scan the fields of nature and the books of science in search of gaps – gaps which they fill up with God. As if God lived in gaps!" Coulson insisted that God was to be discerned through the ordering and beauty of the world, not hiding in its recesses. What was the point in believing in a God who "sneaks in through the loopholes," having been excluded from everything and everywhere else?

Coulson's unitary vision of reality led him to reject any notion of strictly demarcated "scientific" and "religious" domains of reality. His criticism of this idea can be seen as an important anticipation of the problems associated with Stephen Jay Gould's idea of "nonoverlapping magisteria" (NOMA), discussed in chapter 6:

> This [separation] is a fatal step to take. For it is to assert that you can plant some sort of hedge in the country of the mind to mark the boundary where a transfer of authority takes place. Its error is twofold. First it presupposes a dichotomy of existence which would be tolerable if no scientist were ever a Christian, and no Christian ever a scientist, but which becomes intolerable while there is one single person owning both allegiances. And second it invites "science" to discover new things and thence gradually to take possession of that which "religion" once held. (Coulson, 1958, p. 19)

History makes clear that science advances, and has a marked propensity to fill gaps once held to be "religious" in nature. "There is no 'God of the gaps' to take over at those strategic places where science fails; and the reason is that gaps of this sort have the unpreventable habit of shrinking" (Coulson, 1958, p. 32). Yet why look to the gaps in scientific understanding? For Coulson, reality as a whole demanded explanation. "Either God is in the whole of Nature, with no gaps, or He's not there at all" (p. 28).

In a sermon preached at Cambridge a few months before his death, Coulson continued to press home the weaknesses of the "God of the gaps" approach. This, he insisted, reduced God's activity to the "loopholes" left by scientific principles, and belittled God by reducing him to the level of "a tiny little mouse that scuttles in and out of the holes in the wainscoting and escapes us whenever we look too closely." While there was rather more to God than what is found expressed in the order of nature, Coulson argued that preachers should not be afraid of pointing out that "what we find in the order of Nature is a certain likeness to God."

For Coulson, the biblical account of creation points to the universe possessing and demonstrating a meaningful and ordered pattern, which can be uncovered by the natural sciences. It is in this area that Coulson sees a strong convergence between science and Christianity. Rather than seek God in those things which cannot be explained, Coulson argues that God is to be found in the remarkable beauty and ordering of the world. "We can trace in what we call the Order of Nature the working out of an almost unbelievably grand purpose."

## For Further Reading

### Primary Sources

Coulson, Charles A. *Christianity in an Age of Science*. London: Oxford University Press, 1953.

Coulson, Charles A. *Science and Christian Belief*. London: Oxford University Press, 1955.

Coulson, Charles A. *Science and the Idea of God*. Cambridge, UK: Cambridge University Press, 1958

## Significant Secondary Studies

Hawkin, David and Eileen. *The World of Science: The Religious and Social Thought of C. A. Coulson*. London: Epworth Press, 1989.

Hough, Adrian. "Not a Gap in Sight: Fifty Years of Charles Coulson's *Science and Christian Belief*." *Theology*, 109 (2006): 21–7.

Simões, Ana. "Textbooks, Popular Lectures and Sermons: The Quantum Chemist Charles Alfred Coulson and the Crafting of Science." *British Journal for the History of Science* 37 (2004): 299–342.

# Chapter

# 28    Ian G. Barbour (born 1923)

Ian G. Barbour is widely regarded as one of the most important and positive influences on the growing interest in the interface between science and religion. Indeed, many would argue that the emergence of the field of "science and religion" as an area of study in its own right dates from 1966, when Barbour's landmark work *Issues in Science and Religion* made its appearance. Barbour has played an enormous role in catalyzing the emergence of this distinct field, and has had considerable personal influence on shaping its dynamics – most notably, in appealing to A. N. Whitehead's process thought as a tool of inquiry in the field (see chapter 12).

Barbour was born on October 5, 1923 in Beijing, China, and initially focused his studies on the field of physics, gaining his PhD from the University of Chicago in 1950. His first academic appointment was at Kalamazoo College, Michigan, as professor of physics. However, he had a strong interest in religion, which he was able to pursue through studies at Yale University, leading to a BD in 1956. He served for many years in various roles, including Chairman of the Department of Religion and Professor of Physics, at Carleton College, Northfield, Minnesota (1955–81). He finally became Winifred and Atherton Bean Professor of Science Technology and Society at the college (1981–6).

Barbour's characteristic concern to relate science and religion developed during the 1960s, and led to the publication of the book for which he is best known – *Issues in Science and Religion* (1966). This book reflected his experience of teaching in both the areas of science and religion – teaching interests which he was able to maintain

**Figure 28.1** Ian G. Barbour (Carleton College News Bureau)

throughout most of his academic career. During the 1970s, Barbour developed his interests further through a program on ethics, public policy, and technology, which identified and engaged with a series of religious issues.

*Issues in Science and Religion* – widely regarded as an authoritative, clearly written, and learned book – introduced many to the fascinating questions which were associated with this field. Since then, Barbour has authored or edited a series of works dealing with issues on the interface of science and religion (most notably *Religion in an Age of Science*, which appeared in 1990, based on the Gifford lectures given at the University of Aberdeen in 1989). He is widely regarded as the doyen of dialogue in this field, and was honored for this by the American Academy of Religion in 1993. Barbour was awarded the Templeton Prize for Progress in Religion in 1999 in recognition of his efforts to create a dialogue between the worlds of science and religion.

However, it is important to appreciate that Barbour has done more than encourage dialogue in this field. He has given considerable attention to the development of an intellectual basis for the facilitation and consolidation of this dialogue. Far from being a pragmatic response to the need for two powerful cultural forces to engage in dialogue, Barbour argues, there is an intellectual bridge between the two, which makes the dialogue necessary and proper. Barbour claims that there are important continuities (though not identities) in terms of epistemology (the kinds of knowledge we have), methodology (how this knowledge is obtained and justified), and language (how this knowledge is expressed). Taken together, these commonalities provide a "bridge" between science and religion which is capable of sustaining significant intellectual traffic between them.

One of the most influential aspects of Barbour's approach is the appropriation of the ideas developed in what is known as "process thought" or "process theology" for the engagement between science and religion. As this approach has been touched on earlier (chapter 12), we shall limit this discussion to considering the particular use which Barbour makes of process theology in relation to the field of science and religion.

The key aspect of process theology which Barbour appropriates is the rejection of the classic doctrine of God's omnipotence: God is one agent among many, not the sovereign Lord of all. As Barbour points out, process thought affirms "a God of persuasion rather than compulsion" who "influences the world without determining it" (Barbour, 1990, pp. 29, 224). Process theology thus locates the origins of suffering and evil within the world to a radical limitation upon the power of God. God has set aside (or simply does not possess) the ability to coerce, retaining only the ability to persuade. Persuasion is seen as a means of exercising power in such a manner that the rights and freedom of others are respected. God is obliged to persuade every aspect of the process to act in the best possible manner. There is, however, no guarantee that God's benevolent persuasion will lead to a favorable outcome. The process is under no obligation to obey God. As Barbour comments, process theology thus calls into question "the traditional expectation of an absolute victory over evil" (1990, p. 264).

God intends good for the creation, and acts in its best interests. However, the option of coercing everything to do the divine will cannot be exercised. As a result, God is unable to prevent certain things happening. Wars, famines, and holocausts are not things which God desires; they are, however, not things which God can prevent, on account of the radical limitations placed upon the divine power. God is thus not responsible for evil; nor can it be said, in any way, that God desires or tacitly accepts its existence. The metaphysical limits placed upon God are such as to prevent any interference in the natural order of things.

Barbour finds this approach (especially as it is set out in the writings of Whitehead himself) valuable in illuminating the manner in which science and religion interact. It allows God to be seen as present and active within nature, working within the limits and constraints of the natural order. It would be fair to categorize Barbour's views as "panentheism" at this point (meaning "God is present in all things," and not to be confused with "pantheism," the view that all things are divine).

Perhaps the most interesting way in which Barbour uses the distinctive ideas of process thought relates to the theory of evolution. Barbour argues that the evolutionary process is influenced by – but *not* directed by – God. This allows him to deal with the fact that the evolutionary process appears to have been long, complex, and wasteful. "There have been too many blind alleys and extinct species and too much waste, suffering, and evil to attribute every event to God's specific will" (Barbour, 1990, p. 174). God influences the process for good, but cannot dictate precisely what form it will take. It is here that Barbour's influence has been particularly significant, with many contemporary works exploring the religious implications of evolutionary suffering appealing to the principles of process thought to make the point that God does not directly determine the precise form of the evolutionary process. He suffers, along with others within that process.

While Barbour's distinct approach to the relation of science and religion is important in its own right, it is generally thought that his greatest contribution to the field is his demonstration of its intellectual autonomy and interest.

## For Further Reading

### Primary Sources

Barbour, Ian G. *Issues in Science and Religion*. Englewood Cliffs, NJ: Prentice-Hall, 1966.

Barbour, Ian G. *Myths, Models and Paradigms: A Comparative Study in Science and Religion*. New York: Harper & Row, 1974.

Barbour, Ian G. *Religion in an Age of Science*. San Francisco: HarperSanFrancisco, 1990.

### Significant Secondary Studies

McFague, Sallie. "Ian Barbour: Theologian's Friend, Scientist's Interpreter." *Zygon*, 31 (2005): 21–8.

Russell, Robert John (ed.). *Fifty Years in Science and Religion: Ian G. Barbour and His Legacy*. Aldershot. UK: Ashgate, 2004.

Polkinghorne, John. *Scientists as Theologians: A Comparison of the Writings of Ian Barbour, Arthur Peacocke and John Polkinghorne*. London: SPCK, 1996.

# 29 Arthur Peacocke (1924–2006)

Arthur Robert Peacocke went up to Exeter College, Oxford University in 1942 to study chemistry. At that stage, the Oxford University chemistry course lasted four years. After the initial three years of teaching, the final year consisted of a substantial research project. Peacocke chose to work under the guidance of the Nobel laureate Sir Cyril Hinshelwood (1897–1967) in the Physical Chemistry Laboratory for this final year of his undergraduate work, and remained with him for his doctoral research. Although Hinshelwood was a physical chemist who had received the Nobel Prize for his work on chemical kinetics (that is, the study of the rates of chemical reactions), he subsequently extended his interests to include the growth rates of living organisms. Peacocke's doctoral work focused on the manner in which bacterial growth was inhibited by certain chemical substances.

After his doctoral work, Peacocke accepted a lectureship in physical chemistry at the University of Birmingham, England, where he further developed an interest in aspects of the physical chemistry of DNA. During his time at Birmingham, Peacocke developed his interests in Christian theology by studying for the Bachelor of Divinity. Reading the works of leading English theologians of the time (such as William Temple, Ian Ramsey, and G. W. H. Lampe) encouraged him to explore further the relation of science and religion. After a period as a lecturer at Oxford University and fellow of St Peter's College (1968–73), he accepted the position of Dean of Clare College, Cambridge, which allowed him to develop his interest in the interface of science and religion. He served from 1985 to 1999 as director of the Ian Ramsey Centre at Oxford, which has a special interest in fostering study of issues at the interface of science and religion.

**Figure 29.1** Arthur Peacocke

In addition to his many personal contributions to the dialogue between science and religion, Peacocke also played a significant part in founding a number of organizations which have had an important role in facilitating that dialogue. During the early 1970s he was a leading voice in the discussions that led to the formation of the Science and Religion Forum in the United Kingdom, serving as its first chairman. In 1987, Peacocke founded the Society of Ordained Scientists as a means of advancing the development of the field of science and religion. He envisaged this society as a kind of "dispersed religious community," prayerfully linking together the clergy with serious scientific concerns of the age. He was later active in the founding of the European Society for the Study of Science and Theology. He was awarded the Templeton Prize in 2001.

Peacocke's first major publication in the field of science and religion was the result of being invited to deliver the Bampton Lectures at Oxford in 1978. These were published the following year, with the title *Creation and the World of Science*. A stream of publications followed, focusing on aspects of the relationship of religion and science in general, and the biological sciences in particular. One of Peacocke's most distinctive concerns is his belief that Christian theology needs to respond to the challenges posed by the natural sciences in the modern period. His own work can be seen as representing exactly such a response, which often takes the form of a restatement or reinterpretation of its core ideas in response to scientific developments and challenges.

Peacocke's work has many facets. He is one of a group of writers to emphasize that biological evolution is not in conflict with the Christian faith, and endorses the view that evolution is a "disguised friend" of faith. He is also noted for his panentheist account of God, which leads him to offer significant reinterpretations of a number of Christian doctrines using the concept of emergent levels of complex reality with downward efficacy on their constituents. In this brief discussion, however, we shall focus on Peacocke's commitment to critical realism as a tool in the dialogue between science and religion.

In common with many of those working at the interface of science and religion, Peacocke argues the case for a form of "critical realism." Peacocke can be seen as extending the case for critical realism made by Ian Barbour, incorporating themes deriving from the writings of Ernan McMullin, Hilary Putnam, and Ian Hacking.

Noting that some recent writers have argued that the natural sciences are "sociologically and ideologically conditioned," Peacocke (2001) stresses that they attempt to give an account of something which cannot be regarded as conditioned in this manner. Science and theology alike use imagery in an attempt to offer a reliable and responsible picture of the world as it really is.

> I think that both science and theology *aim* to depict reality; that they both do so in metaphorical language with the use of models; and that their metaphors and models are revisable within the context of the continuous communities which have generated them. This philosophy of science ("critical realism") has the virtue of being the implicit, though often not articulated, working philosophy of working scientists who aim to depict reality but know only too well their fallibility in doing so. (Peacocke, 2001, p. 9)

Having argued that some form of critical realism is integral to the scientific method, Peacocke argues that theology also aims to depict reality using models or analogies. The images used to visualize reality may be culturally conditioned, and may require revision. Yet the realization of the provisionality of the representations of reality do not force us to abandon any idea of a real world, which is somehow represented in this way.

> Theology, the intellectual formulation of religious experience and beliefs, also employs models which may be similarly described. I urge that a critical realism is also the most appropriate and adequate philosophy concerning religious language and theological propositions. Theological concepts and models should be regarded as partial, adequate and revisable but necessary and, indeed, the only ways of referring to the reality that is named as "God" and God's dealings with humanity. (Peacocke, 1993, p. 14)

While recognizing the diversity of types of scientific realism, Peacocke argued for a "common core" of claims – most notably, that scientific change is progressive and accumulative, and that the aim of science is to depict reality. He makes a similar case for critical realism in theology. As in science, theological concepts and models are partial, adequate, and revisable. Yet unlike those in science, they include a strong, affective function, engaging the emotions as much as the mind. It will thus be clear that Peacocke believes that both science and religion operate on the basis of a "critical realism" which recognizes that models are partial, adequate, revisable, and necessary means of depicting reality. Each of these terms merits a little further exploration.

*Partial.* Theological models can only allow access to part of the greater reality which they depict. Peacocke thus recognizes that there are limits on what can be known of reality, whether scientific or religious, on account of the mode of representation which has to be used in the process of depiction.

*Adequate.* Peacocke here draws attention to the fact that these models are good enough to allow us to know about the reality which is depicted. The fact that such knowledge does not derive *directly* from reality is not to be seen as implying that it is somehow substandard or second-rate.

*Revisable.* In the natural sciences, models are revised in the light of an accumulation of experimental knowledge which indicates that the model requires revision. Peacocke also suggests that religious models can be revised in the same way. Perhaps this is one of the more controversial aspects of his analysis, in that many more traditional religious thinkers would hold that the religious models are "given." Such thinkers would concede the need for revision, but insist that what is revisable is the interpretation which we place upon these models, not the models themselves.

*Necessary.* A distinction is generally made between "naïve realism" and "critical realism," with the former holding that it is possible to know reality *directly* and the latter that it is necessary to know it *indirectly*, through models. This is fundamentally an issue about how the human mind makes sense of things. Peacocke holds that it is proper to allow the human mind an active and constructive role in the representation of reality. Far from being a passive observer of things, the human mind actively constructs its representations of the external world.

## For Further Reading

### Primary Sources

Peacocke, Arthur. *Creation and the World of Science.* Oxford: Oxford University Press, 1979.

Peacocke, Arthur. *Theology for a Scientific Age: Being and Becoming Divine and Human.* London: SCM Press, 1993.

Peacocke, Arthur. *Paths from Science Towards God : The End of All Our Exploring.* Oxford: Oneworld, 2001.

### Significant Secondary Studies

Murphey, Nancy. "Arthur Peacocke's Naturalistic Christian Faith for the Twenty-First Century: A Brief Introduction." *Zygon*, 43 (2008): 67–73.

Polkinghorne, John. *Scientists as Theologians: A Comparison of the Writings of Ian Barbour, Arthur Peacocke and John Polkinghorne.* London: SPCK, 1996.

Russell, Robert J. "The Theological-Scientific Vision of Arthur Peacocke." *Zygon*, 26 (1991): 505–17.

# Chapter

# 30 Wolfhart Pannenberg (born 1928)

Wolfhart Pannenberg was born in 1928 in Stettin (then part of Germany, now included in Poland), and began theological studies after World War II at the University of Berlin. His early theological studies were subsequently based at the Universities of Göttingen and Basle, where he completed his doctoral thesis (published in 1954) on the doctrine of predestination of the noted medieval scholastic theologian John Duns Scotus. His first teaching appointment was at the University of Heidelberg, where he remained until called to a vacant chair of systematic theology at the *Kirchliche Hochschule* at Wuppertal (1958–61) as a colleague of Jürgen Moltmann. After a period at the University of Mainz (1961–8), he moved to the University of Munich, where he remained until his retirement in 1998.

Pannenberg is one of relatively few professional theologians who developed an interest in the natural sciences. Initially, Pannenberg's interests lay in the area of the importance of the philosophy of history. These issues were explored throughout the 1960s, when the predominance of Marxism in German intellectual culture made an examination of the role of history particularly significant. Marxism emphasized the importance of the correct interpretation of history, and Pannenberg responded by arguing for the grounding of theology in what he termed "universal history."

His views on this issue were developed and justified in the 1961 volume *Offenbarung als Geschichte* ("Revelation as History") edited by Pannenberg, in which these ideas are explored at some length. This volume established Pannenberg as a leading young theologian of the period. This reputation was further consolidated by his 1968 work

**Figure 30.1** Wolfhart Pannenberg (Bundesarchiv, B 145 image-F065001-0017, Photographer: Reinck)

on Christology, in which he set out an approach to the identity and significance of Jesus of Nazareth which made a particular appeal to the resurrection as a public historical event.

Pannenberg's early essay "Dogmatic Theses on the Doctrine of Revelation" opens with a powerful appeal to universal history. Christian theology is based upon an analysis of universal and publicly accessible history. For Pannenberg, revelation is essentially a public and universal historical event which is recognized and interpreted as an "act of God." Pannenberg thus argues that history, in all its totality, can only be understood when it is viewed from its endpoint. This point alone provides the perspective from which the historical process can seen in its totality, and thus be properly understood. The end of history is disclosed in advance (or, to use Pannenberg's term, *proleptically*) in the history of Jesus Christ. In other words, the end of history, which has yet to take place, has been disclosed in advance of the event in the person and work of Christ.

Perhaps the most distinctive, and certainly the most discussed, aspect of this work is Pannenberg's insistence that the resurrection of Jesus is an objective historical event, witnessed by all who had access to the evidence. Whereas writers such as Rudolf Bultmann (1884–1976) treated the resurrection as an event within the experiential world of the disciples, Pannenberg declares that it belongs to the world of universal public history. Revelation is not something that takes place in secret. It is "open to anyone who has eyes to see. It has a universal character." Any concept of revelation which implies that revelation is either opposed to or distinct from natural knowledge is in danger of lapsing into a form of Gnosticism.

Pannenberg's point here is that the distinctively Christian understanding of revelation lies in the way in which publicly available events are interpreted. Thus the resurrection of Jesus, he argues, was a publicly accessible event. But what did it *mean*? Christian revelation concerns the distinctively Christian way of understanding that event, and its implications for our understanding of God. We can see here the foundations of a "critical realist" epistemology, which later informed Pannenberg's approach to the natural sciences. The resurrection of Jesus is a mind-independent reality, a public event, and not something that existed merely within the minds of the earliest followers of Jesus or within the minds of Christian believers.

During the 1970s, however, Pannenberg began to express an interest in the way in which theology relates to the natural sciences. Two papers dating from the period 1971–2 focus on the approach of Pierre Teilhard de Chardin, and show a clear interest in the general issue of the formulation of a "theology of nature." In one sense, this can be seen as a direct extension of his earlier interest in history. Just as he appealed to the publicly observable sphere of history in his theological analysis of the 1960s, so he appeals to another publicly observable sphere – the world of nature – from the 1970s onwards. Where Karl Barth rejected natural theology as subversive of revelation, Pannenberg emphasized the importance of natural theology as a universal possibility. Both history and the natural world are available to scrutiny by anyone; the critical question concerns how they are to be understood. In his essay "Contingency and Natural Law," Pannenberg draws attention to the way in which these two spheres of history and nature interact, exploring in particular the idea of a "history of nature."

Pannenberg is clear that the natural sciences and theology are distinct disciplines, with their own understandings of how information is gained and assessed. Nevertheless, both relate to the same publicly observable reality, and they therefore have potentially complementary insights to bring. The area of the "laws of nature" is a case in point, in that Pannenberg believes that the explanations for such laws offered by natural scientists have a purely provisional status, until they are placed on a firmer theoretical foundation by theological analysis. There is thus a clear case to be made for a creative and productive dialogue between the natural sciences and religion; indeed, had this taken place in the past, much confusion and tension could have been avoided.

Pannenberg's approach becomes clearer when his discussion of miracles is considered. Do miracles represent violations of the laws of nature? Pannenberg concedes that they can indeed be understood in this way, and that this raises some very difficult scientific questions: "The concept of miracle as a violation of natural law subverts the very concept of law" (Pannenberg, 2002, p. 759). Yet this is a modern statement of the question, which can be corrected by considering earlier approaches to the issue. Pannenberg notes with particular approval the approach of Augustine of Hippo (354–430), who

> ... emphasized that events of that type do not occur contrary to the nature of things. To us they may appear contrary, because of our limited knowledge of the "course of nature." But God's point of view is different, because he is the Creator of the nature of things as well as of the events that appear unusual. (Pannenberg, 2002, p. 860 )

Pannenberg advocates the rejection of the notion of a miracle as *contra naturam* – that is, as an event which contradicts or violates the laws of nature. Augustine's approach, as set out in his commentary on Genesis (written in 401–15), rests upon a recognition that we experience or observe certain events as unusual and exceptional in contrast to the accustomed patterns of events: "A miracle is just an unusual event or action, and religious interpretation identifies it as an act of God" (Pannenberg, 2002, p. 761). What is really miraculous, in Pannenberg's view, are the laws of nature themselves. Why is there such ordering in a radically contingent world? "The order of nature itself by natural law is one of the greatest miracles, in view of the basic contingency of events and of their sequence" (p. 761).

Pannenberg takes this emphasis on contingency further, making the point that contingencies are unpredictable. Some would see the hand of God in certain contingencies, interpreting certain events as miracles, not because they violate the laws of nature, but because they stand out as unusual.

> Once in a while, however, contingencies occur that make people aware of the basic contingency that permeates all reality. Such an unusual occurrence may be experienced as a "miracle," and religious persons will take it as an act of God, a "sign" of the continuing activity of the Creator in creation and perhaps of new things to come. (Pannenberg, 2002, p. 761)

For this reason, Pannenberg argues, the Augustinian approach to the miraculous is to be advocated. It does not require any opposition to the order of nature which is described in terms of natural law. "It only requires us to admit that we do not know everything about how the processes of nature work" (2002, p. 762).

## For Further Reading

### Primary Sources

Pannenberg, Wolfhart. *Toward a Theology of Nature: Essays on Science and Faith*. Philadelphia: Westminster/John Knox Press, 1993.

Pannenberg, Wolfhart. "The Concept of Miracle." *Zygon*, 37 (2002): 759–62.

Pannenberg, Wolfhart. *The Historicity of Nature : Essays on Science and Theology*. Philadelphia: Templeton Foundation Press, 2007.

### Significant Secondary Studies

Hefner, Philip. "The Role of Science in Pannenberg's Theological Thinking." *Zygon*, 24 (1989): 135–51.

Holder, Rodney D. "Creation and the Sciences in the Theology of Wolfhart Pannenberg." *Communio Viatorum*, 39 (2007): 210–53.

Shults, F. LeRon. "Theology, Science, and Relationality: Interdisciplinary Reciprocity in the Work of Wolfhart Pannenberg." *Zygon*, 36 (2003): 809–25.

# 31 John Polkinghorne (born 1930)

One of the most significant contributions to the dialogue between natural science and religion is due to the British physicist and theologian John Polkinghorne. Polkinghorne's expertise is in the area of theoretical physics. After studying mathematics at Cambridge, he undertook further studies in theoretical physics in the research group led by Paul Dirac. He eventually went on to become Professor of Mathematical Physics at the University of Cambridge in 1968. In 1979, he resigned his chair in order to train for ordination, and became a priest in the Church of England. After a period spent ministering in two parishes in the south of England, he returned to Cambridge in 1986 to become Dean of Trinity Hall. Three years later, he was appointed President of Queen's College, a position which he retained until his retirement in 1997.

One of Polkinghorne's most significant achievements is to establish a firm place for natural theology in apologetics and theology. Natural theology is, in Polkinghorne's view, perhaps the most important bridge between the worlds of science and religion. Polkinghorne directs attention to the ordering of the world, which is disclosed particularly clearly in the physical sciences. He argues that one of the most significant achievements of modern science has been its demonstration of the ordering of the world. It has disclosed an intelligible and delicately balanced structure, which raises questions which transcend the scientific, and provoke an intellectual restlessness which can only be satisfied through an adequate explanation.

Polkinghorne is quite clear that exploring or speaking of the ordering of the world in this way does not fall into the discredited "God of the Gaps" approach. It was once

**Figure 31.1** John Polkinghorne (© Godfrey Argent Studio)

thought that there were certain gaps in scientific understanding, which could never be filled by subsequent scientific investigation. It therefore seemed to make apologetic sense to invoke God to explain such gaps. These "gaps," however, kept getting filled through scientific inquiry, with the result that God gradually got squeezed out of a series of steadily decreasing gaps. As we have noted, a similar point was made earlier by Charles A. Coulson (see chapter 27).

Polkinghorne argues that a more credible approach is to concentrate upon the scientifically given, rather than the scientifically open. Science discloses the world as having a tightly knit and intricately interconnected structure, which requires to be explained. Yet, paradoxically, the natural sciences are unable to answer such questions, even though this would appear to be an essential aspect of the project of understanding the world. The central question to be considered is the following: where does the ordering of the world come from? An obvious answer, widely canvassed in more secular circles, might be that there is no order within the world, save that which we impose upon it. It is a construct of the order-loving human mind, resting upon no adequate basis in reality.

Attractive though this belief might initially seem, it rests upon a series of historical improbabilities. Time and time again, it is the neat and ordered theories of human beings which have come to grief against the sheer intractability of the observational evidence. The ordering which the human mind seeks to impose upon the world proves incapable of explaining it, forcing the search for a better understanding. The ordering imposed by the human mind is thus constantly being compared with that disclosed in the world, to be amended where it is inadequate.

One feature of the ordering of the universe which has attracted especial attention, and which is dealt with fully in Polkinghorne's works, is the *anthropic principle* (see chapter 19). In order for creation to come into being, a very tightly connected series of conditions had to apply. Polkinghorne thus draws attention to

… our increasing realization that there is a delicate and intricate balance in its structure necessary for the emergence of life. For example, suppose things had been a little different in those crucial first three minutes when the gross nuclear structure of the world got fixed as a quarter helium and three quarters hydrogen. If things had gone a little faster, all would have been helium; and without hydrogen how could water (vital to life) have been able to form? (Polkinghorne, 1983, p. 12)

After listing other aspects in which a significant degree of fine-tuning is indicated, Polkinghorne points to the way in which such considerations lay the foundations for the Christian belief in God. They do not necessarily give rise to that belief; they are, none the less, consistent with it, raising important and disturbing questions which the religious apologist is in a position to exploit.

Having thus laid the foundations of what we might call a "general theistic apologetic" (in other words, an argument for the existence of some divine being in general), Polkinghorne argues that this general idea of a divine being requires to be supplemented with reference to the specifics of the Christian revelation. Having devoted several chapters in his work *The Way the World Is* to a survey of some pointers towards the existence of God, he notes:

> The kinds of consideration outlined in the preceding chapters would, I think, incline me to take a theistic view of the world. By themselves that is about as far as they would get me. The reason why I take my stand within the Christian community lies in certain events which took place in Palestine nearly two thousand years ago. (Polkinghorne, 1983, p. 33)

More recently, Polkinghorne has developed his emphasis on the capacity of the Christian faith to account for the way in which humanity experiences the world, including – but not being limited to – the successes of the natural sciences. A Trinitarian view of reality, he argues, offers a lens through which the scientific enterprise, along with human culture and experience, can be satisfactorily explained. Science raises questions which it cannot answer, thus pointing the way to the need for a renewed theological engagement with nature. For Polkinghorne, this points to the need for a renewal of the traditional theological discipline of natural theology.

So what needs to be explained? Polkinghorne points to six observed aspects of human experience which he believes need explanation, and argues that in each case a Trinitarian vision of reality offers the best explanatory framework.

1 The intelligible order of the universe;
2 A fruitful cosmic history;
3 A relational universe;
4 A universe of true becoming;
5 The universe as the womb of consciousness and the carrier of value;
6 A universe of eventual futility.

The capacity of a Trinitarian theology to explain things, Polkinghorne argues, must be judged by agreed criteria of metaphysical excellence. He identifies four such criteria as being of particular importance (Polkinghorne, 2003, pp. 38–47).

1  *Economy.* Preference is to be given to a small number of explanatory principles of wide applicability. This, he suggests, corresponds to "an intuition that profound theories are not miscellanies of ideas but they can be expected to display an integrated character that reflects a unitary aspect present in reality."

2  *Scope.* The ultimate goal of the natural sciences is a "Theory of Everything." Yet this task, Polkinghorne argues, lies beyond the limited capacities of physics, and involves the recognition that reality is "rich and many-layered," involving dimensions of the "physical, mental, moral, aesthetic, and sacred, that are each to be taken with equal seriousness."

3  *Elegance and simplicity.* Noting that there is a "deep human intuition" that some fundamentally coherent principles lie beneath the apparent complexity of experience, Polkinghorne notes the importance of development explanations that are not contrived or forced, but which emerge naturally from observation and reflection.

4  *Fruitfulness.* Here, Polkinghorne notes that a successful theory often succeeds in giving "enhanced intelligibility and extended understanding" which go beyond the observations which were involved in its original formulation. The capacity of a theory to generate both understanding and future research programs is thus affirmed.

## For Further Reading

### Primary Sources

Polkinghorne, John. *One World: The Interaction of Science and Theology.* Princeton, NJ: Princeton University Press, 1986.

Polkinghorne, John. *Belief in God in an Age of Science.* New Haven, CT: Yale University Press, 1998.

Polkinghorne, John. "Physics and Metaphysics in a Trinitarian Perspective." *Theology and Science,* 1 (2003): 33–49.

### Significant Secondary Studies

Avis, P. D. L. "Apologist from the World of Science: John Polkinghorne, FRS." *Scottish Journal of Theology,* 43 (1990): 485–502.

Polkinghorne, John. *Scientists as Theologians: A Comparison of the Writings of Ian Barbour, Arthur Peacocke and John Polkinghorne.* London: SPCK, 1996.

Smedes, Taede A. *Chaos, Complexity, and God: Divine Action and Scientism.* Louvain: Peeters, 2004.

Chapter

# 32 Nancey Murphy
(born 1951)

One of the more significant voices in the dialogue between science and religion is Nancey Murphy, presently Professor of Christian Philosophy at Fuller Theological Seminary, Pasadena, in California. The academic foundations for Murphy's engagement with the field of science and religion were firmly laid before her first publication in this field. Murphy's undergraduate degree in psychology and philosophy at Creighton University, Nebraska, led her on to study for a PhD in the philosophy of science at the University of California, Berkeley, where she studied with Paul Feyerabend (1922–94). Finally, she went on to receive a Doctorate of Theology at the Graduate Theological Union, Berkeley.

Murphy's doctoral research led to her first substantial publication, *Theology in the Age of Scientific Reasoning* (1990). In chapter 16, we noted the importance of the work of Imre Lakatos (1922–74) for the development of the philosophy of science, noting particularly his distinction between the "core" of a scientific theory, and its "auxiliary hypotheses" (p. 132). In this work, Murphy set out a major defense of the theological significance of Lakatos's theory of scientific rationality, emphasizing the importance of "research programs." The real significance of the book, in the view of many, lies in its emphasis upon the need for rigorous thinking, particularly in relation to epistemological issues, in the engagement between science and religion. The book justifiably attracted considerable attention, and won prizes from both the American Academy of Religion and the John Templeton Foundation.

Murphy's subsequent writings in the field have explored a number of issues of importance. However, one aspect of her work is often singled out as being of particular importance: the notion of "nonreductive physicalism." To understand both Murphy's approach to this question, and its importance, we need to set this in context by looking at a critical question: how do Christians understand human nature? What are the essential features of a Christian anthropology? Murphy has contributed significantly to what she terms the "debate over the 'ontological constituents' of human beings" (Murphy, 1999, p. 551).

The traditional Christian answer to this question, which received its definitive statements in the Middle Ages, is to draw a distinction between "body" and "soul" (Latin: *anima*). Humans, it was argued, were distinguished from all other animals and inanimate objects by the possession of this spiritual entity. This approach was held to be justified on biblical grounds, in that the New Testament generally speaks of "body and soul," and occasionally of "body, soul, and spirit." References to the "body" were generally understood by medieval writers to refer to the physical and material parts of humanity, whereas the "soul" was understood as an immaterial and eternal spiritual entity, which merely resided within the human body.

There are two questions that cannot be avoided here. First, is this really how we ought to interpret the biblical anthropological statements? Many scholars in the twentieth century pointed out that the notion of an immaterial soul was a secular Greek concept, rather than a biblical notion. The Hebraic vision of humanity was that of a single entity, an inseparable psychosomatic unit, with many facets or aspects. The Old Testament conceives of humanity "as an animated body and not as an incarnate soul" (H. Wheeler Robinson, cited in Murphy 2006, p. 8). Second, what challenges are posed to this traditional view by modern neurosciences, which offer no place for such notions as a "soul"? How are we to conceive human nature, in the light of both recent trends in biblical interpretation, and developments in neuroscience?

Murphy's work engages both these questions, especially the second. She follows the British New Testament scholar James D. G. Dunn (born 1939) in holding that the biblical authors were not concerned to catalogue the metaphysical components of human beings, such as body, soul, spirit, or mind. Their interest was primarily in relationships, and especially a person's relationship with God. Murphy insists on the need for a *physicalist* account of humanity, which does not invoke or presuppose spiritual or immaterial components. She correctly notes, for example, that biblical terms for aspects of human existence came to be translated by, and eventually elided with, Greek philosophical terms, thus coming to be understood as referring to constituents of humanity.

So does this lead to a reductionist account of human nature? Murphy rightly points out that this question needs a careful response. Many "are reluctant to accept physicalist accounts of the person, because these often seem to deny the existence, meaning, or value of those aspects of human life that we hold most dear" (Murphy, 1999, p. 552). Reductionist accounts of human nature seem to call into question many traditional concerns and beliefs about the dignity and theological position of the human person. Murphy helpfully distinguishes a number of senses in which the word "reductionist" is used:

1   *Methodological reductionism* is a research strategy of analyzing the thing to be studied into its parts.
2   *Ontological reductionism* is the view that no new kinds of metaphysical "ingredients" need be added to produce higher-level entities from lower-level ones. This rejects, for example, the views of Henri Bergson (1859–1941) and Hans Driesch (1867–1941), who respectively held that an additional "vital force" or "entelechy" was needed to produce living beings from nonliving materials.
3   *Causal reductionism* is the view that the behavior of the parts of a system (ultimately, the parts studied by subatomic physics) is determinative of the behavior of all higher-level entities. If this thesis – that all causation in the hierarchy is bottom-up – is true, it follows that the laws pertaining to higher sciences in the hierarchy should be reducible to the laws of physics.

Murphy uses the phrase "nonreductive physicalism" in a specific sense – namely, on the one hand accepting ontological reductionism, but on the other rejecting causal reductionism and reductive materialism.

Murphy's position thus involves reclaiming the biblical idea of humanity as an inseparable psychosomatic unit, which is clearly consistent with the modern neuro-scientific consensus. Yet her most significant achievement is to show how this "non-reductive physicalism" can avoid the reductionist pitfalls that its critics might anticipate. This involves the development of two ideas: supervenience and "downward causation" (also known as "top-down causation," or "whole-part causation.")

The notion of supervenience was introduced in a 1970 essay "Mental Events" by Donald Davidson (1917–2003) to describe the relation between mental and physical characteristics. Since it is widely regarded as implausible that ideas, minds, and so forth do not exist at all, physicalists often assert instead that ideas and minds "supervene" on material objects. Murphy adopts this idea to show how the behavior of any given higher-order system may be influenced strongly, but not completely determined by, the behavior of its lower-order components. Neither the freedom of the human mind nor the human will are thus abolished by their physical natures and contexts.

Murphy also appeals to the notion of "downward causation" to defeat reductionism. The importance of this approach has been noted by other writers in the field of science and religion, including Arthur Peacocke and John Polkinghorne. This approach involves challenging the mechanical model of causation which holds that the lower levels of a system determine its higher-level properties, so that behavior at higher levels is in some sense "explained away" by the lower-level systems. On this approach, consciousness is explained by physics. Yet this can easily be challenged. Even if the lower levels of a system were deterministic, the behavior of the system *as a whole* is shaped by the configuration of its individual components. The case of biological evolution is an excellent example, where the relation of organisms to their environments plays a significant role in natural selection, which cannot be predicted on the basis of a mechanical model of "upward causation."

This very brief account of Murphy's approach does not even begin to do justice to her research interests and programs. However, it indicates how the research program generated by the engagement of science and religion is raising some important questions, especially in the philosophy of religion, and also pointing towards some productive and potentially significant outcomes.

## For Further Reading

### Primary Sources

Murphy, Nancey C. *Theology in the Age of Scientific Reasoning.* Ithaca, NY: Cornell University Press, 1990.

Murphy, Nancey C. "Postmodern Apologetics, or Why Theologians Must Pay Attention to Science." In W. Mark Richardson and Wesley J. Wildman (eds), *Religion and Science: History, Method, Dialogue*, pp. 104–20. New York: Routledge, 1996.

Murphy, Nancey C. *Bodies and Souls, or Spirited Bodies?* Cambridge, UK: Cambridge University Press, 2006.

### Significant Secondary Studies

Bielfeldt, Dennis. "Nancey Murphy's Nonreductive Physicalism." *Zygon*, 34 (1999): 619–28.

Clayton, Philip. "Shaping the Field of Theology and Science: A Critique of Nancey Murphy." *Zygon*, 34 (1999): 609–18.

# Chapter

# 33

## Alister E. McGrath
## (born 1953)

The British theologian Alister McGrath began his academic studies in 1971 with an undergraduate degree in chemistry at Oxford University. He continued his scientific research at Oxford under the supervision of Professor Sir George Radda, working on the biophysical properties of biological membranes. At the same time, he began the study of Christian theology, and was awarded the Denyer and Johnson Prize by Oxford University for the best performance in the Final Honour School of Theology in 1978. McGrath then transferred to Cambridge University, where he researched historical theology, as preparation for a more detailed engagement with the field of science and religion. He returned to Oxford University in 1983, and remained there until 2008.

After a series of publications dealing with the development of Christian doctrine, especially in the sixteenth century, McGrath began to engage with the field of science and religion. His initial publication in this field, *The Foundations of Dialogue in Science and Religion* (1998), was followed by *Thomas F. Torrance: An Intellectual Biography* (1999), a detailed study of the methods and approaches of Thomas F. Torrance (1913–2007), one of the pioneers of the dialogue between the natural sciences and Christian theology.

In the period 2001–3, McGrath published a three-volumed work entitled *A Scientific Theology*. These volumes set out to explore how the working methods and assumptions of the natural sciences could enrich and sustain a systematic Christian theology. To use a traditional way of speaking, how could a natural philosophy act as an *ancilla theologiae*, "handmaid of theology"? This exploration of the methodological and conceptual convergences between the natural sciences and Christian theology involved detailed engagement with three broad areas: the status of "nature," the reality of the external world, and the necessity of theoretical representations of this world. In each case the convergences of the natural sciences and Christian theology are identified and emphasized. The work represents the first theological application of the form of "critical realism" developed by Roy Bhaskar (born 1944), which allows the recognition of a degree of social construction in the human representation of reality, while at the same time insisting that ontology determines epistemology.

One theme which emerged from this major work was the potential role of a renewed natural theology as an interface between Christian theology and the natural sciences. McGrath developed this in his 2008 Riddell Lectures at the University of Newcastle, published as *The Open Secret: A New Vision for Natural Theology* (2008). This work set out an approach to natural theology which represented a move away from that of William Paley. The approach can be summarized as follows.

The work opens with an analysis of the concept of the "transcendent," noting how empirical studies indicate that this remains meaningful to most people, even in a supposedly secular western culture. Natural theology is to be set against this continuing cultural interest in the transcendent. The core notion is that the natural world is in some way capable of pointing to, or perhaps even mediating, this transcendent reality. Four different ways of exploring pathways from nature to the transcendent are considered:

1  Ascending to the transcendent from nature;
2  Seeing the transcendent through nature;
3  Withdrawing from nature to find the transcendent within oneself;
4  Discerning the transcendent in nature.

Yet it is important at this point to note that the concept of nature is open to multiple interpretations. In the last 50 years, there has been a growing consensus that "nature" and "the natural," far from being the objective, autonomous entities assumed by the Enlightenment, are actually conceptually malleable notions, open to multiple interpretations. Historical surveys of how humanity has understood and defined "nature" reveal a surprisingly large range of options, most of which lie beyond empirical verification. To note this point is not to lapse into some form of relativism or offer a purely social constructivist account of things. It is to confront the inescapable fact, which can easily be accommodated within a critical realist outlook, that "nature" is now understood to be a contested notion.

"Nature" denotes ways in which human observers choose to see, interpret, and inhabit the natural, empirical world. The process of observation is "theory-laden"

(Hanson, 1958), involving existing schemas or "mental maps" of reality. There are many concepts of nature, in that nature itself is essentially tractable and indeterminate, highly susceptible to conceptual manipulation by the human mind. Recognition of this point is of critical importance for a renewed "natural theology," especially if undertaken from a critical realist perspective. It acknowledges – contrary to the predominant view of the Enlightenment – that the term "nature" does not designate an objective reality that requires interpretation. It is already an interpreted entity, which requires *reinterpretation*, by being "seen" in a new way.

Natural theology is thus understood to be the action of "seeing" nature from a specifically Christian perspective. This involves rejecting the Enlightenment's version of natural theology as a generic attempt to demonstrate the existence and attributes of a putative God from an appeal to the natural world. Instead, nature is viewed from the perspective of the Christian tradition, with its distinct notions of God, nature, and human agency. McGrath argues that a significant degree of resonance or consonance is observed between theory and observation. In other words, there is a high degree of empirical fit between a Trinitarian vision of reality and what is actually observed.

This is not held to constitute a "proof" of the Christian belief in God. The point being made is that what is observed is consonant with the Christian vision of God, *which is believed to be true on other grounds*, in that it offers a significant degree of intellectual resonance at points of importance. Natural theology is not to be understood as an attempt to deduce the existence of God from observing nature, but of the capacity of the Christian faith to make sense of what is observed. Natural theology emphasizes the resonance between the intellectual framework offered by the Christian faith and observation, and does not set out to prove any core element of that faith from an appeal to nature.

> Contrary to the Enlightenment's aspirations for a universal natural theology, based on common human reason and experience of nature, we hold that a Christian natural theology is grounded in and informed by a characteristic Christian theological foundation. A Christian understanding of nature is the intellectual prerequisite for a natural theology which discloses the Christian God. (McGrath, 2008, p. 4)

In that natural theology involves "seeing" nature, the empirical question of how human perception takes place is identified as having considerable theological significance. Natural theology therefore demands an informed understanding of the psychology of human perception, especially its recognition that perception involves thinking about, affective responding to, and enactive interaction with, the world. *The Open Secret* thus appeals to contemporary psychological theories of perception to illuminate how human beings make sense of things. This requires moving on from the

Enlightenment's inadequate and misleading understanding of how the process of perceiving nature takes place. Furthermore, the Enlightenment regarded natural theology fundamentally as a sense-making exercise. In place of this inadequate account of perception, McGrath argues that the so-called "Platonic triad" of truth, beauty, and goodness offers a helpful heuristic framework for natural theology. This takes account of the rational, aesthetic, and moral dimensions of the human engagement with nature.

McGrath developed this approach further in his 2009 Gifford Lectures, published as *A Fine-Tuned Universe: Science, Theology, and the Quest for God* (2009). This work is best seen as a case study in natural theology, focusing on "anthropic phenomena" and cosmic "fine tuning." What explanations may be offered for these? And which is the best of these explanations? The fundamental argument is that the capacity of the Christian faith to accommodate such phenomena must be regarded as an indication of its truth, though not constituting a deductive "proof" of God's existence.

It remains to be seen whether this way of conceiving and applying natural theology will find acceptance, or whether it has any value for the dialogue between science and religion. Yet there is no doubt that there is a growing interest in natural theology in scientific circles, suggesting that the time is right for a renewal of this traditional discipline, even if that renewal leads to the forging of new approaches, or the reappropriation of older ones.

## For Further Reading

### Primary Sources

McGrath, Alister E. *A Scientific Theology*, 3 vols. London: T&T Clark, 2001–3

McGrath, Alister E. *The Open Secret: A New Vision for Natural Theology*. Oxford: Blackwell, 2008.

McGrath, Alister E. *A Fine-Tuned Universe: Science, Theology, and the Quest for God*. Louisville, KY: Westminster John Knox Press, 2009.

### Significant Secondary Studies

Colyer, Elmer. "Alister E. McGrath, *A Scientific Theology*." *Pro Ecclesia*, 12 (2003): 226–31, 492–7; 13 (2004): 244–40.

Keating, James F. "The Natural Sciences as an *Ancilla Theologiae Nova:* Alister E. McGrath's *A Scientific Theology*." *The Thomist*, 69 (2005): 127–52.

Myers, Benjamin. "Alister McGrath's *Scientific Theology*." *Reformed Theological Review*, 64 (2005): 15–34.

# Chapter
# 34 Philip Clayton (born 1956)

The final recent voice that we shall consider in the contemporary dialogue between science and religion is Philip Clayton, presently Ingraham Professor of Theology at Claremont School of Theology, and professor of philosophy and religion at Claremont Graduate University, California. After his undergraduate studies at Westmont College, Santa Barbara, Clayton studied theology at Fuller Theological Seminary. His doctoral work at Yale University focused on the concept of explanation in science and theology. Unusually, Clayton's PhD was awarded by both the faculties of the philosophy of science, and of religious studies. Clayton has held a number of visiting professorships, most notably as Visiting Professor of Science and Religion at Harvard Divinity School for the academic year 2006–7. He also served as Principal Investigator of the "Science and the Spiritual Quest" program at the Center for Theology and the Natural Sciences, Graduate Theological Union, Berkeley. A prolific author, he is having a significant impact on the shaping of the contemporary landscape in science and religion, particularly on account of his work on emergence.

Clayton's first major published work was a study of explanation in science and religion. *Explanation from Physics to Theology: An Essay in Rationality and Religion* (1986) is widely regarded as having made a powerful case for retaining the notion of "explanation" as religiously meaningful. Clayton countered the trend to treat religion as lacking any explanatory potential, which was then prevalent within the philosophy of religion. This view is found in the writings of Ludwig Wittgenstein (1889–1951), especially his caustic remarks on Sir James Frazer's *Golden Bough*, and has had a significant impact on the philosophy of religion. An excellent example of this "religion without explanation" approach is found in the writings of D. Z. Phillips (1934–2006), who held the Danforth Chair in Philosophy of Religion at Claremont Graduate University for the final period of his career.

Responding to this challenge, Clayton pointed out that religious belief systems could indeed be said to offer "explanations," when this term was properly defined. At this stage, explanation was still primarily understood in causal terms. For example, philosopher of science Wesley Salmon argued that "to give scientific explanations is to show how events and statistical regularities fit into the causal network of the world" (Salmon, 1998, p. 104). Yet Clayton rightly pointed out that causal notions of explanation were being displaced by their coherentist counterparts. In other words, an "explanation" could be understood in terms of the provision of an intellectual framework which proved capable of the maximum accommodation of observations. Clayton's approach to explanation is reflected in his emphasis upon the theological importance of the notion of "inference to the best explanation," which does not necessarily depend upon a causal account of explanation. The critical question is which of a group of potential explanations of a given set of observations seem to offer the best "fit."

While noting that religious explanations often focused primarily on the way in which individuals making sense of their experience, Clayton pointed out that religious intuitions are not limited to the domain of what might be called specifically *religious* experience. Indeed, religious explanation has a capacity to make sense of experience as a whole. Thus the believer or mystic senses (or "sees") that things fit together, that there is an underlying coherence – or, to use the familiar phrase of Julian of Norwich (1342–c.1416), that "All shall be well, and all manner of thing shall be well."

Clayton's emphasis on the holistic aspects of religious explanation can be seen as underlying his interest in the concept of *emergence* – the development of novel unpredictable properties and behaviors at increasing levels of complexity. This notion is coming to play an increasingly significant role in the dialogue between science and religion, with Clayton being one of the most significant advocates of its importance.

"Emergentism" came to be of particular importance in the first part of the twentieth century in Great Britain. Two British emergentists are of particular importance: Samuel Alexander (1859–1938) and C. D. Broad (1887–1971). The general approach of British emergentism, as found in Broad's landmark *The Mind and Its Place in Nature* (1925), can be summed up as follows. Nature is understood as a stratified or layered reality, with each "layer" or "stratum" corresponding to the science which attempts to investigate it. These layers are, in ascending order, physics, chemistry, biology, and psychology. Certain properties "emerge" at higher levels which are not found at lower levels.

There are, however, significant differences between the British emergentists concerning the causal implications of this approach. Broad takes what Clayton terms a "strong" view of emergence, holding that genuine new causal processes emerge at higher levels of a system, supplementing those that are found at lower levels. Alexander, however, holds what Clayton terms a "weak" view, arguing that new patterns of causality appear at higher levels, which do not displace or supersede those of lower levels.

It will be clear that this approach has significant implications for the dialogue between science and religion. For example, where is theology located on this "layered" approach? And how does this impact on our understanding of how the mind works (an issue addressed, as noted earlier, by Nancey Murphy). One of Clayton's most significant achievements is to develop a comprehensive theory of emergence, which is both scientifically informed, and theologically relevant.

In his 2006 Boyle Lecture, Clayton pointed out the strongly antireductionist character of emergence:

> So what, in the simplest possible terms, is emergence? It is the hypothesis that reduction, or "reductionism", is false. An emergentist theory of human thought and action, for example, argues that the reduction of the human sciences to biology or physics is false. A non-reductive theory of religious belief argues that the reduction of religious belief to its psycho-social functions is false. (Clayton, 2006, p. 294)

Clayton thus argues that empirical reality is naturally divided into multiple levels, and that over the extended course of natural history, new emergent levels evolve. These emergent wholes are more than the sum of their parts, and require new types of explanation adequate to each new level of phenomena. Furthermore, such emergent wholes manifest new types of causal interaction. To give an example: biological systems are not "nothing more than" microphysical interactions; they include irreducibly biological interactions and must therefore be explained in biological terms.

Although there are some variations in definition of the concept of "emergence," Clayton's understanding of the notion has four general features.

1  Everything that exists in the world of space and time is ultimately composed of the basic fundamental particles recognized by physics. However, physics proves inadequate to explain how this material comes to be structured.
2  When ensembles or aggregates of material particles attain an appropriate level of organizational complexity, genuinely novel properties begin to emerge.
3  These emergent properties cannot be reduced to, or predicted from, the lower level phenomena from which they emerge.
4  Higher level entities exercise a causal influence on their lower-level constituents.

The overall picture which Clayton discerns is that of the emergence of complexity from simpler previous physical structures, leading to the creation of higher levels with properties not possessed by lower levels.

Clayton draws an important distinction between "weak" and "strong" concepts of emergence, and locates the difference between them in causal terms. For Clayton, strong emergence implies that genuinely new causal processes or causally effective agents come into existence as systems evolve. Weak emergence makes the somewhat more modest claim that only new patterns emerge, without the appearance of novel causal processes or agents. Clayton himself advocates "strong" emergence, which buttresses the antireductionist emphasis of his position. He illustrates the importance of this point by noting a divergence between two evolutionary biologists – Richard Dawkins and Stephen Jay Gould. Clayton rightly points out that a recognition of the role of environmental influences in triggering gene expression has led to a move away from the radical reductionism of Dawkins. Gould's move away from the reductionist model in the late 1970s was due in part to his recognition of the role of the environment not only in selecting for or against structures, but also in causing its development.

Clayton's approach clearly has much to offer the dialogue between science and religion. Its antireductionism clearly offers theology conceptual space which was denied it by certain older approaches to the natural sciences, which often amounted to the uncritical adoption of reductive physicalism as a metaphysical program. Yet perhaps more importantly, Clayton offers a framework within which complex traditional questions – such as God's action in the world – can be approached in a new manner. While much further exploration remains to be done, it is clear that this approach has much to offer the dialogue between science and religion.

## For Further Reading

### Primary Sources

Clayton, Philip. *Explanation from Physics to Theology: An Essay in Rationality and Religion*. New Haven, CT: Yale University Press, 1989.

Clayton, Philip. *Mind and Emergence: From Quantum to Consciousness*. Oxford: Oxford University Press, 2004.

Clayton, Philip. "The Emergence of Spirit: From Complexity to Anthropology to Theology." *Theology and Science*, 4 (2006): 291–307.

### Significant Secondary Studies

Drees, Willem B. "God and Contemporary Science: Philip Clayton's Defense of Panentheism." *Zygon*, 34 (1999): 515–25.

Gregersen, Niels Henrik. "Emergence in Theological Perspective: A Corollary to Professor Clayton's Boyle Lecture." *Theology and Science*, 4 (2006): 309–20.

Haag, James W. "Between Physicalism and Mentalism: Philip Clayton on Mind and Emergence." *Zygon*, 41(2006): 633–47.

# Conclusion

This short book has offered a brief and simple overview of the increasingly important field of science and religion, with particular reference to Christianity. The work is an introduction to the field, not a thorough treatment of its many aspects. It has tried to introduce you to the historical landmarks, theoretical issues, contemporary debates, and some of the contributors to the field. It has also given you some guidance about how to develop your thinking in each of the topics covered, through the provision of short reading lists. By the time you finish this book, you should be able to get the most out of your further studies in this field, and enjoy conferences on these themes. Finally, this work has also attempted to whet your appetite to know more, so that you will finish the book feeling dissatisfied. This is probably all that a short book can hope to achieve when dealing with so rich and complex a subject as the interaction of science and religion.

So where might you go next? What might you do to develop your interest in the field? If you are using this book for a taught course in the field, it is likely that your instructor may have helpful suggestions to make. If you are using it by yourself, the following pointers may be of use in taking your studies further.

1   Deepen your understanding of one particular historical issue, in which science and religion play a major role. One obvious possibility is to master one specific debate – such as the Darwinian controversy. As scholarly understanding of the issues associated with this debate increases, so does its fascination. It seems certain to

remain a topic of debate for some time. Although this work has provided an introduction to the three "landmark" debates in science and religion, there are others that repay study.

2   Explore some theoretical question in much greater detail. For example, how can we think of God acting within the world? Does it matter that the existence of God cannot be proved scientifically? In what sense can the Christian faith be said to explain anything? Each of these questions has been explored very briefly in this book, and can be opened up in much greater depth by following through on the suggested reading.

3   Consider exploring one contemporary thinker in detail. A number of possibilities have been mentioned in this work. If you are coming from a theological background, you might find it particularly helpful to explore Thomas F. Torrance or Wolfhart Pannenberg in more detail. Those with a background in physics might appreciate a detailed engagement with John Polkinghorne, just as those with a background in the biological sciences might enjoy reading Arthur Peacocke. There are other writers, not included in this work, whose works are also well worth exploring further. For example, those with an interest in philosophy will enjoy interacting with Ernan McMullin of Notre Dame University, whose work on critical realism is particularly rigorous.

4   You may find it helpful to visit websites of organizations that are interested in encouraging discussion of issues in science and religion. This will allow you to learn of forthcoming conferences and new publications in this field. Many also include online articles on topics of interest. The following are especially recommended: the Center for Theology and the Natural Sciences, Berkeley; the Faraday Institute, Cambridge; and the Metanexus Institute, Pennsylvania. These also include links to other sites of interest, allowing you to use the web to open up and develop your specific interests. The Faraday Institute website is especially useful, as it includes audio recordings of more than 200 lectures of relevance to the field.

5   A number of journals are dedicated to the field of science and religion, and are available in print or online through academic libraries. The three most important of these are: *Zygon*, *Theology and Science*, and *Science and Christian Belief*. These include both academic articles and book reviews, and occasionally news of conferences and public lectures.

But wherever you chose to go next, it is hoped that you will have found this work useful in introducing you to the field. The publisher and author would welcome comments on this book, so that future editions can be responsive to user feedback.

# References

Al-Ghazali, Moderation in Belief, trans. Michael Marmura. In "Al-Ghazali's Chapter on Divine Power in the Iqtisād." *Arabic Sciences and Philosophy*, 4 (1994): 279–315.

Alston, William P. "The Inductive Argument from Evil and the Human Cognitive Condition." *Philosophical Perspectives*, 5 (1991a): 29–67.

Alston, William P. *Perceiving God: The Epistemology of Religious Experience*. Ithaca, NY: Cornell University Press, 1991b.

Ayala, Francisco J. "Teleological Explanations in Evolutionary Biology." *Philosophy of Science*, 37 (1970): 1–15.

Ayer, A. J. (ed.) *Logical Positivism*. New York: Free Press, 1959.

Barbour, Ian G. *Myths, Models and Paradigms: A Comparative Study in Science and Religion*. New York: Harper & Row, 1974.

Barbour, Ian G. *Religion in an Age of Science, 1989-1990*. San Francisco: Harper, 1990.

Barrett, Justin. *Why Would Anyone Believe in God?* Lanham, MD: AltaMira Press, 2004.

Barrett, Justin. "Cognitive Science of Religion: What Is It and Why Is It?" *Religion Compass*, 1 (2007): 1–19.

Barrow, John, and Frank J. Tipler. *The Anthropic Cosmological Principle*. Oxford: Oxford University Press, 1986.

Baumeister, Roy F. *Meanings of Life*. New York: Guilford Press, 1991.

Blackwell, Richard J. *Galileo, Bellarmine and the Bible*. Notre Dame, IN: University of Notre Dame Press, 1991.

Boyer, Pascal. "Religious Thought and Behavior as By-products of Brain Function." *Trends in Cognitive Sciences*, 7 (2003): 119–24.

Cantor, Geoffrey, and Chris Kenny. "Barbour's Fourfold Way: Problems with His Taxonomy of Science–Religion Relationships." *Zygon*, 36 (2001): 765–81.

Carr, B. J., and M. J. Rees, "The Anthropic Principle and the Structure of the Physical World." *Nature*, 278 (1979): 605–12.

Chadwick, Owen. *From Bossuet to Newman: The Idea of Doctrinal Development.* Cambridge, UK: Cambridge University Press, 1957.

Clayton, Philip. "The Emergence of Spirit: From Complexity to Anthropology to Theology." *Theology and Science*, 4 (2006): 291–307.

Conway Morris, Simon. *Life's Solution: Inevitable Humans in a Lonely Universe.* Cambridge, UK: Cambridge University Press, 2003.

Coulson, Charles A. *Christianity in an Age of Science.* London: Oxford University Press, 1953.

Coulson, Charles A. *Science and Christian Belief.* Chapel Hill, NC: University of North Carolina Press, 1958.

Craig, William Lane, and Quentin Smith. *Theism, Atheism, and Big Bang Cosmology.* Oxford: Clarendon Press, 1993.

Cupitt, Don. *Only Human.* London: SCM Press, 1985.

Darwin, Charles. *On the Origin of the Species by Means of Natural Selection.* London: John Murray, 1859.

Darwin, Charles. *The Descent of Man.* London: John Murray, 1871.

Darwin, Charles. *On the Origin of the Species by Means of Natural Selection*, 6th edn. London: John Murray, 1872.

Davies, Paul. *God and the New Physics.* New York: Simon and Schuster, 1983.

Davies, Paul. *The Mind of God: Science and the Search for Ultimate Meaning.* London: Penguin, 1992.

Dawkins, Richard. *The Blind Watchmaker: Why the Evidence of Evolution Reveals a Universe Without Design.* New York: W. W. Norton, 1986.

Dawkins, Richard. *The Selfish Gene*, 2nd edn. Oxford: Oxford University Press, 1989.

Dawkins, Richard. *A Devil's Chaplain: Selected Writings.* London: Weidenfeld & Nicholson, 2003.

Dawkins, Richard. *The God Delusion.* Boston: Houghton Mifflin, 2006.

Dennett, Daniel C. "Back From the Drawing Board." In Bo Dahlbom (ed.), *Dennett and His Critics: Demystifying Mind*, pp. 203–35. Oxford: Blackwell, 1993.

Dennett, Daniel C. *Darwin's Dangerous Idea: Evolution and the Meaning of Life.* New York: Simon & Schuster, 1995.

Devitt, Michael. *Realism and Truth.* Oxford: Blackwell, 1984.

Dirac, Paul. "The Evolution of the Physicist's Picture of Nature." *Scientific American*, 208, 5 (1963): 45–53.

Dyson, Freeman. *Disturbing the Universe.* New York: Harper and Row, 1979.

Dyson, Freeman. "The Scientist as Rebel." In John Cornwell (ed.), *Nature's Imagination: The Frontiers of Scientific Vision*, pp. 1–11. Oxford: Oxford University Press, 1995.

Edwards, Jonathan. *The Images of Divine Things.* New Haven, CT: Yale University Press, 1948.

Flew, Antony, "Theology and Falsification." In Antony Flew and Alasdair MacIntyre (eds), *New Essays in Philosophical Theology*, pp. 96–9. London: SCM Press, 1955.

Freud, Sigmund. *Leonardo da Vinci and a Memory of His Childhood*. In *Complete Psychological Works*, ed. James Strachey, vol. 11, pp. 57–137. London: Hogarth Press, 1957.

Freud, Sigmund. *The Future of an Illusion*. In *Complete Psychological Works*, ed. James Strachey, vol. 21, pp. 1–56. London: Hogarth Press, 1961.

Freud, Sigmund. *Moses and Monotheism*. In *Complete Psychological Works*, ed. James Strachey, vol. 23, pp. 1–137. London: Hogarth Press, 1964.

Gould, Stephen Jay. "Impeaching a Self-Appointed Judge." *Scientific American*, 267, 1 (1992): 118–21.

Gould, Stephen Jay. "Nonmoral Nature." In *Hen's Teeth and Horse's Toes: Further Reflections in Natural History*, pp. 32–44. New York: W. W. Norton, 1994.

Gould, Stephen Jay. "Nonoverlapping Magisteria." *Natural History*, 106 (March 1997): 16–22.

Gould, Stephen Jay. *Rocks of Ages: Science and Religion in the Fullness of Life*. London: Jonathan Cape, 2001.

Hanson, N. R. *Patterns of Discovery: An Inquiry into the Conceptual Foundations of Science*. Cambridge, UK: Cambridge University Press, 1958.

Hick, John, "Theology and Verification." In John Hick (ed.), *The Existence of God*, pp. 252–74. London: Macmillan, 1964.

Hooykaas, Reijer. *Religion and the Rise of Modern Science*. Edinburgh: Scottish Academic Press, 1972.

James, William. *The Varieties of Religious Experience: A Study in Human Nature*. New York: Longmans Green, 1917.

James, William. *The Will to Believe and Other Essays in Popular Philosophy*. New York: Dover, 1956.

James, William. *Essays in Radical Empiricism*. Cambridge, MA: Harvard University Press, 1976.

Jastrow, Robert. *God and the Astronomers*. New York: Norton, 1978.

Kuhn, Thomas S. *The Structure of Scientific Revolutions*, 2nd edn. Chicago: University of Chicago Press, 1970.

Mayr, Ernst. *Toward a New Philosophy of Biology: Observations of an Evolutionist*. Cambridge, MA: Harvard University Press, 1988.

Mayr, Ernst. *Evolution and the Diversity of Life: Selected Essays*. Cambridge, MA: Harvard University Press, 1997.

McCauley, Robert. "The Naturalness of Religion and the Unnaturalness of Science." In Frank C. Keil and Robert A. Wilson (eds), *Explanation and Cognition*, pp. 61–85. Cambridge, MA: MIT Press, 2000.

Medawar, Peter. *The Limits of Science*. Oxford: Oxford University Press, 1985.

Midgley, Mary. *Beast and Man: The Roots of Human Nature*. London: Methuen, 1980.

Mitchell, Basil. *The Justification of Religious Belief*. London: Macmillan, 1973.

Murphy, Nancey. "Physicalism Without Reductionism: Toward a Scientifically, Philosophically, and Theologically Sound Portrait of Human Nature." *Zygon*, 34 (1999): 551–71.

Murphy, Nancey C. *Bodies and Souls, or Spirited Bodies?* Cambridge, UK: Cambridge University Press, 2006.

Nagel, Ernest. *The Structure of Science: Problems in the Logic of Scientific Explanation*. London: Routledge and Kegan Paul, 1979.

Numbers, Ronald L. "Science and Religion." *Osiris*, 1 (1985): 59–80.

O'Donovan, Oliver. *Resurrection and Moral Order*. Grand Rapids, MI: Eerdmans, 1986.

Pannenberg, Wolfhart. "The Concept of Miracle." *Zygon*, 37 (2002): 759–62.

Peacocke, Arthur. *Theology for a Scientific Age: Being and Becoming Divine and Human*. London: SCM Press, 1993.

Peacocke, Arthur. *Paths from Science Towards God: The End of All Our Exploring*. Oxford: Oneworld, 2001.

Pittendrigh, C. S. "Adaptation, Natural Selection, and Behavior." In A. Roe and George Gaylord Simpson (eds), *Behavior and Evolution*, pp. 390–416. New Haven, CT: Yale University Press, 1958.

Plantinga, Alvin. *The Analytic Theist: An Alvin Plantinga Reader*, ed. James F. Sennett. Grand Rapids, MI: Eerdmans, 1998.

Plantinga, Alvin. *Warranted Christian Belief*. Oxford: Oxford University Press, 2000.

Polkinghorne, John. *The Way the World Is*. London: SPCK, 1983.

Polkinghorne, John. *One World: The Interaction of Science and Theology*. Princeton, NJ: Princeton University Press, 1986.

Polkinghorne, John. *Science and Creation: The Search for Understanding*. London: SPCK, 1988.

Polkinghorne, John. *Reason and Reality*. London: SPCK, 1991.

Polkinghorne, John. "Physics and Metaphysics in a Trinitarian Perspective." *Theology and Science*, 1 (2003): 33–49.

Popper, Karl R. *The Logic of Scientific Discovery*. New York: Science Editions, 1961.

Popper, Karl R. *Conjectures and Refutations: The Growth of Scientific Knowledge*. London: Routledge & Kegan Paul, 1963.

Popper, Karl R. *Realism and the Aim of Science*. London: Hutchinson, 1983.

Putnam, H. *Mathematics, Matter and Method: Philosophical Papers*, vol. 1. Cambridge, UK: Cambridge University Press, 1975.

Quine, W. V. O. *From a Logical Point of View*. Cambridge, MA: Harvard University Press, 1953.

Raven, Charles E. *Natural Religion and Christian Theology*, 2 vols. Cambridge, UK: Cambridge University Press, 1953.

Redhead, Michael. *From Physics to Metaphysics*. Cambridge, UK: Cambridge University Press, 1995.

Rowe, William L. "The Problem of Evil and Some Varieties of Atheism." *American Philosophical Quarterly*, 16 (1979): 335–41.

Salmon, Wesley C. *Causality and Explanation*. New York: Oxford University Press, 1998.

Tennant, F. R. *Philosophical Theology*, 2 vols. Cambridge, UK: Cambridge University Press, 1930.

Torrance, Thomas F. *Theological Science*. London: Oxford University Press, 1969.

Torrance, Thomas F. "The Problem of Natural Theology in the Thought of Karl Barth." *Religious Studies*, 6 (1970): 121–35.

Torrance, Thomas F. *Reality and Scientific Theology: Theology and Science at the Frontiers of Knowledge*. Edinburgh: Scottish Academic Press, 1985.

Van Fraassen, Bas C. *The Scientific Image*. Oxford: Oxford University Press, 1980.

Van Till, Howard. "Theistic Evolution." In J. P. Moreland and John Mark Reynolds (eds), *Three Views on Creation and Evolution*, pp. 159–218. Grand Rapids, MI: Zondervan, 1999.

Watts, Fraser. "Cognitive Neuroscience and Religious Consciousness." In R. J. Russell, N. Murphy, T. Meyering, and M. Arbib (eds), *Neuroscience and the Person*, pp. 327–46. Vatican City: Vatican Observatory, 1999.

Weinberg, Steven. *Dreams of a Final Theory: The Search for the Fundamental Laws of Nature*. London: Hutchinson Radius, 1993.

Wilson, Edward O. *Sociobiology: The New Synthesis*. Cambridge, MA: Belknap Press, 1975.

Wright, N. T. *The New Testament and the People of God*. London: SPCK, 1992.

# Index

*Note:* Page references in italics indicate photographs and diagrams.

*Index compiled by Meg Davies (Fellow of the Society of Indexers)*